ROUTLEDGE LIBRARY EDITIONS:
CURRICULUM

Volume 9

EUROPEAN DIMENSIONS AND THE SECONDARY SCHOOL CURRICULUM

EUROPEAN DIMENSIONS AND THE SECONDARY SCHOOL CURRICULUM

IVOR GOODSON AND VERONICA MCGIVNEY

LONDON AND NEW YORK

First published in 1985 by Falmer

This edition first published in 2019
by Routledge
2 Park Square, Milton Park, Abingdon, Oxon OX14 4RN

and by Routledge
711 Third Avenue, New York, NY 10017

Routledge is an imprint of the Taylor & Francis Group, an informa business

British Library Cataloguing in Publication Data
A catalogue record for this book is available from the British Library

ISBN: 978-1-138-31956-1 (Set)
ISBN: 978-0-429-45387-8 (Set) (ebk)
ISBN: 978-1-138-31850-2 (Volume 9) (hbk)
ISBN: 978-1-138-32160-1 (Volume 9) (pbk)
ISBN: 978-0-429-45454-7 (Volume 9) (ebk)

Publisher's Note
The publisher has gone to great lengths to ensure the quality of this reprint but points out that some imperfections in the original copies may be apparent.

European Dimensions and the Secondary School Curriculum

Ivor Goodson
and
Veronica McGivney

The Falmer Press
A member of the Taylor & Francis Group
London and Philadelphia

UK The Falmer Press, Falmer House, Barcombe, Lewes, East Sussex, BN8 5DL

USA The Falmer Press, Taylor & Francis Inc., 242 Cherry Street, Philadelphia, PA 19106-1906

First published in 1985

Library of Congress Cataloging in Publication Data

Goodson, Ivor
European dimensions and the secondary school curriculum.

Includes index.
1. Europe—History—Study and teaching (Secondary)—Great Britain. I. McGivney, Veronica. II. Title.
D16.4.G7G59 1985 940′.07′1241 85-4590
ISBN 1-85000-045-X
ISBN 1-85000-046-8 (pbk.)

Typeset in 10/12 Caledonia by
Imago Publishing Ltd, Thame, Oxon

Jacket design by Leonard Williams

Printed in Great Britain by Taylor & Francis (Printers) Ltd, Basingstoke

Contents

Abbreviations

Throughout the book the following abbreviations for examination boards have been used:

Associated Examining Board	AEB
East Anglian Examinations Board	EAEB
Joint Matriculation Board	JMB
North West Regional Examinations Board	NWREB
Oxford and Cambridge Schools Examination Board	OX/CAM
Oxford Delegacy of Local Examinations	OXF
South East Regional Examinations Board	SEREB
South Western Examinations Board	SWEB
Southern Regional Examinations Board	SREB
Southern Universities' Joint Board for School Examinations	SUJB
University Entrance and School Examinations Council, University of London	LON

Acknowledgements

The authors would like to acknowledge the European Cultural Foundation and the European Commission for their help in funding much of the research from which this study derives.

The major projects from which data is taken were directed by Dr Goodson at the Schools Unit, University of Sussex, between 1977 and 1981. The first project, the *European Parliament Study*, was funded solely by the European Cultural Foundation and ran between 1977 and 1979. The part-time research fellow was Dr F. Lawrence. The second project, a much larger undertaking — the *Europe in the School Project*, was funded both by the European Cultural Foundation and the European Commission and ran from 1979 to 1981. The full-time research fellow was Dr V. McGivney. The Europe in the School Project was a seven member state project and a good deal of the work was co-ordinated by the Sussex Unit. The data reported in this study comprises only the United Kingdom section of the work of the project.

In the course of investigations, help and information was sought from a large number of schools, local education authorities, further and higher education institutions, examination boards and individuals. Our sincere thanks go to all of those who responded so generously with information and time. We are particularly grateful to the many teachers who gave up their precious free time to talk to us and provide us with their classroom materials.

We thank Eileen Daffern for her help with the section on modern languages, and Simon Duncan for his useful comments on the geography section.

Finally many thanks are due to Sheila Lee and Mary Hoar for their painstaking help in typing several versions of the text.

Introduction: European Dimensions and the Secondary School Curriculum

'Europe' and the EEC seem to be virtually synonymous for the majority of our population, and the ambivalent feelings many people have about the Community together with the consistently bad press it has received in the UK in recent years, seem to have engendered a certain hostility in educational circles towards teaching about Europe as a whole. However if one of the aims of education is to increase children's awareness, tolerance and understanding of the world about them; to widen their experience and horizons, then teaching about the wider world must have a place in the curriculum.

The 1980 DES consultative paper *A Framework for the School Curriculum* listed six possible aims 'to comprehend the whole range of desirable school curricular activity'. The fourth and fifth of these are:

> to instil respect for religious and moral values, and tolerance of other races, religions and ways of life;
> to help pupils understand the world in which they live, and the interdependence of individuals, groups and nations

The DES consultative paper went on to suggest what the components of a core curriculum should be but of these only the learning of one or two European languages would go any way towards fulfilling the aims quoted. This is in spite of a growing feeling among informed members of the public that global awareness should be one of the essential aims of the secondary school curriculum. Although the DES paper on the curriculum posited a number of laudable and wide-ranging aims, its subsequent recommendations for a core curriculum seemed to relegate global awareness to a fringe or optional activity since there is little evidence to show that learning foreign languages (at least as they are taught at the moment) gives pupils more than a slight and superficial insight into the wider world

Yet we live in an increasingly interdependent world. We cannot restrict education to purely nationalistic concerns while the most important and pressing issues of our time are so patently of global dimensions. An important part of the wider world is the continent of Europe and Europe should have an prominent place in the curriculum for a number of reasons: cultural, geographical, linguistic, economic and political. Our relationship with Europe in all these spheres has shaped much of our past and, whether we like it or not, is influencing much of our present and future. Because of this, teaching young people about our European neighbours with whom we have so many long-established and varied links should, logically, be an educational priority.

If our geographical, historical and cultural links with Europe are not considered valid enough reasons for teaching about the continent, we now have, whatever the controversy they arouse, strong economic and political ties with a substantial and growing body of European countries. If only for practical reasons we need to instruct our future policy-makers, economists, exporters and businessmen not merely in the languages but also in the way of life, culture, institutions and recent history of at least some of those parts of Europe with which we are, at least in an economic sense, partners.

Yet these arguments for broadening the focus of the school curriculum are fiercely resisted. To some extent this resistance is understandable and the fundamental political issue is whether coverage of European issues is to be desired within the nation-state. This raises huge questions about 'national identity' and 'political autonomy'. Such bedrock political considerations are beyond the orbit of a book on European education although it can develop our understanding of the fact that European issues may be taught in ways that develop critical awareness as well as tacit acceptance. But the fact of potential pedagogic flexibility cannot preempt questions that are perceived in terms of national and political destinies.

It is not possible to talk about European education in Britain without considering the general position which Europe occupies in our national and political consciousness. In many ways Europe is a deeply alien concept, often for very understandable reasons. The basic reasons are twofold: they are chronologically distinct but mutually reaffirming. The first reason is that our school curriculum as in any other country, is an historical artefact. Hence school subjects reflect our national and imperial past. History, to take the most obvious example, provides a wealth of evidence of past imperial activities. In a country whose navy 'ruled the waves' the major terms of celebration in foreign policy were once 'splendid isolation'. Whilst the rest of Europe records the 'Age of Napoleon', English textbooks deal with the 'Age of Nelson'. In short, our deep-grained insularity as an island race is both celebrated and reinforced by our school curriculum. The second reason carries on from this imperial legacy and is related to our ambivalence about modern Europe, expecially the EEC, which in this country is held largely responsible for higher food prices and is remembered more for much-publicised petty bureaucratic regulations and rumours of profiligacy than for its positive measures such as social reforms. There is, however, a world of difference between an unthinking rejection of all things European (and the EEC in particular) and *a constructive yet critical understanding* of Europe. Nevertheless, our geography and our historical legacy lead to a psychological predilection for isolation from and rejection of Europe. Such a psychological predilection acts against any understanding of the relationship between Britain and Europe in spite of the fact that Britain's experience has always been closely related to that of Europe. Yet it is perfectly possible to view Britain as a distinct, and indeed Sovereign entity, and at the same time concede that much of the historic, cultural and economic milieu of Europe is part of a common experience shared by Britain. Any balanced judgment of Britain's relationship with Europe and the wider world requires as a pre-requisite that we abandon the imperial insularity that is reflected still in much of our school curriculum and indeed national psychology.

Hence in this book we are arguing for education *about* Europe, not education necessarily in favour of Europe. We see European education as part of a long overdue process of breaking down the national insularity of the UK curriculum and using Europe as one convenient 'window on the wider world'.

At the present time the only subject concerned specifically with the study of Europe is European Studies. This subject was created partly as an initial curriculum response to Britain joining the EEC and to date it has presented the only opportunity in the school curriculum for providing a sequential and unified approach to the study of Europe. Unfortunately, however, the subject presented comprehensive schools with a solution to the problems created by pupils experiencing difficulty with learning foreign languages. The subject therefore developed in response to this problem, often hastily, without resources and to suit the conditions prevailing in individual schools. This has led to some *less able* students taking European Studies while other less able students receive no European Studies at all. Among more academic students, apart from those students taking the few courses available at 'O' level or 'O/A' level, no European Studies are taught. Able pupils depend for their information about Europe largely on history, geography and modern languages courses. As has been noted, these subjects, history in particular, often stress Britain's imperial isolationist past at the expense of her European present. How much longer this situation will prevail remains to be seen: certainly there are few initiatives under way which promise substantial change.

To summarize, in the United Kingdom secondary school curriculum *some* less able children are taught European Studies, largely in a haphazard and ill-resourced manner. The children who are given these courses may be stigmatized as 'less able' because they have difficulty learning languages and hence European Studies are perceived and received as a 'badge of failure'. Able pupils meanwhile receive no specific teaching about Europe and their knowledge must be mainly distilled from history, geography and modern languages which only a minority take and which often stress imperial or isolationist factors. *This means that in our secondary schools most children, and the majority of able children, receive no specific teaching about Europe.* This is an absurd and wholly unjustifiable situation. The object of the research on which this book has been based is to see how this situation can be rectified and what kind of teaching about modern Europe is currently on offer to pupils in our secondary schools.

Defining a Research Strategy

When we review recent British curricular history, we find that a traditional response of curriculum projects has been to produce curriculum materials about the issue in question. This response was characteristic of curriculum projects in the 1960s. But materials development *with no understanding of school context* or existing teacher strategies proved in the 1960s to be an approach with severely limited pay-offs. Materials sent into schools by curriculum projects were often misused, abused or quite simply not used. In short, a more complex response was and is needed.

If this is true of those curriculum projects operating in fairly well-known and high-status areas of the UK curriculum, it clearly applies with even more force to less well-understood, lower status areas. At the moment our knowledge of the main contexts and strategies for education about Europe within the UK is limited. This is partly because we are dealing with a relatively new area of the curriculum. It is also because it is a curriculum area characterized by chaos and confusion. For this reason, above all, UK curriculum projects concerned with educating about European issues needed to begin by identifying the major strategies through which European 'messages' were being transmitted in our school curriculum. A second reason for focussing attention on strategies and contexts was that issues of current European importance change over time. To ensure a permanent return from curriculum projects it was crucial that the main areas of educating about Europe were identified and tentatively evaluated (rather than beginning by preparing materials on current, but possibly ephemeral, European issues).

As well as pursuing objectives within the domestic curriculum the researchers conducted multilateral curriculum projects which sought to further understanding of European education in other educational systems. Members of the Schools Unit at the University of Sussex had been working closely with Dutch counterparts since 1976 and in later years with five other member states. This was in keeping with a point made by Hywel Jones, a leading member of the European Commission. It is impossible to work in the field of European educational systems, he said, without becoming:

> deeply aware of the tensions which exist between central and decentralized structures in the field of education, and the differing reactions to governmental or central interventions in the world of curriculum. In a very real sense, education lies in the heartland of political and personal sensitivities . . . it provides an important indicator of the real willingness of the participating countries to transform a Common Market into a community.

In this respect Jones saw a crucial need to 'underline the importance of increasing mutual understanding of each other's educational systems, so that practitioners can be more sensitive and open to the endeavours made by their counterparts in other countries.'[2]

Once again if mutual understanding of each other's educational systems is a goal, research is required which moves beyond materials (which might be the same for all countries) to an appreciation of the diversity of curriculum strategies within the member states. Thus for both national and European reasons the curriculum projects took as their priority the scrutiny of the strategies at present employed in educating about Europe in United Kingdom secondary schools.

Preliminary Investigations: The Survey

The first problem confronting the researchers was to establish where education about Europe was in fact taking place in the curriculum. A large amount of anecdotal evidence was available and the researchers became accustomed to the confident assertion that 'everybody already knows where Europe is dealt with in the timetable.' When all the anecdotes were assembled it became clear that they were mutually contradictory. A survey was therefore designed to elicit information from a sample of all categories of secondary schools in the United Kingdom and Northern Ireland. Besides building up a general picture of education about Europe in the United Kingdom's secondary schools, the national survey was intended as an important first stage in the research work. The survey was expected to pinpoint the major curriculum areas where European education might be maximized. The intention was then to focus other stages of the research on these strategic areas of investigation.

Syllabus Analysis

In the light of the survey findings, subjects which appear to have the most existing and potential modern European content were investigated: European Studies, history, geography, modern languages and economics. In addition to these, Modern Studies was scrutinized as a good example of a successfully established interdisciplinary subject with an integral modern European content. The syllabus analyses concentrated on GCE and SCE courses, partly because of the very large number of syllabuses that would have been involved had CSE mode 1 been included. Another reason was that, rightly or wrongly, it is the GCE examination which confers status upon a subject and, where a new subject is concerned, ensures its survival. It therefore seemed appropriate to concentrate as a priority on GCE courses both to analyze their existing modern European content and to investigate the possibilities they offer for changing the scope and emphasis of education about Europe in the curriculum.

During the investigation of the syllabuses, particular attention was paid to the amount and nature of the European content of the syllabuses, the experiences of teachers already teaching or wanting to teach courses with a modern European content and the possibilities for modifying or strengthening the modern European content of the examination syllabuses.

Case Studies

Following a series of syllabus analyses in the areas identified, a range of exemplary case studies were planned. From this two-pronged approach it was considered that the practising teacher could be given practical syllabus guidelines alongside some related examples of 'good practice'. However, so as not to prejudice the 'purer' research purpose of presenting a picture of practice 'as it was' as well as 'as it might be', a number of case studies were pursued to highlight some of the dilemmas and problems confronting teachers in this problematic area of the curriculum.

The syllabus analyses and case studies conducted during the research were very long and detailed. In this report they have necessarily been condensed. Brief summaries are given of the syllabus analyses and only relevant extracts taken from the case studies.

Redefining the Problem: New Strategies

Whilst the sequence from survey to syllabus analysis and case studies was followed, the research was conducted against a background of crisis and fluidity in the educational system. A good example here is the introduction of the common examination which at the time of the research seemed to be blocked for the foreseeable future. As a result the original intention of dispassionately 'mapping' curriculum areas had to be rapidly abandoned. Maps are of little use when the world is changing. As the research progressed the researchers began to develop a 'theory of curriculum feasibility.' This had the effect of substantially changing the focus of the work away from an original preoccupation with European Studies (of which a whole range of case studies had been collected), towards the European dimension in traditional (ie. politically well-established) subjects.

The ebb, flow and ebb, of European Studies is characteristic of many innovative interdisciplinary courses. In *School Subjects and Curriculum Change* a similar evolution has been recently discerned for Environmental Studies.[3] Hence surveys provided estimates of 11 per cent of schools undertaking European Studies in 1972 (before we joined the European Community) rising rapidly to 33.3 per cent in 1977 (when the research began) but falling back to 23.3 per cent by 1980. In 1980 only 2.7 per cent of schools were taking European Studies at 'O' level.

Assessing Curriculum Feasibility

European Studies emerged in English secondary schools in the wake of comprehensivization. Most often European Studies courses were taught to those students who failed to come to terms with the foreign languages courses that they were offered. The low status which thereby accrued to European Studies by association with the less able clientele for whom the subject was originally destined has been a continuing problem in mobilizing support for the subject. In short the low status of European Studies has posed central problems in terms of both its feasibility as a subject for all abilities and its capacity to attract finance and resources. The question which any theory of curriculum feasibility must address, however, is why low status, apart from concerns of teachers' pride and dignity, should be such an overwhelming problem. To explain this requires some detailed understanding of the major traditions inside the English curriculum and some passing knowledge of the evolutionary profiles of school subjects.

To develop our study further a tentative model of the evolution of school subjects is required. As will be seen, this evolutionary profile is of considerable use in analyzing the prospects for European Studies as a separate subject.

The Evolution of School Subjects and Curriculum Traditions

David Layton, writing in 1972, tentatively defined three stages in the evolution of a school subject. In the first stage:

> the callow intruder stakes a place in the timetable, justifying its presence on grounds such as pertinence and utility. During this stage learners are attracted to the subject because of its bearing on the matters of concern to them. The teachers are rarely trained specialists but bring a missionary enthusiasm of pioneers to their task. The dominant criterion is relevant to the needs and interests of the learners.

In the interim second stage:

> a tradition of scholarly work in the subject is emerging, along with a corps of trained specialists from which teachers may be recruited. Students are still attracted to the study, but as much by its reputation and growing academic status as by its relevance to their own problems and concerns. The internal logic and discipline of the subject is becoming increasingly influential in the selection for organisation of subject matter.

And finally in the third stage:

> the teachers now constitute a professional body with established rules and values. The selection of subject matter detailed in large measure by the judgments and practices of the specialist scholars who lead enquiries in the field. Students are initiated into a tradition, their attitudes approaching passivity and resignation, a prelude to disenchantment.[4]

Layton's view of school subject evolution indicates that the pattern of aspiration for a school subject is to move away from pedagogic and utilitarian traditions towards the academic tradition. The pattern thereby discerned suits aspiring subjects like European Studies especially well. Modern Studies, as will be seen in chapter 7, has also closely followed Layton's evolutionary pattern. It should be noted, however, that there are considerable problems in generalizing the model too far. 'Applicable' subjects, like computer science for instance, seem to follow a more rapid route. Moreover not all subjects have followed this route, whilst others like Classics have risen only to fall later. In fact Layton's work has been mainly concerned with the history of scientific school subjects. Yet his evolutionary theory would fit subjects like English or geography equally well. Placing European Studies in this evolutionary pattern elucidates both the problems and pressures under which the subject at present labours.

As will be seen in chapter 2, European Studies is quite clearly confined at present to stages 1 and 2 of Layton's scheme. The claims to 'pertinence and ability' are of course often negatively couched in that the subject is devised for those who fail to cope with traditionally taught modern languages. Nonetheless, some of the pioneers do bring a 'missionary enthusiasm' to the task of teaching about Europe even though they have not been trained for such work. Moreover, a certain tradition of scholarly work has emerged from the new European Schools set up in the universities (mostly the new universities).

To appreciate why subjects aspire to follow Layton's maturational process we need to understand the links between the academic tradition and the flow of status and resources in the educational system. An understanding of the forces behind curriculum conflict over academic status will hopefully elucidate the problems encountered by contenders like European Studies.

Examinations and Academic Subjects

The linkage between the main subjects taught in school and external examinations was established with the birth of the School Certificate in 1917. The School Certificate rapidly became the major concern of grammar schools and because of the subjects thereby examined, confirmed that *academic* subjects would dominate the school timetable.

The years after 1917 saw a range of significant developments in the professionalization of teachers. With the establishment of specialized subject training courses teachers began to see themselves as part of a 'subject community'. The associated growth of subject associations both derived from and confirmed this trend. This increasing identification of secondary teachers with subject communities tended to separate them from each other, and as schools became larger, departmental forms of organization arose which reinforced the separation. Norwood summarizes the position by saying that 'subjects seem to have built themselves vested interests and rights of their own.'[5] In explaining the continuing connection between external examinations and academic subjects the part played by the vested interests of the subject groups needs to be analyzed. The dominance of academic subjects with high-status examination credentials would need to be in close harmony with the vested interest of subjects groups to explain the strength of this alliance over so long a period.

The 'subject' label is important at a number of levels: obviously as school 'examination' category, but also as title for a 'degree' or 'training course'. Perhaps most important of all, the subject defines the territory of a 'department' within each school. The subject is the major reference point in the work of the contemporary secondary school: the information and knowledge transmitted in schools is formally selected and organized through subjects. The teacher is identified by the pupils and related to them mainly through his subject specialism. Given the size of most comprehensive schools a number of teachers are required for each subject and these are normally grouped into subject 'departments'. The departments have a range of 'graded posts' for special responsibilities and for the 'Head of Department'. In this way the teacher's subject provides the means thereby his salary is decided and his career structure defined.

Within school subjects there is a clear hierarchy of status. This is based upon assumptions that certain subjects, the so-called 'academic' subjects, are suitable for the 'able' students whilst other subjects are not. In her study of resource allocation in schools Eileen Byrne has shown how more resources are given to these able students and hence to the academic subjects. She writes:

> two assumptions which might be questioned have been seen consistently to underly educational planning and the consequent resource-allocation for the more able children. First, that these necessarily need longer in the school, than non grammar pupils, and secondly, that they necessarily need more staff, more highly paid staff and more money for equipment and books.[6]

Byrne's research ended in 1965 before widespread comprehensivization and therefore refers to the tripartite system. However, referring to the new comprehensive system she wrote in 1974:

> there is . . . little indication that a majority of councils or chief officers accept in principle the need for review and reassessment of the entire process of the allocation of resources in relation to the planned application, over a period of years, of an approved and progressive policy, or coherent educational development.[7]

If Byrne's judgment is correct, then the discrimination in favour of academic subjects for the able pupils continues within the comprehensive school.

A range of studies confirm the status hierarchy between subjects. For instance, Warwick[8] reported that a 1968 survey showed that over seven per cent of the male teachers who had studied within the languages and literature group (forming just over nineteen per cent of the total sample) had become headteachers, compared with less than one per cent of those who had studied in the field of technology and handicraft (who formed just over eleven per cent of the total sample). Similarly, among male teachers 'former students of languages and literature had apparently four times as many chances as former students of music and drama, and one and a half times the chances of former students of science and mathematics of becoming headmasters'.

The hierarchy of subjects is clearly derived from traditional grammar school preferences. Stevens reports that here:

> English, Science, Languages and Mathematics are in general the subjects in which success or lack of it is significant for the children. The fact that practical subjects come low on the scale does not in itself support a assumption that more intelligent children are weak, even comparatively, at practical subjects ... The figures are rather as indicating the degree of importance with which several people but chiefly the staff, invest subjects for the children.[9]

European Studies and Academic Traditions

European Studies, like all school subjects, comprises communities of people with differing interests and intentions. Certain common factors unite these sub-groups within the subject community.

The self-interest of subject teachers is closely connected with the status of the subject in terms of its examinable knowledge. Academic subjects provide the teacher with a career structure characterized by better promotion prospects and pay than less academic subjects. More resources are given to the academic subjects which are taught to 'able' children. The conflict over the status of examinable knowledge is therefore essentially a battle over the material resources and career prospects available to each subject community.

Bringing together the notion of curricular traditions and evolutionary profiles of school subjects generates a number of hypotheses about European Studies which the research aimed to test.

A *Internal Patterns of Change*

1 European Studies whilst beginning with a stress on pertinence and ability will attempt to seek a place as an academic subject in its own right. This will be mainly because the teacher groups involved will hope to attract finance and resources in this way. Moreover status and career projects will be provided if the subject were to be widely accepted as a separate academic entity.

2 The moves to define the new subject will focus on the need for 'O' level and 'A' level academic examinations. Those involved in university scholarship in

European Schools or departments will be expected to cooperate. However, at this point, the internal changes will run into conflict with external factors and groups.

B External Conflict

3 The moves to define European Studies as a new academic subject will be opposed by those subjects already having academic status.
4 The Examination Boards (which define 'O' levels) are inevitably dominated by those trained in traditional academic subjects. Similarly university departments are organized around the traditional academic subjects.

For these reasons it is likely that any moves to establish European Studies as a new academic subject will fail.

C Regression to the traditional

If European Studies is not accepted as a new academic subject the pressures on its teachers will be rapidly perceived. With no career prospects or internal school finance the subject will be unattractive as a vehicle for individual teachers building careers. Ambitious teachers would therefore, be wise to return to their parent disciplines. In the universities the recruitment of able students will not be possible from European Studies, and the new European Studies Schools will suffer from low status by association. The same pressure to return to the parent discipline may be felt in the university sector. Abandoned by ambitious secondary teachers and losing its tertiary base, European Studies would return to its orginal base — in a pedagogic and utilitarian enclave for those who reject academic modern languages.

The New Climate of Opinion

The emergence of a 'back to basics' ideology, together with the reassertion of the divine status of traditional subjects, virtually ensures the marginality of any interdisciplinary subjects like European Studies. This tendency is reinforced by the growing lobby in favour of a 'protected curriculum' made up of 'core' subjects and echoed inside the Examination Boards by moves to reduce the 'proliferation of subject titles'.

Alongside these ideological changes are associated and complementary economic and demographic trends. A climate of public expenditure cuts and general retrenchment is linked with falling school rolls. The Briault Report[10] in 1980 from the University of Sussex clearly defines the results of these interlinked tendencies within secondary schools. The Report notes a contraction in interdisciplinary subjects because they are thought 'inefficient' in comparison with traditional subject. Certainly interdisciplinary subjects may well be less cost-effective if judged by solely financial criteria and in this sense they may come to be viewed as dispensable luxuries from the period of economic expansion which began to falter in the early 1970s.

Judgments about the curriculum feasibility of European Studies are therefore based on an underpinning theory and an assessment of an evolving political 'climate'. It should be stressed that the theory of curriculum feasibility advanced is specific to interdisciplinary 'subjects' like European Studies which pursue acceptance as 'academic' subjects. In the following chapter early surveys of European Studies are presented in abbreviated form because of the judgment about future potential for implementation. However, there is considerable evidence that problems of implementation and teacher career promotion were widely perceived by the late 1970s. The fact that so much of the comment about the difficulty of implementing interdisciplinary study will now seem commonsensical if not anachronistic is, in one sense, evidence of how far the debate about curriculum has shifted in the 1980s.

Notes

1 DES (1980) *A Framework for the School Curriculum*, London, HMSO, p. 3 para. 9.
2 Jones, H. (1977) 'Britain and Europe: A forward look' in Clatter, R. (Ed.) *Control of the Curriculum: Issues and Trends in Britain and France*, NFER, Slough, p. 126.
3 Goodson, I. (1983), *School Subjects and Curriculum Change: Case Studies in Curriculum History*, Beckenham, Croom Helm.
4 Layton, D. (1972) 'Science as General Education' *Trends in Education*, January.
5 Norwood Report (1943) 'Curriculum and Examinations in Secondary Schools'. Report of The Committee of the Secondary School Examination Council appointed by the President of the Board of Education in 1941, London, HMSO, p. 61.
6 Byrne, E.M. (1974) *Planning and Educational Inequality*, Slough, NFER, p. 29.
7 *Ibid* p. 311.
8 Warwick, D. (1976) 'Ideologies, integration and conflicts of meaning' in Flude, M. and Ahier, J. (Eds) *Educability, Schools and Ideology*, London, Croom Helm, p. 101.
9 Stevens, F. (1972) *The Living Tradition: the Social and Educational Assumptions of the Grammar School*, London, Hutchinson (3rd edition) pp. 117–118.
10 Briault, E. and Smith, F. (1980) *Falling Rolls in the Secondary School*, Slough, NFER.

1 *The National Survey*

The Europe in the School survey[1] was sent in 1980 to 400 sample secondary schools in England, Wales, Scotland and Northern Ireland. Though small because of the tight research schedule, the sample nevertheless was sufficiently representative to give a *general* impression of the role of Europe in secondary school curricula in the UK. Of the 400 schools 316 were in England: 40 in Scotland, 24 in Wales and 20 in Northern Ireland. The latter three figures represent a slightly higher ratio of regional schools to English schools than is proportionately accurate. The enlarged number was suggested by a DES statistician as necessary to ensure a better spread of types of secondary schools in Wales, Scotland and Northern Ireland.

The questionnaire[1] was composed of a section for headteachers asking them to identify the subjects in their curricula which had a modern twentieth century European content, and a section for teachers of the relevant subjects asking for details of courses with a modern European element. Just under 65 per cent of the questionnaires were completed of which about 5 per cent for various reasons, were unusable. The results are therefore based on 240 returned questionnaire, 60 per cent of the sample. The following is a breakdown of these returns by region:

	Approximate per centage of sample schools returning completed questionnaire
England	58
Wales	56
Scotland	55
N. Ireland	45

Table 1 Numbers of different institutions that returned questionnaires.

Type of School	*England*	*Wales*	*Scotland*	*N. Ireland*	*Total*
Comprehensive	133	13	15	1	162
Grammar	18	—	—	3	21
Secondary Modern	2	—	1	5	8
VIth Form College	6	—	—	—	6
Independent	25	1	6	—	32
Total	184	14	22	9	229

Eleven headteachers did not identify the type of school.

Headteacher Responses

(a) *Subjects with a European Dimension*
(N.B. separate questions were asked about European Studies)

In the headteachers' section of the questionnaire the subjects most often identified as having a modern European content are the following:

	Percentage of headteachers making mention of subject
History	78.9
Geography	75.7
Modern Languages	70.6
Economics	35.8
Social Studies (or Sociology)	14.7
Modern Studies	6.4
World Studies	5
Other subjects (in order of frequency of mention: general studies, commerce, or business studies, religious studies, government and politics, liberal studies, current affairs, humanities, theatre studies; music).	10.6

Table 2 breaks down in terms of type of school, the subjects mentioned as having a modern European content.

The few variations among the most frequently mentioned subjects have several implications: that geography courses at sixth form level frequently do not have a European content (or teachers do not select European options or examples in syllabuses); that geography courses in secondary modern schools tend to have a modern European content while history courses in the same type of school often do not.

The results for the other subjects suggest, not surprisingly, that the newer

Table 2

Subject	*Comprehensive*	*Grammar*	*Secondary Modern*	*Independent*	*Sixth Form*
History	79.2%	81.0%	57.1%	83.3%	83.3%
Geography	73.0%	85.7%	100.0%	90.0%	33.3%
Modern Languages*	72.2%	76.2%	85.7%	63.3%	66.7%
Economics	33.3%	42.9%	42.9%	50.0%	16.7%
Social Studies	19.4%	—	14.4%	6.7%	16.7%
Modern Studies	6.3%	—	14.3%	10.0%	—
World Studies	19.4%	—	14.3%	6.7%	16.7%
Other Subjects	11.1%	4.8%	—	3.3%	66.7%

*In this context modern languages has to be treated with some caution since some teachers considered that teaching a European language is *per se* teaching about modern Europe while others, more accurately, only referred to modern languages if they included a significant background or civilization element. Consequently the figure which suggests that a large number of schools are teaching about modern Europe through the medium of modern languages is probably misleading.

subjects with potential European dimensions, such as Social Studies and World Studies, are more prevalent in comprehensives, secondary moderns and sixth form colleges than in the traditional, academically-oriented grammar schools and independent schools.

In addition, the large percentage of sixth form colleges teaching about modern Europe through 'other subjects' reflects the wider range of subjects and non-examination courses such as General Studies taught in institutions dealing with sixth formers from the whole ability range. General Studies in the sixth forms of comprehensive schools was also the most frequently mentioned 'other subject' for teaching about modern Europe.

Table 3 shows regional variations where the different subjects are concerned.

Table 3

Subject	*England*	*Wales*	*Scotland*	*Northern Ireland*
History	78.0%	100.0%	80.0%	62.5%
Geography	72.3%	83.3%	100.0%	87.5%
Modern Languages	68.9%	75.0%	80.0%	87.5%
Economics	34.5%	58.3%	45.0%	12.5%
Social Studies	16.4%	16.7%	5.0%	—
Modern Studies	1.1%	—	60.0%	—
World Studies	4.5%	8.3%	—	12.5%
Other Subjects	12.4%	8.3%	—	—

Worthy of note here is that in all responding Welsh secondary schools history was considered to have a modern European dimension and in all the responding Scottish schools geography was thought to contain European content (reflecting the requirements of SCE syllabuses). The results also show that schools in Scotland and Wales more often mentioned economics as a vehicle for teaching about modern Europe than schools in England and Northern Ireland, while the newer subjects, with the exceptions of Modern Studies which was developed in Scotland, and World Studies taught by 12.5 per cent of the Northern Irish schools, were more often mentioned by English and Welsh schools than by Scottish and Northern Irish ones. General Studies, for example, was exclusively mentioned by English and Welsh schools as a vehicle for education about Europe.

The most obvious result of this part of the survey is that in all of the schools circularized throughout the British Isles the headteachers considered history, geography and modern languages, in that order, to be the principal subjects in their curricula through which education about modern Europe was taking place. There was a very large gap between the number of heads specifying these subjects and those identifying other subjects as having a significant modern European content.

(b) *European Studies*

The questions relating to separate European Studies courses on the headteachers' questionnaire yielded the following results: 23.3 per cent of all responding schools had a separate European Studies course. This figure represented roughly 27.1 per cent of the responding English schools; 15.4 per cent of the Welsh schools; 9.1 per cent of the Scottish schools and a rather surprising 33.3 per cent of the Northern Irish schools (N.B. Northern Irish schools also had the largest percentage of World Studies courses). A further 8.1 per cent of headteachers said they had formerly run a European Studies course which had been dropped. The schools which initiated then discontinued separate European Studies courses were all comprehensive all of which were in England. 37.5 per cent of the responding secondary modern schools had European Studies courses; 33.6 per cent of the comprehensives and 20 per cent of the sixth form colleges. Only 4.8 per cent of the grammar schools had the subject and none of the independent schools (which represented 13.3 per cent of the schools which returned questionnaires).

The quality and ethos of European Studies courses depend very largely on why and how they were developed in a school. In this respect it was important to know in each case which subject group had been responsible for developing and coordinating the course. Consequently the questionnaire included a question asking headteachers to identify the department in their school responsible for European Studies. The results of this are as follows:

In 75 per cent of the schools where European Studies was taught the main teacher responsible came from modern languages; this breaks down regionally as follows: 73.9 per cent of European Studies teachers in England, and 100 per cent in both Scotland and Northern Ireland.

The overall percentage of European Studies teachers coming from other subjects was, by contrast, very low. In 9.6 per cent of all the schools with the subject the teacher responsible was a historian (8,7 per cent of the European Studies teachers in the responding English schools and 100 per cent of the teachers of the subject in the Welsh schools). Geography provided only 5.8 per cent of European Studies teachers overall (6.5 per cent of teachers of the subject in English Schools) and subjects such as social studies, general studies and humanities were specified in 7.7 per cent of cases (8.7 per cent of the English European Studies teachers). At one of the English schools European Studies was the responsibility of the Remedial Department (an individual example of a trend subsequently made clear in the case studies: the interconnection between European Studies and 'less able' pupil clienteles).

In Wales, in all the responding schools with European Studies, the responsible teacher was drawn from history (which seems to reflect the importance of the modern European dimension in Welsh secondary school history courses suggested in the earlier subject responses).

Table 4 Shows variations between types of school:

Table 4

European Studies Teachers drawn from the following subject areas:	*Type of School*			
	Comprehensives	*Grammar*	*Secondary Modern*	*Sixth Form*
Modern Languages	73.3%	100%	100%	50%
History	8.9%	—	—	50%
Geography	0.7%	—	—	—
Other subjects	8.9%	—	—	
(missing observations)	2.2%			

This shows that at the time of the survey European Studies teachers were being drawn from a greater variety of subjects in comprehensive schools than in other types of school, even though modern language departments provided by far the most. In sixth form colleges, on the other hand, European Studies teachers were equally divided between linguists and historians.

Teacher Responses

The second section of the questionnaire required teachers within the schools circulated to fill in details of any courses they are involved in teaching which have a modern European content. Of the 750 responses: 26.3 per cent were from teachers of history; 25.2 per cent geography; 21.4 per cent modern languages; 10.3 per cent economics; 6.6 per cent European Studies; 4.2 per cent Social Studies; 1.8 per cent Modern Studies; 3.2 per cent other subjects (mainly general studies). History, geography and modern languages, therefore, made up the bulk of the responses — 72.9 per cent – with all the other subjects combined representing only 26 per cent of the teachers' sections returned.

Age Groups

78.3 per cent of the responding teachers gave details of courses with a European content taught to the 14–16 age range and 52 per cent of them referred in addition to courses taught to sixth form pupils. *Table* 5 shows what percentages of the courses mentioned are taught to these two age groups:

Table 5

	SUBJECT								
AGE GROUP	*Econ*	*Euro Studs*	*Geog*	*Hist*	*Mod Langs*	*Mod Studs*	*Soc Studs*	*Wld Studs*	*Other*
14–16	39.7	87.0	87.2	73.8	92.9	100	93.3	57.1	50.0
Sixth Form	91.8	15.2	45.1	49.7	58.9	66.7	16.7	42.9	60.0

This table shows that traditional subjects together with World Studies, Modern Studies and General Studies etc. were well represented at both 14+ and 16+, while European Studies and Social Studies were taught predominantly at 14+ level. A very large proportion of the economics courses mentioned were taught to the older age group. The courses with a modern European content taught to the 16+ group were predominantly found, unsurprisingly, in the sixth form colleges followed by grammar schools (71.4 per cent of courses detailed) and independent schools (68.2 per cent).

Examination Courses

The teachers responding for each subject gave details of both examinable and non-examinable courses. Of the seven hundred and fifty teachers' sections returned 49.1 per cent detailed courses leading to CSE; 61.2 per cent to GCE 'O'-level or SCE 'O' grade; 6 per cent to GCE 'A/O' level; 2.2 per cent to CEE and 48.3 per cent to GCE 'A' level or SCE 'H' grade. By comparison with the other examinations the numbers of subjects being examined at CEE and 'A/O' level was negligible.

Table 6 gives a percentage breakdown, according to teacher responses, of the number of courses within each subject with a European content which led in 1981 to the available range of public examinations. The percentages reflect the fact that teachers indicating specific subjects in the questionnaire may have done so at a number of examinable levels.

The table indicates that newer subjects in the school curriculum such as Social Studies, European Studies and to a lesser extent General Studies etc. are mainly examined at CSE level. A large proportion, too, of the modern language courses detailed are also examined at CSE (some of these referred to language studies courses which have a considerable background or civilization content — more than can be found in many GCE modern language courses).

Table 6

	SUBJECT								
EXAMINATION	*Econ*	*Euro Studies*	*Geog*	*Hist*	*Modern Langs*	*Modern Studies*	*Social Studies*	*World Studies*	*Other*
CSE Modes 1, 2 or 3	20.0	86.5	41.3	43.8	65.9	18.2	88.5	50.0	52.9
GCE (O) Level or SCE (O) Grade	55.7	2.7	70.3	69.3	72.9	100.0	19.2	—	17.6
GCE (A/O) Level	1.4	2.7	9.0	4.5	7.8	—	3.8	50.0	5.9
CEE	1.4	13.5	0.6	1.7	0.8	—	3.8	—	5.9
GCE (A) Level or SCE (H) Grade	77.1	—	45.8	54.5	61.2	81.8	11.5	—	41.2

The 'O' level figures are consistent with earlier findings: a high percentage of courses in the more traditional subjects mentioned — geography, history and modern languages led to this examination. A sizeable proportion of the economics courses mentioned also led to 'O' level while all of the modern studies courses mentioned led to SCE 'O' grade.

By contrast the survey showed the smallest percentage by far of all courses examined at 'O' level to be within European Studies — only 2.7 per cent of all the European Studies courses detailed in the completed questionnaires. This was in sharp contrast to the 86.5 per cent of European Studies courses leading to CSE. This was mainly due to the paucity of available 'O' level examinations in European Studies but it probably also reflected a tendency within schools to offer the subject to the lower ability bands. In addition, a very low percentage of the specified subjects were taken at CEE level (2.2 per cent) but of these a much higher proportion of courses were in European Studies than in any other subject: 13.5 per cent of European Studies courses, therefore, according to this survey were almost exclusively examined at CSE and CEE with only a tiny percentage of courses leading to 'O' and 'A/O' level. (Currently there are still no 'A' levels available in the subject but a new 'O' level has been developed by the Associated Examining Board [see Appendix 1].)

At GCE 'A/O' level the subject which leads the field is World Studies which, according to the teacher responses, was examined mainly at this level and at CSE.

The highest proportion of courses with a modern European element taken to GCE 'A' level or SCE 'H' grade were in Modern Studies, economics and modern languages. The lowest occurred within Social Studies (or sociology): only 11.5 per cent of courses which led to 'A' level as opposed to the 88.5 per cent leading to CSE. Although the survey revealed that Social Studies courses can be taken to both GCE 'O' and 'A' levels, the general impression of the subject created by these statistics is not unlike the one created by European Studies, both these subjects being mainly taught to the 14–16 age group and leading predominantly to CSE.

Table 7 shows how the percentage of courses leading to the different examinations differed according to type of school.

Table 7

	INSTITUTION				
EXAMINATION	*Comprehen-sive*	*Grammar*	*Secondary Modern*	*Indepen-dent*	*Sixth Form College*
CSE Mode 1, 2 or 3	61.6	21.2	57.1	9.5	—
'O' Level	59.8	65.2	76.2	69.8	23.8
'A/O' Level	6.0	4.5	9.5	3.2	9.5
CEE	2.9	—	—	—	4.8
'A' Level	41.7	72.7	33.3	74.6	71.4

These findings confirmed that independent schools and grammars are likely to have fewer CSE courses in subjects with a European dimension that comprehensives and secondary modern schools, and teach principally to GCE 'O' and 'A' level. The responding secondary modern schools seemed to have a high proportion of 'O' level courses (but this could be a misleading picture of secondary modern school practice since only a small number figured in the sample and returned questionnaires). The greatest percentage of 'A' level courses were in independent schools, sixth form colleges and grammar schools.

According to the survey, only sixth form colleges and comprehensive schools were taking the subjects mentioned to the CEE examination.

Table 8 shows the regional variations in the percentage of courses leading to the different public examinations.

This suggests that the largest percentage of CSE courses in the various subjects were being taught in England and Northern Ireland followed by Wales, whereas very few courses led to this examination in Scotland where

Table 8

	REGION			
EXAMINATION	*England*	*Wales*	*Scotland*	*Northern Ireland*
CSE Modes 1, 2, 3	54.5	47.8	10.7	59.3
GCE 'O' Level	58.7	60.9	72.0 (SCE 'O' Grade)	77.8
'A/O'	5.2	6.5	12.0	3.7
CEE	2.8	—	—	—
GCE 'A' Level	43.0	71.7	61.3 (SCE 'H' Grade)	55.6

subjects were mainly examined at SCE 'O' and 'H' grade (72 per cent and 61.3 per cent of the courses mentioned by responding Scottish teachers). A large percentage of the subjects led to 'O' level in Northern Ireland while the responses for Wales revealed the largest proportional number of 'A' levels.

Proportional European Content

Attempts to elicit information on the actual proportions of courses devoted to the study of modern Europe created problems since it proved impossible to find a question formula which would fit all cases and take equally into account the considerable variations in school practice and the great diversity of existing syllabuses and school based courses. In addition, so many practical factors affect the time allocated to the different components of a single course, that unless they are extremely rigidly structured and timetabled they are difficult to quantify. In consequence teachers understandably found this question difficult to answer and added many unanalysable comments and provisos.

For all these reasons the proportions of European content per subject, given in *Table 9* are very approximate.

Table 9

Approximate European Content	*Economics*	*Geography*	*History*	*Modern Languages*	*Modern Studies*	*Social Studies*	*World Studies*	*Other Subjects*
100% of the course	—	11.0%	17.9%	31.2%	—	—	—	—
50%	—	15.2%	49.7%	10.6%	—	10.7%	28.6%	15.0%
33.3%	5.5%	17.7%	13.3%	5.0%	15.4%	3.6%	28.6%	20.0%
25%	2.7%	25.0%	8.7%	5.0%	15.4%	—	—	10.0%
Less	91.8%	29.3%	7.5%	46.1%	69.2%	85.7%	42.9%	55.0%

The general picture revealed here is that in all subjects except history (and obviously European Studies which it was not necessary to include), the study of modern Europe most often accounted for less than a quarter of the total course. Inevitably history, geography and modern languages are presented as the subjects which have the largest European component. The 56.1 per cent of modern language teachers who said they were spending a third or less of their courses on teaching about Europe were probably the ones accurately interpreting European content as meaning background or civilization elements. History therefore has the largest proportional modern European content of all the subjects which feature in the survey returns, followed by geography.

At the bottom of the scale economics and Social Studies seemed to have the smallest modern European element (reflecting the fact that syllabuses in these subjects are related to Great Britain rather than elsewhere). World Studies on the other hand appeared to have a sizeable European content with 57.2 per cent of teachers devoting a third or more of their course to it.

Modern Studies has an obligatory modern Europe element at 'O' grade but it composes 25 per cent or more of only 30.8 per cent of the courses referred to in the survey, probably because in the Modern Studies syllabuses Europe has to compete with many other course components.

Teacher Training Courses

Teachers of all relevant subjects were asked whether they had received any special training or attended any courses on teaching about Europe; 41 per cent answered in the affirmative, 26.1 per cent specifying universities;0.8 per cent polytechnics; 10.6 per cent colleges of education and 3.3 per cent other institutions.

The 26.1 per cent university figure is possibly misleading since some responding teachers often considered a university degree in a subject with a European dimension to constitute special training in teaching about Europe.

The percentage of teachers from each type of school who said they had received training or attended courses on teaching about Europe at the different institutions is given in *Table 10.*

Table 10

INSTITUTION OF HIGHER OR FURTHER EDUCATION	*SCHOOL*				
	Comprehensive	*Grammar*	*Secondary Modern*	*Independent*	*Sixth Form College*
University	25.2	36.1	25.0	26.9	27.3
Polytechnic	0.6	1.4	4.8	—	—
College of education	14.3	6.9	8.3	5.6	—
Elsewhere	3.1	1.4	4.2	—	18.2

This shows that even allowing for reference by some teachers to their university degree as specialized training about Europe, universities predominate as the institutions where most responding teachers from all types of school, particularly grammars, have attended courses on Europe and European issues.

Colleges of education which are the next most frequently mentioned institutions have provided European-oriented courses for a much smaller number, while polytechnics seem to have done little in this field. In-service training and day courses on European education in other centres and institutions seem to attract considerably more teachers from sixth form colleges than from other types of school.

Regionally, the percentages of all responding teachers who received some training about Europe at the different institutions breaks down as given in *Table 11*.

Table 11

INSTITUTION OF HIGHER OR FURTHER EDUCATION	*REGION*			
	England	*Wales*	*Scotland*	*Northern Ireland*
University	25.1	26.9	34.1	46.4
Polytechnic	0.9	—	—	—
College of education	10.7	3.8	25.9	17.9
Elsewhere	3.8	—	1.2	—

This shows universities and colleges of education predominating throughout the country as the institutions where most teachers have received training about modern Europe. Again the possibility of some considering a first degree or teacher training within a specialist subject as training in teaching about Europe cannot be ruled out, although the majority of teachers responding to this question specified special conferences or day, weekend or longer courses on Europe in the curriculum.

Of the teachers from the different subject areas who attended courses or received special training about Europe, the largest number specialized in history, geography and Modern Studies followed by World Studies, economics and modern languages. Again, the figures may refer in part to teachers' first degrees. Interestingly European Studies teachers are the only subject group to attend more special courses in other institutions than in universities. *Table 12* shows the precise percentages of teachers per subject to have received special training about Europe in the different institutions.

Table 12

	INSTITUTION			
SUBJECT	*University*	*Polytechnic*	*College of education*	*Elsewhere*
Economics	24.6	—	9.6	2.7
European Studies	8.5	2.3	6.8	12.8
Geography	29.6	—	20.1	1.1
History	34.2	0.5	10.2	4.3
Modern Languages	25.7	0.7	7.2	3.3
Modern Studies	30.8	—	23.1	—
Social Studies	10.0	3.7	16.7	—
World Studies	28.6	—	—	—
Other Subjects	13.6	4.5	13.6	—

Survey Conclusions

According to the survey, history was the subject consistently claimed to have the strongest modern European dimension, followed by geography. This, together with some of the other main findings of the *Europe in the School* survey, reflects the findings of three other surveys, regional, national and international undertaken during the 70s[2]. In all three of the earlier surveys history and geography head the list of subjects with a modern European content while modern languages, which comes next is mentioned with the same provisos that are made in the *Europe in the School* survey. Of the subjects with a smaller modern European content, economics was the most frequently mentioned, another finding which is duplicated in the *Europe in the School* survey. The earlier surveys also found Modern Studies to be the most frequently mentioned subject after history and geography in Scotland

Where separate European Studies courses are concerned, the earlier surveys found an increase in such courses between 1972–77, mainly in comprehensive and secondary modern schools. They also found a strong relationship between the development of European Studies and the reorganization of schools into the comprehensive system. In the 1972 national survey 11 per cent of responding schools had the subject and in the 1977 regional survey, 33.3 per cent of schools (which is probably a larger than average figure because of the area's proximity to the Continent). Nevertheless this shows a sharp increase, and all three earlier surveys refer to European Studies as a 'growth area'. The *Europe in the School* survey shows this increase to have stabilized and even started to drop slightly with 8 per cent of responding comprehensive schools reporting that they have discontinued the subject.

The age groups to which the subject is offered and the examinations to which it leads appear to have changed very little in the last eight years, i.e. in all of the surveys the subject is taught predominantly to the 14–16 group, with the regional survey schools offering it also to low ability 11–14 pupils. There appears to have been little development in the subject at sixth form level, a fact confirmed in the *Europe in the School* findings. On the evidence of the three earlier surveys and the *Europe in the School* findings, CSE mode 3 continues to be the main examination for European Studies.

Where the different subject areas responsible for European Studies are concerned, the 1972 survey showed European Studies teachers to be drawn from miscellaneous disciplines. The 1977 regional survey, however, found a marked preponderance of modern language teachers, (80 per cent of the European Studies teachers responding), a phenomenon which was also marked in the *Europe in the School* survey (75 per cent of European Studies teachers).

Another regional survey, *The Study of Europe in Secondary Schools in Cumbria and Lancashire* 1978–79, also shows this trend: '26 out of the 33 schools mounting courses in European Studies, French Studies or German Studies, left responsibility for devising and teaching such courses in the hands of Modern Languages Departments'[3]

Another finding of the Cumbria and Lancashire survey is that: 'in all but *one* instance European Studies was taught to less able pupils who had shown themselves to be apparently incapable of making satisfactory progress in the learning of a modern foreign language'[4]. The survey reported that 62.5 per cent of the schools doing European Studies 'taught the subject to pupils in years 2 and/or 3, as an alternative to the study of a modern language or, in one case, as a supplement to the study of a modern language.'

In his concluding comments following the summary of the survey findings, the author warned of the possible future consequences of leaving so much concentrated teaching about Europe in the hands of modern linguists:

> unless steps are taken to resolve the confusion (about the precise place of studies of Europe in the curriculum), it would seem likely that the whole field of European education in the secondary curriculum will become discredited and, with the advent of effective methods of Modern Language teaching to pupils of average and low ability, will cease to feature as a serious element in secondary education in all but a minority of schools.[5]

Current developments in modern language teaching across the ability range do indeed suggest the possibility of a gradual undermining of the principal rationale for separate European Studies courses. As a result, other subjects in the curriculum may have to take total responsibility for teaching about modern Europe. The most appropriate subjects seem, on the evidence of the *Europe in the School* and earlier surveys, to be history, geography, modern languages and economics. These, therefore, are the subjects which need to be examined as a priority in order to see what contributions they are already making, or could make, to education about Europe in secondary schools.

In the following chapters analyses will be made of current trends in European Studies and these four subjects in an attempt to pinpoint their potential for study of Europe. In addition, there will be a section on Modern Studies which is an example of a new multidisciplinary subject with a strong European dimension.

* This report concentrates on European Studies courses and French and German Studies courses in secondary schools

Notes

1 The questionnaire for the *Europe in the School* survey was designed and dispatched with the guidance of the Schools Council *Impact and Take-up* project team, the DES statistics department and the Computer Centre at the University of Sussex. The returns were analysed by the University of Sussex Arts & Social Sciences Research Support Unit & the Computer Centre.

2 Wheatcroft, M. and Freeman, P. (1972) *Patterns of Teaching about contemporary Europe in Secondary Schools*, CCES, University of Sussex.
European Studies in East and West Sussex, LEA survey 1977
Freriks, W. (1977) *The European Dimension in the Secondary School Curriculum in EC(9).*

3 Peacock, D. (1980) *The Study of Europe in Secondary Schools in Cumbria and Lancashire*, Lancaster, St. Martin's College.

4 *Ibid.* p. 38.

5 *Ibid.* p. 42.

2 *European Studies*

As we have noted in the Introduction, the research methods derive from an underlying theory of curriculum feasibility. The major testing ground for this theory is the curriculum area in secondary schools which concentrates solely on teaching about Europe: European Studies as a separate subject.

European Studies became a fashionable curriculum innovation in the 1960s. The new synthesis originated from two quite unconnected events: firstly, the growth of the European movement expressed through agencies like the European Commission and the Council of Europe which encouraged the development of education about Europe. Essentially the messiahs of the new Europe were concerned to encourage an awareness of a common European heritage and European governments associated with the European Cultural Convention in 1966 were exhorted to do everything within their power to ensure that all disciplines concerned — for instance history, geography, literature, modern languages — contributed to the creation of a European consciousness.[1] Secondly, the changing organization of the British secondary school system and curriculum during the 1960s encouraged the development of European Studies. The interdisciplinary or integrated approach was a major element in the curriculum reforms initiated in the 1960s and 1970s to meet the new pedagogical demands created by comprehensivization of schools, mixed ability classes and the Raising of the Schod Leaving Age to 16 in 1972.

The co-existence of newer interdisciplinary subjects with established separate subjects within a single school has led, however, to a two-tier approach within the educational system, i.e. traditional academic subjects leading to external examinations tend to be regarded as 'high status knowledge', and newer integrated or interdisciplinary subjects as 'low status' knowledge.[2]

The continuing division in British curricula between the two nations of 'the able' and the 'less able' is very pertinent when considering European Studies. Most courses in the subject have been initiated and developed in modern languages departments as shown in a number of different surveys undertaken during the 1970s, and the 1980 *Europe in the School* survey indicates that the majority of courses remain the responsibility of modern language teachers. This happened initially because, with the introduction of the comprehensive system, modern language departments were faced by an enormous challenge: how to teach their subjects to the whole ability range. In the past, three-quarters of the school population had gone to secondary modern schools. The 1963 Newsom Survey had noted that just under a third of the modern schools provided some foreign language teaching, mainly in French and largely confined to the ablest pupils. Thus, for a section of the comprehensive school population, somewhere over half the intake, defined as 'less able', learning a modern language was to be very much a new experience.

What was needed, it was therefore argued, was to inform these pupils about the background and lives of the foreign people whose language was to be studied. Thereby the interest of the less able might be engaged and their motivation to learn enhanced. A number of teachers have tried out this idea. Though in a sense these teachers represent a 'second wave' in the introduction of European Studies, since their efforts are well documented, they throw light on the general position of modern language pioneers introducing the new subject. Basically, they confirm Michael Williams' contention that:

> many European Studies courses have begun with the feeling of modern language teachers that a small 'pill' of language will be taken by weak pupils if it is strongly dissolved in a heavy surfeit of jam, i.e. non-language study.

Williams also argues that:

> without doubt the teaching of European Studies to pupils in the first two years of comprehensive schools has become part of the debate over equality of curricula opportunity. If French is to be taught to one child, then some would argue it should be taught to all. To make it palatable to the academically weaker pupils, especially when they are taught in mixed ability groups, much time must be spent arousing their interest, motivating them to learn the language by using non-language studies.[3]

The desire to use European Studies as a vehicle for motivating the less able inevitably inverts the normal process by which school subjects are defined. In the traditional manner the 'intellectual disciplines' of the subject are defined and the pedagogic strategies with which to teach these disciplines are then formulated. European Studies, introduced because pedagogic strategies to teach languages could not be formulated, has in many cases evolved using pupil interest as the major criterion for content selections. For example, Barry Jones described in 1975 a project with the bottom 'streams' in the fourth and fifth year of two comprehensive schools in Cambridgeshire. The major aim of the project was to improve the teaching of modern languages to the 'less able' and the first strategy was 'to list the topics which the pupils stated and demonstrated were of interest to them in their everyday lives'. This was justified so that teachers could 'create situations in which the second language (French) could be perceived by the pupils as a means of communicating information in which they showed a stated interest'. The themes which thereby emerged in order of popularity were:

1 Pop Stars: their appearance, their lives, their travels, their concerts.
2 Horoscopes.
3 'Problem page'.
4 Shops and markets.
5 Camping holidays.
6 Eating and drinking.
7 Advertisements.
8 Entertainment: films, television programmes and discotheques.
9 Clothes.
10 Fairgrounds.
11 Sport: football, cars and motorcycling.
12 Make-up and hairstyles (girls).
13 Slimming (girls).
14 Cartoons: films and 'comic strips'.

The course thereby focussed on this range of content to substantiate the teachers' claim to be 'concentrating our efforts on what interested the pupils'.[4]

A number of European Studies examination courses have been developed over the last decade. These are mainly CSEs although there are some pilot 'O' level and alternative ordinary level syllabuses. An analysis of some of these illustrates the range and diversity of content that exists within the subject.

Syllabus Commentary

A review of European Studies syllabuses reveals a range of aims and objectives which veer from the brutally honest to the extremely optimistic — with very little in between! In the first category comes the following example:

> to provide children for some reason unable to follow a language course with a corpus of basic knowledge about the main countries of Western Europe and their inhabitants.

This is coupled with the desire:

> to complement, as far as possible, the teaching of the history, geography and commerce departments insofar as these are concerned with European affairs.

An optimistic syllabus provides for the following aims and objectives:

Aims

To encourage the student to achieve an understanding of contemporary European societies. To use and develop the skills and concepts already being fostered in the pure disciplines within the context of an interdisciplinary mode of enquiry.

Objectives

Knowledge of: (1) the dimensions of the countries of Europe and of how the boundaries of Europe have altered through history; (2) the geographical features of Europe and how they affect the communications systems of the different countries; (3) the (recent) history of Europe expressed through some of the central events and characters; (4) the legacy of European culture expressed in art, architecture, literature and music. An understanding of: (5) contemporary European society through national studies which concentrate on the life of the people of particular nations; (6) one or more European languages sufficient for survival in the particular country whose language is being studies; (7) current problems and prospects for Europe.

Neither of these polarized versions of European Studies is in any sense wrong. However, syllabus analysis reveals that both versions carry within them a range of potential pitfalls. Examination boards' scrutiny of exam syllabus submissions are much concerned with the internal logic of the proposal: does the course proceed in a way that is likely to implement the stated aims and objectives? As Frances Lawrence has noted:

> it often seems that authors, once having set out aims and objectives as a ritual preamble, proceed to construct the syllabus without further reference to either. Such internal confusion is not only likely to arouse the hostility of Examination Boards if the syllabus is submitted for their approval, but it also endangers the efficiency with which the syllabus can be taught.[5]

It is, of course, easy to indicate contradictions, and anybody who has tried to draw up a syllabus is only too aware of the difficulties. Nonetheless, a few examples will clarify the point. Some syllabuses give their major aim as the development of certain individual study skills and the acquisition of concepts, but then set out examinations solely based on straight factual recall:

'EEC stands for . . . .'

'The original members of the EEC were . . .'

'The EEC has its headquarters in . . .'

The polarities evidenced in syllabus aims and objectives can also be found in their statements of content. Some syllabuses are characterized by a small number of very generalized themes: 'work and leisure', 'society' or 'conflict', etc. Such themes give little or no indication of what ideas are to be put across. Such generalized schemes require a close definition of the concepts that are assumed to be known and those that are to be developed. This conceptual analysis is seldom forthcoming. Moreover, thematic content often focusses on pupil-chosen topics, even though the clientele of the courses are often so thoroughly disillusioned with any sort of school subjects that any such choice is a non-starter.

Syllabuses which focus more on the definition of a body of knowledge titled 'European Studies' are often characterized by a frightening overload of content. This is probably the most common fault in European studies courses: an observer is left wondering how some syllabuses could be reasonably covered in ten years, let alone the two years allocated in most schools. Like the students, the syllabus makers have found that one of the most difficult tasks is selection.

Individual Syllabus Analysis

In 1980 a small number of syllabuses which demonstrate the range of examinations available were selected for detailed analysis. The full analyses are to be found in *Europe in the School Interim Report* Vol. 2 which was produced specifically for the use of teachers. The syllabuses selected were the following:

North West Regional Examinations Board (NWREB)	Pilot CSE Mode 1
Southern Regional Examinations Board (SREB)	Proposed CSE Mode 1
South East Regional Examinations Board (SEREB)	Draft CSE Mode 1
South Western Regional Examination Board (SWREB)	Proposed CSE Mode 1
University of Cambridge Local Examinations Syndicate (CAM)	GCE Pilot 'O' Level (devised for Ingatestone School)
Associated Examining Board (AEB)	Proposed GCE 'O' level
Associated Examining Board (AEB)	GCE 'A/O' level[6]
University of London Examination Board (LON)	GCE 'A/O' level

Individual Syllabus Commentary

Assessment

The syllabuses are similar in that they all have a main section devoted to a core content which is to be terminally examined by written paper. The exam papers related to this main section account for most of the final marks in all cases except the Ingatestone Paper 1 which has a 50 per cent weighting and the SREB and SEREB Common Core external examinations which are both weighted 40 per cent.

All of the syllabuses have a final section involving a choice of topics or themes to be either examined by terminal written examination or assessed as course or project work. Choice of options varies widely between syllabuses, for example the NWREB Pilot CSE offers a choice between three special topics for school-based work whereas the AEB 'A/O' level gives pupils a completely free choice of topic provided they are based on areas relevant to the main body of the syllabus. The final optional paper on course work is usually weighted lower than the core syllabus paper except in the case of the SREB proposed CSE mode 1 in which the two chosen options account for 60 per cent of the final marks.

The SEREB draft CSE also has an important course work element with course work assessment on the common core accounting for 40 per cent and the option, for which there is a choice of assessment procedures 20 per cent.

The most school-based syllabus is the Cambridge 'O' level developed for Ingatestone School, for which Paper 1 is externally set and marked to the school's own syllabus; Paper 2 is internally set and marked by the school and externally moderated; and Paper 3 (Project) is marked by the school and externally moderated.

Pedagogic Orientation

All of the syllabuses require candidates to display a combination of descriptive, analytic and evaluative skills. The CSE courses tend to lay stress on the first of these and usually have a written examination section devoted to short answer and data response questions, several of which may be compulsory. These are generally followed by a second section and sometimes a second paper involving longer answers of an essay type. The options or course work essays require more in-depth analysis (for example SWREB CSE 'a single extended piece or two or three shorter pieces of a comparative and analytical nature'), nevertheless in most courses option work is usually weighted lower than the examination papers involving descriptive and factual recall skills.

More stress is put on understanding, analysis and evaluation in the GCE syllabuses. The AEB 'A/O' course, for example, is at pains to specify that:

> it is not intended that the syllabus and the examination papers shall stress exclusively factual recall, but that candidates shall understand the current state of Europe, recognize relationships that exist, and perceive factors that have caused evolution, change and modifications, and that may do so in the future.

This can be contrasted with the SEREB draft CSE which unequivocally emphasizes factual recall which comes first on its list of objectives and which rates 30 per cent on the assessment chart as opposed to 10 per cent for analysis and evaluation. Similarly the NWREB Pilot CSE syllabus specifies in its aims factual knowledge as the first requirement of the candidate, followed by the development of study skills. Assessment and evaluation of material come last in the list of eight objectives.

Content

There is a prescribed core syllabus in all the examination courses analyzed. Only the NWREB draft CSE offers a choice of core content (four units to be studied out of eight).

All the core syllabuses stress historical, geographical, political and economic aspects of the development of modern Europe with only the Ingatestone Cambridge 'O' level course having additional social and cultural sections which are of equal importance to the historical, political and economic elements.

The SREB proposed CSE has a more focussed core syllabus than most with the content divided into four 'situations' including, unusually a study of *People and Languages in Europe.*

Three of the courses have a modern language element: the *Ingatestone* syllabus in which it is compulsory though limited to text comprehension; the *SEREB* draft CSE in which it is an option and limited to very basic vocabulary; and the SREB proposed CSE where it is more developed (French, German or Spanish, to be assessed by oral test, aural comprehension test and reading comprehension test).

The option sections in most of the syllabuses offer choices from a very wide field, NWREB being the exception as it offers only three specified options.

In the other syllabuses the option sections are characterized by very generalized themes, the SEREB section being fairly typical:

> 1. European Diary. 2. A comparative study of People in Europe (to include two contrasting countries and the UK). 3. A detailed study of the significance of one or more internationally famous Europeans.[7] 4. Environmental problems. 5. Minority and Nationalist Groups. 6. A study of a town area elsewhere in Europe linked or twinned with one in the UK. 7. The Arts. 8. Language option.

The AEB 'A/O' goes even further by giving complete freedom of choice of course work topics provided they form part of the European Studies, while the SWREB CSE asks only for selected course work of a comparative and general nature reflecting the aim of the examination'.

All of the syllabuses seem generally ambitious in what they wish to achieve and the ground they aim to cover. Some show a tendency to overload their content in an attempt to cover every possible aspect of modern Europe. The University of London 'A/O' syllabus is an example of this. Paper 1 Section B states:

> candidates will be expected to have a general knowledge of the physical and human geography of Europe. Awareness of the following regional differences will be expected; climate, landscape, resources endowment (especially energy), population distribution and urban development. National and regional contrasts in affluence, life style and types of farming should be considered. There should be some understanding of the factors influencing industrial location and of the environment and society, with the possible creation of social and economic problems, e.g. migrant workers, pollution.

Area of Europe Covered

The University of London syllabus is the most explicit listing twenty eight countries from both East and West Europe. (This, like the content of the syllabus, suggests an overambitious attempt to cover *all* aspects of contemporary Europe.) However, in all of the syllabuses Western Europe inevitably predominates, probably for the reasons suggested in the AEB 'A/O' introductory section: 'the syllabus is intended to cover the whole of Europe, but it is understood that the range of material available and the greater ease of arranging visits may well result in a primary emphasis on Western Europe'.

Most of the syllabuses make some reference to Eastern Europe in their historical, political and economic sections and the Ingatestone in particular includes detailed study of East European countries (Yugoslavia and Romania). Two of the courses (SWREB CSE and London 'A/O') have sections on Europe and the rest of the world.

Conclusion

Of all the syllabuses the SEREB draft CSE is most emphatic in its aims to foster a sense of European identity in pupils:

1 To develop pupils' awareness of themselves as Europeans.
2 To develop an awareness and understanding of the different ways

of life of Europeans.

3 To encourage an understanding of the different aspects of Europe and its peoples.

Most of the courses lay more stress on factual knowledge and understanding of contemporary European events and issues than on developing a sense of 'Europeanness' in pupils.

All of the syllabuses include sections on European moves to unity, cooperation and integration. In most cases these sections, for reasons of chronology, come after others on division and conflict in Europe although in the NWREB 1982 pilot CSE syllabus, section 6: *Political Life* changes to *Unity and Division* — a reversal in the usual order of the wording which suggests a welcome change in emphasis. Similarly the proposed AEB 'O' level puts 'an awareness of movements towards unity within Europe' high on its list of aims which contrasts with the stress laid by most of the other European Studies courses on problems, conflict and diversity.

On the whole the courses examined all make a serious attempt to inform and encourage awareness of contemporary European history, geography, political and economic life, with occasional emphasis on sociological and cultural factors, particularly in the options, but these are usually secondary in importance to the main core elements.

Inevitably some courses seem over-ambitious in scope, seeking to cover geographical areas and fields of knowledge which are perhaps too wide to be fitted into the time available and, in the case of some CSEs, containing concepts which are too demanding of the student clientele with which European Studies courses are usually associated. This may be inevitable with a subject entitled European Studies which encompasses so many countries and concepts as to be almost impossible to limit and define. Some kind of breakdown into manageable areas and topics, as in the SREB CSE, is essential to avoid overloading of content.

The range of syllabuses available highlights the paradox that the bulk of European Studies pupils, children who are often deemed incapable of formulating the most elementary phrase in a foreign language, are considered perfectly able to assimilate a whole wealth of facts and concepts of a sophisticated, thought-provoking nature from a wide spectrum of areas of knowledge, the diversity of which they will find in few other subjects.

School Case Studies

This section examines the problems and possibilities faced by individual schools in establishing European Studies. The section starts by briefly summarizing teachers' views on the introduction of the subject and its subsequent development. This is followed by a case study of the introduction of a European Studies course in a comprehensive school. The study was mainly put together by the teacher involved, Mr. K. Boyden, and therefore substantially employs his terms and perspectives. The second case study looks at the examples most normally found in schools: European Studies for the less able.

The major concern of this section is to illuminate the internal school processes whereby European Studies becomes established as a CSE and 'O'-level option and as a separate school 'department'. In this way the research begins to focus on problems of curriculum feasibility.

Case Study 1

The Introduction of European Studies Courses

Initially, research focussed on observation, interviews, correspondence and documentary analysis. The focus was mainly on established comprehensive schools, but case studies were also undertaken of a grammar school going comprehensive and a sixth form college. A number of common problems and perceptions can be tentatively defined which relate to certain major 'issues' in the emergence and evolution of European Studies in all of the case study schools.

The dominant perception among teachers recalling the beginning of their courses is of haphazard and idiosyncratic reasons for introducing European Studies:

> at the time I was head of geography in the Faculty of Social Studies. In the summer the headmistress suddenly decided we would have European Studies. It was to be non-exam only.
>
> In my school languages were going down badly with whole sets of kids. The Deputy Head decided something new was needed . . . for the 'C' set anyhow . . .

The theme of or the 'non-exams' was most common among language teachers:

> My head of languages gave me the responsibility for devising it (the European Studies course). He wanted something fairly broad, fairly wide for the non-exams. Something to be taught from Macdonald's Atlas . . . that was the only book we had that was of any use . . . there were mutinies in the ranks . . . the teachers had seldom seen this band of kids. He introduced it just like that on the first day of September.
>
> I think it came from the staff originally, I mean the Head was very keen on it to start with and there were certain members of departments like myself, liberal studies, history and modern languages and geography . . . Basically, students were saying 'we've had enough of this'. Universal apathy reigned and we just felt like giving them

something else ... and European Studies came up. At the same time the Head was very helpful indeed and was looking for an expansion of the sixth form option thing ... we've got, you know, a very wide range of 'A' level students, and we wanted one year courses for the people who had a lot of free time ...

A number of teachers described their awareness of the dangers which flowed from hasty considerations of what to do with the less involved pupils. In several instances this led to a more positive view developing of the potentialities and position of European Studies:

Well you see ... I think as far as we were concerned this was a conscious turning away from what was beginning to develop and that was people starting to say 'what are we going to do with the youngsters who are not learning French or German?' ... From the point of view of timetable convenience they ought to be doing something associated ...' let them learn about Germany, you know, and what you have for tea in Brussels or something' ... We were so frightened that this was what European Studies was going to become, some sort of dustbin ... I think we have consciously turned away from that and although I think we haven't got to lose sight of it eventually, I think we've got to come back to terms with this after we've done the other things ... I think we've got to go ahead from our middle school into our sixth form first and get that thing right and get the subject established with status ... then we may be able to add on these less able youngsters.

All teachers involved in the introduction of European Studies referred to the important role played by parental opinion. One of the problems consistently faced by new subjects in the secondary school is parental unfamiliarity and distrust:

When we offered this subject at first there was considerable resistance. Parents saying 'my child is not doing this new-fangled invention' ...

Several teachers speculated on the reasons for parental distrust:

I think that people are suspicious you know ... I think that they think this is not going to be academically acceptable ... this is something that somebody has dreamt up, this is an artificial thing, contrived ... it isn't something I can easily understand like geography or history, French and things ...

And I think another thing — I think people are tired of hearing things with Studies on the end. I think we'll end up teaching something with a better title ... we could do with a new term.

The most common problem I had was parents saying 'My child is not doing this because it is a CSE' ... and the fact that Grade 1 is equivalent to 'O' level doesn't cut any ice ...

> Above all, the parents judge what's going on at school from their own experience, and their own experience was the three 'Rs' plus if they were lucky drawing in the afternoon ... and anything that's outside of that is extravagant.

Partly, the parental opposition to innovational curricula is shared by the employers; and indeed the parents' opposition derives in part from an awareness of employers' likely antipathy:

> Our local employers have got a built-in prejudice against CSE — they want 'O's and 'A's to prove the child is good.

Several of the teachers, appreciating the crucial importance of gaining parental support, opted for a policy of positive canvassing:

> I campaigned in the third year at the Parents' Open Meeting ... The Head always talks, not usually the staff ... Anyhow, I stood up and talked about the new subject. I said it will offer an 'O' level pass for suitable candidates in the option scheme beginning in the fourth year.
>
> I went to the parents' evening with copies of the aims and objectives of my European Studies course. I handed it out at the door ... Well, I had to make it sound attractive ... the staff all made jokes, said it was the 'hard sell' ... but it must have worked. I got twenty-six children and at the time it was badly paired ... 'A' band had 'O' level History paired against it.

Developing the Course

The origins of European Studies as a haphazard, often impulsive and desperate, response to the problem of involving the 'less-able' linguists meant that many courses were ephemeral. Perhaps the most common answers to enquiries as to the way European Studies are organized were of the following kind:

> Well, it may well be that in various years depending on the staff there, one of the CSE unit options will be a European Studies Course with geography, history and all the rest of it ... but very hotchpotch and off-the-cuff.
>
> Well, when I became Head of Humanities they also made me Head of European Studies ... which had been taught on and off for several years to the 'dumbos' in languages ...
>
> So I organised a meeting to discuss it as a subject — only the young assistant teachers were interested. I went to the Head and asked for money. I was given £150.
>
> We drafted out a syllabus based on 'what can we reasonably do with them' — we then worked out a few aims ... mainly based on bits of the local environment, like the ferries, identity cards ... we were

> fighting to make it broad but sometimes we had to draw the line ... glacial deposits, that was too technical. I didn't mind much what went on as long as the teachers could make it work. We built up our courses mainly on the basis of what had worked in the first 'panic' year.

Whilst in the first school quoted European Studies has since died out, in the latter school there is now a well-established department preparing children not only for the CSE but also for 'O' level. Clearly European Studies began in most cases along the lines of the syllabus quoted earlier 'to provide children for some reason unable to follow a language course with a corpus of basic knowledge'. The crucial research question is to understand why in some instances European Studies take root, broaden in adequately formulated interdisciplinary courses and eventually become institutionalized as separate departments.

Three, or exceptionally four, stages can be discerned in the maturation of European Studies. Although, of course, many schools remain firmly rooted at Stages 1 and 2:

Stage 1

Ephemeral courses in European Studies organized on a piecemeal basis from year to year dependent on the dynamics of the fourth year option system and the number of non-linguists which languages departments have allotted to them.

Stage 2

Permanent courses for less-able linguists normally taught by the young assistant teachers of the departments, under-resourced and under-developed. Such permanent courses most often emerge if languages are a 'core' subject rather than an option.

Stage 3

(A) The language department seek the aid of other departments. notably history and geography, to teach an inter disciplinary course.
(B) The Head, perceiving a continuing need to provide for the less able, creates permanent 'less able' options and departments (e.g. European Studies, Environmental Studies, Parentcraft).

Stage 4

The European Studies department, having attracted some of the more messianic or enthusiastic teachers, attracts increasingly numbers of able students. The Head agrees to begin an 'O' level course and provide a responsibility post and extra resources.

To ensure that Stage 4 can be sustained and institutionalized, it is important that higher education defines European Studies as a discipline. The last section of this chapter will deal with this issue as it is central to lasting curriculum feasibility.

Case Study 2 (Stage 3)

European Studies for the Less Able: the Dominant Model

The school started in 1972 with the amalgamation of two single-sex secondary modern schools (now the upper and lower schools). It is fully comprehensive with an all-ability range of pupils, and operates fine setting (high ability banding) in the upper school. It is 12-form entry with 1850 pupils altogether. There are 1170 pupils in the present sixth form.

European Studies became an experimental option in 1974 for children in years 2 and 3 not doing German. At the same time French Studies was started as an alternative to French but this was later abandoned as a failure. European Studies, however, proved popular and successful and as a result it was suggested to the coordinator that it could be offered as a fourth year option combined with Integrated Studies within which it would be one of two options leading to CSE mode 3. In the fourth and fifth years pupils take compulsory maths, English, some RE and one 'Moral Education' lesson a fortnight. In addition to those, they are allowed to select six options from a wide range of practical and academic subjects. The option choice is ostensibly free but, according to the headmaster, in practice it is 'guided' and pupils are unable, for example, to combine Integrated Studies (which counts as two options) with history or geography.

European Studies can also be taken to CEE level and this has proved the most popular option in the sixth form where it attracts a good ability mix.

Bob, the coordinator of European Studies and a geographer by training, has been at the school for seven years. He outlined his extensive European Studies programme in the Lower School:

> there are approximately 400 children taking European Studies in years 2 and 3 where it is opted against German. It covers four 70-minute periods a fortnight. It takes up more time in years 2 and 3 than history or geography. It's second only to French, English and Maths. They're the three top-line subjects then European Studies comes next in order of time available.

In the Upper School, however, the picture isn't quite so rosy and Bob's principal aim is to get European Studies upgraded in years 4 and 5. At the moment the subject is offered as a combined option with Integrated Studies but he sees this as a millstone, attributing to it the fact that he is getting very low-ability pupils in European Studies in the fourth year:

> We got European Studies into years 4 and 5 married to Integrated Studies and I was happy with that because it got us into the 4th and 5th years. The big problem is now that not a lot of children want to do Integrated Studies, maybe because they don't know anything about it, maybe because it suddenly appears in the 4th year. They have no

experience of Integrated Studies but they *do* have experience of European Studies and they either like it or they don't . Integrated Studies has always had a tradition of taking the not-so-academic. Consequently European Studies gets levelled with it as an option. A lot of people would like to do European Studies but they don't want to do the other half of it. They think they're committing themselves to something they really don't want to do. Now I want to go the next step and get European Studies divorced from Integrated Studies and set up on its own.

In order to do this, however, Bob needs to get the option system changed which has turned out to be anything but easy:

The option system is desperate at the moment. It just doesn't satisfy enough people. It never satisfies everybody. The timetable is set up independently almost of the wishes of departments. You put forward your requirements but perhaps 70 per cent of them are met and it's the 30 per cent we can't fit in anywhere that makes a problem within the option system.

This view was later confirmed by the Deputy Headmistress responsible for the option system, who remarked somewhat drily: 'the problem with the options has nothing to do with the children. The problem is the staff.'

For Bob the main difficulty with the option system is that although children can in theory choose any combination of subjects, European Studies is to all intents and purposes opted against history and geography. The reason for this, according to the headmaster, it that 'skills overlap'. As a geographer himself Bob refutes this:

I get no complaints about European Studies from the history and geography departments in the Lower School so I can't see why they complain in the Upper School . . . I know as a geographer that I'm not duplicating anything in European Studies.

However Bob seemed to be aware that the reason for European Studies being opted against history and geography was more complex than just the fear of overlapping content and skills:

I think it's a slight worry that people are treading on each other's toes. In a place like this departments are huge and they like to keep their legality. It's all a problem of trying to cross barriers which have been there for a long time. However well you get on with people it's still a thought in the back of their mind that their empire could be being chipped away at. Interdisciplinary Studies are always going to be in that situation.

The history department are pretty forward looking and progressive and prepared to accept what's happening I think. But the new head

> of geography ... he's young but very much of a tradionalist; and he sticks very much to the line.

The Deputy Headmistress sees the problem in terms of competition between subject groups for better ability pupils:

> Heads of department want at least one fine set to do exam work. I don't see why European Studies shouldn't be out on it's own but it would mean that probably history and geography numbers would go down. Fewer children would opt for them. It would cut down their fine setting.

In Bob's opinion this competition gives an unfair advantage to the history and geography departments:

> The problem is that the children who adapt best to European Studies in the Lower School are the humanities-type children who obviously do history and geography. In the Upper School they can get 'O' levels in history and geography so they're obviously going to opt for them ... I can see that an 'O' level is going to be of far more use to them than a CSE which they can get for European Studies so we're stuck between the devil and the deep blue sea.

The problem therefore for Bob, where the upgrading of European Studies in the Upper School is concerned, is basically a dual one: timetabling and option problems on the one hand; the preservation of subject boundaries on the other: 'it's a combination of crossing barriers and the timetable. The two make it a big problem.'

Although ruefully admitting 'I'm fighting a lone battle here', he has put two proposals to the headmaster and his deputies. The first is that European Studies should be a separate option and the second is that it should be opted against German.

> I'm suggesting it should be now opted against German as it is in years 2 and 3, because the children who did German want to carry on doing it anyway. We're not likely to get many children who did German doing European Studies. But at least it would be on the same footing as it was in the lower School.

He has written a letter to the Deputy Headmistress making a formal request that European Studies should be offered as an option in its own right against German and asking that a meeting should be held to discuss the matter. As he hasn't yet received a reply he seemed rather anxious and pessimistic about the outcome:

> To date I've had no answer. I want to look for a syllabus to start in September but I can't do that until I know what the situation is.

Bob feels that the changes he proposes are crucial to the survival of European Studies in the school:

> if it doesn't find its place as a free option completely standing on its own then it won't have a hope I don't think. And if European Studies disappears I don't know what they would replace it by in the Lower School.

At the time of the interview in 1980 the Deputy Headmistress had not yet sent Bob a formal reply to his request but later, in private, she expressed sympathy with his position:

> I see the strength of Bob's argument that European Studies doesn't tread on history's and geography's toes in the 2nd and 3rd year so why suddenly discriminate at this level? That is the strength of his argument.

She also seemed favourably disposed towards offering European Studies as a separate option:

> I hope Bob will be seeing the Head about it very soon. He may put it on as a separate 'O' level which would mean another set. I would like to see it because it gives extra scope for the children.

Bob described how he visualized European Studies if he were able to offer it as a separate option:

> Once it's on its own it's got slightly more chance of picking up children if they haven't got to opt for two subjects as they do with Integrated Studies. I think we can get round the problem by following a CSE syllabus. The head said he wants a CSE Mode 1 syllabus first so it's got to be the CSE. We're not going to get into an 'O' level syllabus straight away. He won't accept that. Mode 1 carries more weight anyway. I'm prepared to accept it just leading to a CSE for the first couple of years on its own. We can only hope that it leads to an 'O' level . . . so first, Mode 1 CSE to make sure it can prove itself: if it can't prove itself then it'll have to disappear.
>
> The trouble is these Board 'O' levels are very history-oriented and (a) I'm not a historian, (b) it *would* be treading on the toes of the history department. Most European Studies people want a contemporary syllabus. We don't want to drag through the coals all the geography and history syllabuses. We want a European syllabus — the contemporary life we lead — and that's the problem.

Bob sees the paucity of 'O' level exam courses as a stumbling block to any future development and upgrading of European Studies:

> Really now we're held up by the exam boards because they haven't produced any worthwhile syllabuses. The subject has established itself

> . . . most schools now have European Studies departments, but even so I'm still sceptical about its survival simply because there are no public examinations to keep it moving . . . We've got a CEE syllabus in the sixth form. It's a super syllabus but again it doesn't carry any weight.

The link between exams and the high or low status of a subject was more bluntly stated by the Deputy Headmaster:

> I have every sympathy with Bob's need to get high status for the subject. The problem is the cash value of a subject. How marketable a subject is depends on the cashable value of its qualifications. The children are very aware of this.

The problem of being associated with a 'low-status' subject has career implications which have become painfully clear to Bob:

> I'm very disillusioned about my own future. Well it hasn't given me a future after five years so I can't see that it will suddenly give me a future in the next few years. I don't think I could have done much more than I have done. I got involved with the County syllabus, had a lot of contacts with the European Resources Centre, one thing and another, and I thought this can only be of benefit to my career. But it's been going on and I've been doing things and doing things and it's done me no good whatsoever. You know I'm still where I was when I came here and that was 7 years ago! I just don't know really . . . obviously I've become disillusioned, disheartened. I may have to move out of the subject altogether . . . go back to geography or the pastoral side. But it's not what I really want to do . . . If you go looking for a job and say you've been head of European Studies you don't get very far!

Because of his own experience Bob is rather pessimistic about the future of European Studies not only in his own school but in general:

> European Studies is always going to survive here I think . . . as long as I'm here, but I'm very doubtful about its future unless it becomes a common core subject. There's a lot of curriculum change going on at the moment and the possibility of the Common Core is very much the in-thing. European Studies appeared at a time when the rationale was for huge, wide-open options which we still operate here as a matter of fact. The number of subjects available here is incredible yet they can only choose 6 to follow. As things start being chiselled down as it were, I think European Studies has got to find its place as a free option soon otherwise it will disappear. I don't think it's got a tremendous future, if only because it won't be accepted by other departments . . . it's sort of . . . tainted in some way. It's got the mark on it . . . the voodoo sign!

Bob's situation and his comments highlight what perhaps is the crucial factor militating against any large-scale future development of European

Studies: that being associated with a subject which has not achieved full academic respectability and comparability with the established disciplines can adversely affect a teacher's career prospects and consequently his or her morale. Unfortunately this could result in the most energetic, committed and enthusiastic teachers such as Bob, reluctantly abandoning a subject they have painstakingly built up to return to former specialisms which seem to hold greater chances of future advancement.

The loss of such teachers would ultimately deal a devastating and perhaps irreversible blow to the survival prospects of European Studies.

Case Study 3 (Stage 4)

European Studies as an 'O' Level: Success Story

This study attempts to portray the major events and issues that were behind the successful introduction of a European Studies course into the upper school of a large secondary school (which has since become a comprehensive). It is designed to form an historical case study of implementation, rather than exploring the advantages of integration of learning methods, of course content, or of teachers.

Within the institution under consideration, a Group 12 school, obtaining the support or consent of many different teachers was paramount in elevating the subject of European Studies to a position where it would be established within the school. This study explores the strategy employed by a teacher in pursuit of this end, and was largely derived from the teacher involved, Mr K. Boyden.

Section 1 — The Role of the Head

Although larger comprehensives are witnessing a change in management style, such as the creation of multiple deputy headship roles, whereby 'innovative' heads are deploying deputies as 'change agents' with specific responsibilities for curriculum studies, the centrality of the Head's role in innovation is vital.

This centrality can possibly be traced to four main factors:

1 *the traditional authority of the Head*: in this respect the development of European studies within the school was solely initiated by the Head;

2 *the perception of the Head*: in comparison with other positions in the overall structures, the Head holds a unique opportunity to view the school as a whole, and thereby can perceive any 'need' for innovation. Clearly, the Head saw a 'need' for European studies.

Subsequent factors 3 and 4 are more intuitive than concrete, deriving from observation than experience;

3 *the Head as innovator*: there are expectations of others (LEA?) that the Head will innovate; and
4 *external connections*: the Head has greater facility to make contact with people who are promoters, change-agents, field-officers or whatever of current curriculum knowledge.

The extent to which a Head innovates is a combination of receptivity (which is bound up with the personality of the Head), administrative and leadership style. Although most writers accept that there is a clear distinction between administration (the maintenance of existing structures, procedures and goals) and leadership (the changing of structures and procedures for attaining goals), what clearly emerged were the varying strategies of the Head to implement change:

(a) *autocratic*: the initial decision to implement was entirely the Head's;
(b) *positive leadership*: setting a good example with support and encouragement;
(c) *persuasive*: as opposed to the official authority position, using personal qualities in persuading staff to make it work;
(d) *establishing suitable administrative procedures*: especially the need for flexibility in approach. The Head holds a unique position in 'obstacle' clearance.

Section 2 — A Model for Change

In keeping with the general shift in emphasis; the school favoured a school-based innovation, with all the associated transactions and negotiations. The range of discussions held were far-reaching and covered a vast spectrum of educational issues. The steps taken were flexible and adaptable, and thereby responsive to the variety of complex forces in operation (See *figure 1*).

Figure 1

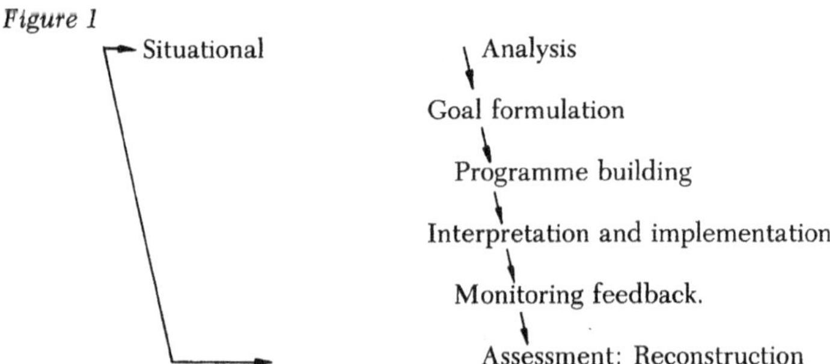

The different stages should not be thought of as separate entities but as running concurrently. Considering each of these stages separately, the main issues, which are discussed, were as follows:

Stage 1: Situational Analysis

(a) *External* (i) Cultural and social changes and expectations, for example common experiences: expectations of parents, community, employers.
(ii) Examinations.
(iii) External support: resources.
(iv) In-service training.

(b) *Internal* (i) The pupils: abilities, needs
(ii) The teachers: skills, adaptability, values, attitudes.
(iii) Resources.
(iv) Perceived place in existing curriculum.

Stage 2: Goal Formulation

(a) Expression of aims, goals and objectives.
(b) Knowledge of Learning Theory.

Stage 3: Programme Building

(a) Content, method, range, sequence.
(b) Means.
(c) Resources.
(d) Provisions.

Stage 4: Interpretation and Implementation

(a) The learning milieu itself.
(b) Changes: responsive adaptations.
(c) Problems, in general, of diffusion.

Stage 5: Monitoring, Feedback, Assessment, Reconstruction

(a) Continuous assessment — problems } Menus of assessment of goal
(b) Testing. } achievement
(c) Communication.
(d) Sensitivity to feedback data.

Section 3 — Barriers (1)

Although not all change is for the better, it is essential within education if only for the simple reason that it has to adapt and be sensitive to change in other social institutions which affect it. Nevertheless, there exist many barriers which immediately hinder the path of innovation from the outset, the main ones being materials, time and facility.

(a) Materials

Paramount to any development is the question of money. The capitation of £400 initially may seem a lot to the under-privileged, but as the base for the inauguration of a new department it is very little when it has to cover stationery, textbooks, teaching aids etc. for up to 150 children.

The innovation was handicapped by the lack of available materials so it had to look inwards from the start to developing its own. This in turn threw up the old problem of time.

(b) Time

This is without doubt the nearest and dearest thing to the teacher's heart. The teachers who helped initiate the innovation and develop resource materials (along with the frequent course meetings etc.) had to 'find' time, and the fact that they did tells much about them, their enthusiasm and dedication. Nevertheless, it does seem that to give the best possible chance to implementation, it is imperative to alleviate as much of the extraneous duties (for example covering for an absent colleague) as possible, not so much to give the team the extra odd half-hour, but to give a feeling of recognition and support 'from above'.

(c) Facility

This involves the concepts of power, authority and influence. The first two have their place, especially in the status of the role of the innovator, for example in streaming or banding a school. Although power and authority may make for a more attentive audience, unless coercion is used, they alone will not make for successful innovation, as teachers have to be first and foremost, willing. Thus, it may be that a combination of the former can give a greater facility for the last of the triology influence. Possibly the three most important strategies which emerged were:

(i) *personal influence*: this is the capacity to persuade others of the appropriateness/need of the subject;
(ii) *prestige*: to get others to feel the worthwhileness of the innovation, and not merely because of their relationship to the leader.
(iii) *professional expertise*: to give the feeling that this was not only new and exciting (an appeal to the pioneer spirit?) but also it was taking them out of their subject confines and giving a broader perspective.

Section 4 — Towards a 'Team'

Bringing together a 'team' of teachers who would be willing to develop a course, materials and teach the subject was the biggest step in the innovation. It was agreed that a team of six teachers would be necessary if all forms were to be covered adequately at the outset.

The initial step taken was to the Heads of Departments, as it was to be members of their subjects who would be 'tapped' and thereby spend less time teaching their subject. At a Head of Department meeting the following points were made to them:

(a) that a subject had the backing of the Head (an appeal to authority);
(b) that all steps had been taken after consultation with the Head (the seal of approval?);
(c) that only one member of any department could be co-opted to join the European Studies Department;
(d) that the most each member of department would teach would be three periods per week.

Assurances were then made on such points as which subjects would 'lose' out by children opting for European studies; whether their departments would be 'light' in teacher hours, etc.

The next approach was formally, using the opportunistic approach, of attending various departmental meetings and outlining the course and its aims, aspirations etc:

> Nearly all these meetings involved discussions and, gauging which people appeared interested, I hotly pursued them at breaks to have an informal chat as to their receptiveness!
>
> The last strategy was then to follow up the likely respondents with written information about the course, and inviting them to attend a discussion (without obligation — I was quickly learning the salesman's technique!) in the near future.
>
> Success! Without too much cajoling I obtained enough 'volunteers' — and not more than one per department who could be operative. The initial meeting had ten participants, of whom three categorically stated they would prefer not to teach European Studies at that particular time, but were sufficiently interested to come along and perhaps actively involve themselves at a later date.

Section 5 — Barriers (2)

Throughout the innovatory period, opinions were constantly expressed about European Studies. Ostensibly, such utterances are expressions of an attitude, which in turn may be, at the deepest level, part of their basic personality, being either favourable or unfavourable to change in general. Additional complexity may be added if they are thought of as a function of background and previous experience. However, whatever the nature of attitudes, it became patently obvious that the task of changing fundamental attitudes was beyond both personal skill and means, and that the only way of dealing with such was to attempt to create a series of situations in which negative attitudes could, given favourable circumstances, be modified.

From the variety of negative expressions, an attempt has been made to categorize into an identifiable framework, as shown in the following table.

Table 13: Framework for Identification of Responses

	Type	*Response*
1	Hostile	'You're building a nice little empire' 'Here comes Mr. Euro Studies'
2	Sceptical	'That sounds NICE' 'Not more education!'
3	Comparative	'It's not better than what we've got' 'Other things are far more valuable'
4	Ignorance	'But we do French already' 'I suppose it'll help with their geography'
5	Personal	'It's beyond me' 'I'm a mathematician, not a social scientist'
6	Apathetic/ Lethargic	'It sounds a good idea but I'd rather not'
7	Suspended	'I really am too busy, you know' 'If you do get it off the ground then I might join you next year'
8	Situational	'How are you going to fit it in?' 'I can't see parents wanting their children to get a CSE in this!' 'Where are you going to get the money?'

Developing strategies to counter these types were successful to a limited degree in that some marginal improvement in tolerance was discerned, but rarely to the position wherein they became positive:

> The teachers who were most receptive and some of whom eventually made up the team, were those who perhaps had the strongest personal allegiance to me.

This is possibly a crucial point in that not only can attitudes themselves from a barrier, but also that positive or negative attitudes can be built on a personal level. In this situation, the curriculum development was dependent on consensus, on the agreement and collaboration of a number of people. It is self-evident that the people concerned should react favourably towards one another. Thus, in addition to paying attention to promoting an innovation itself, the innovator should give time to developing relationships.

Section 6 — The Team

The 'timetablers' requested the names of those who were going to be actually teaching the subject early in the summer term. The requisite number was only six, but eight names were put forward. These included geographers, the Head of Remedial Department, a mathematician, a linguist and an historian.

Retrospectively, an analysis of these individuals produces a fairly strong typology, embodying a set of values that could be said to epitomize the more progressive teachers. Apart from the physical qualities of being male and under thirty years, they included:

a marked degree of open-mindedness;
had a more tolerant attitude to slow learners;
saw their role more in terms of guidance than as instructor;
untilized less formal lessons than others;
were more permissive;
were more tolerant of movement, noise and talking in the classroom;
made more use of audio-visual equipment;
were inclined to favour mixed ability grouping;
were more sparing in their use of formal testing;
favoured grouping of desks/tables, rather than lines or rows.

(NB. These values were obtained by discussion and observation so to that extent it is personally judgmental. Additionally, the use of comparative words such as 'more', 'less' is in contrast with other teachers who were not interested in European studies.)

Section 7 — Towards an Approach

The approach was principally along the lines outlined in Section 3. However, a basic distinction must be made between those aims and objectives which were superimposed and those that were self-generated.

(a) *Superimposed*
As mentioned in Section 2, an examination course was deemed desirable from the outset, not only as it would be beneficial to the pupils, but also from the department's position. Eventually, the GCE Alternative 'O' level syllabus offered by the Associated Examining Board, was chosen, both for educational reasons (the aims were much akin to the school's own), and for administrative, in that the school as a whole taught this Board and there would, therefore, be few worries of it clashing with other examination dates:

Thus it can be said that we accepted this syllabus — warts and all.

(b) *Self-generated: (Head of Department's Conclusions*
Politically it was felt that we had to tread carefully as 'the eyes of the school were upon us'. Were we the department, the disciples from Brussels, who were going to turn the masses into 'good Europeans'? That was a strong impression we collectively shared, of the sceptical expectation of many of the staff. The problem, as we saw it, was to devise a rhetoric that (a) we all believed in; (b) we could put into practice; and (c) be seen to be doing it.

Thus we tried to avoid using aims formulated in their most bland and generalized sense (for example 'to give an appreciation of') and to list endless objectives (for example 'to be able to write down the countries of the EEC). Obviously, the content of the syllabus, which is open to public inspection, reflects our beliefs, but mostly implicitly. Nevertheless, we articulated a number of aims (which have been criticized for their oblique wording). These are:

(i) fundamentally, to break down the insular perspective that we have traditionally held in respect to the European continent;
(ii) to illustrate the diversification of Europe whilst maintaining each country's particular identity;
(iii) to highlight links between European nations;
(iv) to remove stereotyped conventional wisdom concerning our neighbours;
(v) to provide a balanced framework within which changes, both past, present and future, planning and decisions have led to a considerable interaction in the past, and will continue to do so;
(vi) to give a common 'European experience' to our children.

Case Study 4

Examining Curriculum Feasibility: European Studies as 'a scholarly discipline'.

The majority of European Studies degree courses in 1981 consisted of a combination of one or two compulsory languages and social science subjects, in particular politics and economics. They involved an obligatory period abroad, usually one year. Applicants were often required to have a minimal qualification in a foreign language. Courses of this type were offered at Ealing and La Sainte Union Colleges of Higher Education, the Polytechnics of North London and Wolverhampton, and the universities of Aberystwyth, Bath, Bradford, Brunel, East Anglia, Hull, Kent, Lancaster, Loughborough, UMIST and Ulster (New Univeristy). Within such courses Europe could be a narrow concept because of the few languages offered: invariably French and German; less frequently Italian and Spanish; occasionally Russian, and, in a handful of institutions, one or two other East European languages, Scandinavian languages and Dutch.

It appears from the languages offered and themes outlined in the different registers of courses, that most European Studies BA programmes concentrated mainly on Western Europe, the few exceptions being University of Sheffield BA (Hons) in Modern East European studies; University of Hull BA in European Studies, which included the Politics of Eastern Europe and Politics and Society in Southern Europe; University of Lancaster BA (Hons) in Central and South East European Regional Studies; and University of Bradford where students of German could specialize in Eastern Europe.

Russian could be taken as part of the European Studies programmes of the

Universities of Bath, Brunel, East Anglia, Hull, Lancaster, Queen Mary College, Sussex and UMIST; and at Ealing College, and Wolverhampton Polytechnic. Lancaster and Bradford universities also offered, respectively, Czechoslovakian and Serbo-Croat and Rumanian and Serbo-Croat. However, given that the position of Russian courses in universities is currently precarious because of the programme of cuts recommended by the University Grants Committee (UGC) how long East European languages remain part of European Studies courses is open to question. The elimination of this element could well result in European Studies programmes becoming even more Western-European oriented in their overall emphasis.

A few undergraduate programmes in European Studies did not have a compulsory language element. Courses at Dundee and Loughborough Universities, Queen Mary College and Trent Polytechnic, for example, included languages as course options.

Many degree courses entitled European Studies appeared to differ little but in name from some modern languages degrees since a large part of the prescribed study involved only one language and one country. Kingston Polytechnic BA in Languages, Economics and Politics, for example, seemed to be very similar to many European Studies degrees. The Polytechnics of Leeds, Liverpool, Oxford, Newcastle, Sheffield, Wolverhampton, NE London, Portsmouth, Central London and South Bank also offered BAs in languages/language studies which had strong social science components. Similarly, many university modern languages courses included emphasis on European history, contemporary European institutions, politics etc. (for example Edinburgh, East Anglia, Brunel and Surrey).

European Studies courses which have a wider arts or humanities, as well as social science, orientation avoid the problem of being identical in all but name to some modern languages degrees. Wider courses of this type are offered at the universities of Dundee and Sussex, East Anglia and Ulster (New University). When the survey was conducted, East Anglia, Dundee, Lancaster and Loughborough put emphasis on European history and East Anglia in particular had a wide range of history-based options: twentieth century Europe, European history and economics, social history and sociology, European and economic history, intellectual history and philosophy. East Anglia was also offering about the widest range of languages available within a European Studies course: French, German, Russian, Danish, Norwegian, Swedish, plus at ancillary level, Italian and Spanish.

The University of Sussex School of European Studies combines the greatest number of disciplines from both humanities and the social sciences. Courses are contextual and there is an interdisciplinary approach. By comparison with the wider programmes of European Studies available at Sussex, East Anglia and Lancaster, courses with a limited number of languages (French or German) combined with one or two social science or humanities options (for example Loughborough) seem restricted and narrow in their coverage of Europe. In fact *European Studies* can be an ambitious misnomer in some cases, since any analysis of the range of courses provokes the question whether some of them could not be more aptly or explicitly named. Those which are focussed on just one or two languages and countries might be more appropriately entitled something like contemporary French or German studies; those which involve mainly one discipline (for example politics as at Hull and Edinburgh) might also be renamed.

Certainly there is no single definitive model of a European Studies course in universities, colleges and polytechnics although it is easy to identify the subjects which characteristically contribute most to such courses: languages, social sciences and history. There are in fact a number of different course models: European Studies can for example provide a whole organizing structure within which main degrees are provided (Sussex); it can be an integrated scheme composed of tightly focussed units deriving from European themes and leading to a single European Studies award (UMIST); it can be based on different subjects rather than themes, emphasize basic skills and have a vocational bias (Bath and Bradford). Other models can also be identified.

The range of possibilities, which is inevitable because of the scope of the subject, led one speaker at a UACES conference in Lancaster in 1981 to refer to European Studies as a 'Humpty Dumpty' subject, i.e. it can mean whatever people choose it to mean. Another participant pointed out that this can lead to the provision of too many course options which may not necessarily compose a coherent whole.

In spite of all the problems currently besetting higher and further education interest in interdisciplinary courses on Europe does not seem to have waned to quite the same extent that it has in schools. Although several institutions have dropped European Studies in the last few years, in 1981 others were still submitting course proposals in the subject to CNAA and other validating bodies. Vocational courses on Europe were also slowly increasing; for example, Hull College of Higher Education had a new European Business Studies course; Leeds Polytechnic was offering a three-year BA Honours degree in European Studies in finance and acounting, providing qualifications valid in both Britain and West Germany.

How long the present level of course provision can be maintained in either the university or public sector is, of course, open to question. An important consideration is whether separate degree courses entitled European Studies are going to be affected by expenditure cuts and the narrowing of the curriculum, official policies and public attitudes. Might hostility towards the EEC, for example, and any action taken by the present or any future government affecting British membership of the Community, force a change in the name or structure of degrees in the subject?

An additional consideration is whether the subject's continuing 'low status' reputation in schools will have a detrimental effect on the quantity and quality of applicants to courses in higher education. This has caused at least one university school of European Studies to change its name in recent years, as admitted privately by a spokesman:

after the mid-seventies once the attraction of 'new' universities started to decline we suffered a year by year decline in applications and in quality of applicants. We eventually changed the name of our school of European Studies as a result of a new range of language-based courses. But we were influenced in reaching this decision by our own survey in selected secondary schools which almost universally demonstrated the 'low status' of European Studies both amongst teachers and pupils. Our fortunes in both quantity and quality of applications have changed dramatically for the better since that time.

The problem is that there is an unfortunate divergence between what European Studies represents in schools and what it represents in higher education — a mismatch which does not occur with other subjects. European Studies, as discussed earlier, has a generally poor image in schools as a subject for less able, unacademic pupils. As there are few GCE 'O' levels and no 'A' levels, there is no smooth transference of students from sixth forms to degree courses in the same subject as there would be for, say, history or geography. In other words, pupils who do European Studies at school will not be those who take the subject in higher education. Furthermore, schools or departments of European Studies in colleges, polytechnics or universities usually require applicants to have at least minimal qualifications in modern languages. But since in many secondary schools European Studies is presented as a lower status *alternative* to modern languages, the very pupils the subject needs to attract in higher education may be prejudiced against it from the start.

Additionally, European Studies programmes in secondary and tertiary education tend to differ fundamentally in course content and emphasis. Schools courses tend to focus on historical, geographical and cultural aspects of Europe with little or no compulsory language work, while higher education courses often concentrate on political, economical and sociological topics often with a compulsory language element. As long as there is no overarching definition of the subject and no comparability of course aims and content, and as long as European Studies programmes at secondary and tertiary levels continue to cater for entirely different students, the quantity and quality of student intake to the latter are likely to be affected.

Conclusions

The emergence of European Studies as a separate synthesis of knowledge has happened in piecemeal fashion over the past two decades or so, mainly in the new polytechnics, universities and institutes of higher education. As a result, there is as yet relatively little agreement as to what constitutes the new synthesis: we are faced with a wide spectrum of competing definitions. Historically this has often been the case in the initial stages in the definition of new school subjects. The inevitable result is that scholars and teachers *trained in other disciplines* come together to focus on the new area of interest. Thus, those advocates who state that European Studies should aim to be interdisciplinary in a sense miss the point. At this stage in its evolution European Studies could not be anything but interdisciplinary.

The resolution of the interdisciplinary problems of European Studies *might* be solved by following the maturational model defined.

In schools at the moment, the subject is very firmly rooted at Layton's Stage 1, stressing 'pertinence and utility' with the 'dominant criterion' as the 'relevance to the needs and interest of the learners'. European Studies is a classic example of a reactive innovation — responding to the problem of less-able linguists in schools. But such change from the bottom needs to bring about the creation of a, 'scholarly discipline' at higher education level to be successful. At the moment there is little evidence of such a scholarly discipline. Although European Studies do exist in various forms in British universities, courses given that title are diverse and idiosyncratic. Consequently no overarching definition of European Studies is currently forthcoming.

With this vacuum at the 'top' effective or permanent change from the bottom is impossible. The universities represent the power elites which can act as 'gatekeepers' to prevent restructuring innovations from entering a social system. Thus European Studies is faced by problems of interdisciplinarity at two levels — there are the problems encountered by the low-status European Studies at present taught in schools and the interdisciplinary problems faced by those attempting to develop more scholarly versions of the subject in higher education.

The failure to develop any coherent definition of European Studies at tertiary level has had several crucial implications for the subject at school level: above all, it has meant that it has largely remained confined in the first stages of the maturational model defined in the introduction. Therefore any strategies for the resolution of the problems faced by European Studies need to focus on improving the current position the subject occupies in schools. The best way this can be achieved is by eliminating the gap between what the subject represents at secondary and tertiary levels, i.e. by the following developments:

1 The setting up of training schemes at tertiary level for those wishing to teach European Studies. This would: (a) offer the prospect of an overarching definition of the subject; (b) provide specialists in the new subject; (c) supply the status and expertise that derive from tertiary practice.
2 The joint involvement of academics and teachers in the development of new GCE examinations. This would provide a bridge between secondary and tertiary teachers and a transitional status escalation for European Studies.

It seems, however, that given the present economic situation, neither of these developments is likely to take place on any substantial scale in the foreseeable future. Moreover, since there seems to be little support among educationalists generally for promoting the study of Europe as a separate curricular activity within either the secondary or the tertiary sector, the best strategy would seem once again to be the addition or reinforcement of the European dimension to established subjects.

Notes

1 Jotterand, R. (1977) Introducing Europe to senior pupils; quoted in Williams, M. *Teaching European Studies*, Heinemann Educational, London, p. 22.
2 Young, M.F.D. (1971) *Knowledge and Control*, New York, Collier-Macmillan.
3 *Op. cit.* Williams 1977 pp. 18–19.
4 Jones, B. (1973) 'Language and the less able' in Daffern, E. and Joy, C. (Eds) *The Language Element in European Studies*, Curriculum Development Series No. 10, Schools Unit, University of Sussex, p. 49.
5 Lawrence, F. *Syllabuses for European Studies*, Schools Unit, Curriculum Development Paper., University of Sussex.
6 The new AEB 'O' level which was approved in 1983, is replacing the 'A'/'O' level. The outline syllabus is presented in Appendix 1.
7 In later drafts this has been replaced by a language option.

3 *History*

The *Europe in the School* survey, together with earlier ones undertaken during the 1970s, indicates the focal importance of history in contributing a modern European dimension to the school curriculum. Just under 80 per cent of schools responding to the questionnaire identified history as the major vehicle for teaching about modern Europe in the secondary school curriculum, and over half of the responding history teachers estimated that 50 per cent or more of their courses for the 14–18 age range are on modern European history.

History therefore is the curriculum area to which special attention must be paid in any study of teaching about Europe in British secondary schools.

In England school history courses have long displayed a tendency to be strongly nationally based. The detailed explanation of separate national experiences and destinies is of course a necessary element in any child's education. Nevertheless there are problems inherent in an overly nationalistic or 'drum and trumpet' approach to history — an approach which, to be fair, predominates not only in British versions of events but also in the versions given by some other European countries. This is clearly not conducive to mutual understanding and cooperation and has been a matter of some concern to organizations and individuals dedicated to the furtherance of European unity. E.H. Dance for example, refers to the harm that can be done through national bias in history courses and textbooks:

> The national bias which has done most harm in Europe and its textbooks is the internal nationalism of the European States themselves . . . this is most obvious in their treatment of the history of their wars and their enemies. For instance, in their account of the Hundred Years War, both English and French histories used to give the victories of their own side much more prominence than to the victories of the other, so that both French pupils (rightly) and English pupils (wrongly) get the impression that their own country had the best of it.[1]

Where modern European history is concerned, courses and syllabuses in England are often negative and problem-centred giving far more prominence to wars, crises, conflicts and problems generally than to post-war moves to cooperation and unity. Thus, there is a danger that modern European history may also be taught in such a way as to reinforce national prejudices and sterotyped views of other nations, with certain of them appearing predominantly in the context of war and conflict, while our own role on the modern European stage may be, implicitly if not explicitly, enhanced by contrast. This applies not only to military but also to political affairs, for the tendency to overstate national, militaristic solutions and successes has been echoed in the treatment of political themes in traditional English history courses. This has led to complacent assumptions of English superiority and the underrating of important political events elsewhere in Europe.

> It is natural that English books should see the history of self-government in Europe as a preponderantly English phenomenon, and should say little about democratic developments else-where. But in doing that they usually ignore other democratic developments, particularly in France since the great revolution, though that revolution gave a turn to democracy which was quite new, and in some respects quite un-English.[2]

The development of wider perspectives in history courses offers the opportunity to correct this imbalance. Wider historical perspectives could lead to a less blinkered view of our national history and enable students to see past events, trends and issues in the broader framework of an interrelated and ever-changing world. The addition of modern European perspectives for example, by putting prominence not only on war and dissension but also on post-war moves towards peaceful cooperation and unity, could help to promote in the next generation more positive attitudes of understanding and tolerance of other nations and races.

There are significant groups among teachers, educationalists and in society as a whole arguing that this is an important, indeed essential part of our children's education. As was noted in the Introduction, of the six broad educational aims referred to in the DES documents *A Framework for the School Curriculum* (1980) and *The School Curriculum* (1981), one is concerned with tolerance of other races, religions and ways of life and another with understanding of the contemporary world.

A practising history teacher interviewed for the research identified ethnocentric history courses 'whether British or European based' as one of the potential contributory causes of what he calls one of the major educational and social problems of our time: the lack of understanding of intolerance of other racial and cultural groups'.

Many of those concerned with this problem now argue persuasively in favour of world history:

> A proper understanding of the history of the mid-twentieth century surely requires a world perspective. Technological and economic developments have produced such a close inter-weaving of interests that a teacher of contemporary history would probably find a national or continental approach more difficult in practise than the global scale. The very nature of recent history forces the teacher into world history.[3]

Within European history itself, there are positive steps which can be taken to reduce national bias and selectivity in history courses. The book published in 1967 by the Council of Cultural Cooperation of the Council of Europe — *History Teaching and History Textbook Revision* was part of an attempt to elaborate and apply 'a new conception of the common past of the European peoples'. This, however, did not prove a easy task for several reasons not the least of which was the number of different education systems existing within the different countries of Europe.

> The widely varying education systems in those countries of the Council of Europe . . . require very varied methods of procedure. The desired advance from purely bilateral to regional cooperation can therefore only be achieved gradually among those countries whose education systems are more or less alike.[4]

Another problem affecting history textbook writing and revision, according to Schüddekopf, is that there are entrenched and powerful interests involved in the dominant national views of history, therefore it is the task of teachers and authors 'simply to provide and use textbooks that correspond to the present position of historical research *and to the political beliefs of our time*' (author's emphasis).

Schüddekopf makes the point that a common European textbook would be worthless if its perspectives and emphases are not reflected in the conviction and outlook of the individual teacher.

Since the major factor, even in inter-European work, is the individual teacher, then clearly it is within the confines of single national educational systems that one must begin to try and make effective changes. The first step is to analyze current British school history courses and syllabuses in order to identify their salient characteristics and the possibilities they offer for studying modern history in a wider European perspective.

Syllabus Commentary

In 1980 there were a very large number of GCE history syllabuses at 'O', 'A/O' and 'A' level — over ninety (including both the current and the new AEB 'O' levels which were first examined in 1983). There were also four SCE history syllabuses at 'O' and 'H' Grade.

Comparatively few of the total number of syllabuses had a compulsory modern[5] European element, about twenty in all. A further twenty-six had some modern European content either as an optional period study or as a special topic.

GCE 'A' Level Examinations

Of the GCE 'A' level examinations the only one to have what amounts to a compulsory modern European dimension is the *London syllabus D* (269), a very detailed syllabus which is divided into *International Problems since 1931* and *The World since 1945*. According to statistics, however, this syllabus seems to attract considerably fewer candidates than the London syllabuses A, B and C; only 383 candidates in 1978 (June) as opposed to 3429, 2588 and 952 for the other syllabuses. This trend is repeated in subsequent annual statistics.

Most of the 'A' level syllabuses with European possibilities offer a number of period or special study options. One which offers good scope for teaching about modern Europe is the AEB 'A' level (630) which has three groups of period options, one of which is European history until 1970, and seven alternative topics including *Totalitarianism in Germany and Italy in the Twentieth Century* and *Imperial Russia and the USSR 1904–1968*. The Board is to revise this syllabus although the Period Studies will remain unchanged with the possible addition of World Affairs since c. 1900.

The *AEB Alternative 'A' level* (Pilot scheme) 673, is a more flexible syllabus with an internal assessment element, but its scope for teaching about modern Europe is limited by the fact that it has seven options in one paper, only one of which covers European history from 1450–1970 — rather too large a period to guarantee coverage of modern history.

Of the remaining 'A' level syllabuses, one with good opportunities for studying modern European history as an option is *JMB Syllabus A* which has a whole section on European history divided into twelve period studies. Three of these are modern periods: *European History 1789–1914*; *European History 1870–1945* and *Europe and the Modern World 1914–1963*. Within each of these options there is a list of political, social, economic and cultural topics.

The Oxford and Cambridge could be another useful syllabus for teaching about modern Europe as it has a choice of European or American history to 1965 for one paper and seven special topic options for the other, one of which is *Hitler and the Third Reich*.

The University of Cambridge has a very large number of options but only two of them offer good opportunities for teaching about modern Europe: *European History to 1964* and *World Affairs since 1945*. In addition there is a topic *The Origins of the Second World War*. This same special topic figures as part of the *Oxford Local A* (9836) for which there are also eight outline period studies the last of which is 1890-1951. An additional topic is *Europe and the Scramble for Africa 1870–1914*.

Of the *WJEC* syllabuses one with considerable modern European potential is the *Economic and Social History 'A' level* which has a paper on the economic and social history of major powers. For this paper candidates can choose France, Germany, USSR or USA, but the period for study does not go beyond 1939.

All of the other WJEC syllabuses have papers on both English and Welsh history and European history. The options in the European sections of syllabuses A and B have only one modern period which again is restricted to 1939. Syllabus C is more promising with two modern European topics out of six: *the Triumph of Nationalism 1871–1920* and *Changing Europe 1918–1957.*

The University of London syllabuses are similar in format to the *WJEC 'A' levels*, being divided into English and European (or foreign) history. The most useful of these where modern Europe is concerned, are syllabus A in the second paper, in which there are three period studies including 1763–1954, and syllabus C which has in paper 2 six period studies including 1870–1954.

Syllabus B has eight topic options two of which have a strong modern European element: *The USA and World Affairs 1917–1953*, and *Dictatorships in Europe 1919 – 1937.*

For the *SUJB 'A' level* (9030, 9031 and 9032) students are asked to study two of the following: British history, European history and history of the USA. In the European history option there is one out of five choices on modern history: 1830–1964.

The SCE Higher Grade syllabuses also have an optional modern European content. The traditional syllabus, like many of the 'A' levels, is divided into British and European history. For the latter there are two period options which can be classified as modern: 1815–1914. The *Alternative 'H' Grade* has a Period Studies paper for which there are four options: option 3 is *History of Europe, USSR and Britain, 1848–1919*, and option 4: *European and World History 1914–1964.* The second paper of this syllabus has eight special subject options two of which have a modern European dimension: *The Collapse of European Security 1931–1939* and *Britain at War and Peace 1939–1951.*

GCE. 'A/O' Level Examinations

Of twelve syllabuses, five have no modern European content; two have an integral modern European element, and five have it as an option.

The two 'A/O' levels with the greatest coverage of modern European History are *AEB World Powers in the Twentieth Century* (181) and *SUJB World Affairs since 1945.* In the first there are four syllabus sections one of which is *the World Powers' Relations since 1945*; another, *the USSR since 1917.* The SUJB covers 'broad themes in world history since 1945' in part and has eight options for part 2 including *Europe and the United Kingdom since the Second World War* and *the USSR since 1953.*

Of the 'A/O's with an optional modern European dimension, the *JMB Historical Studies* syllabus has five varied topics one of which is *European Dictatiorships between 1917 and 1953.*

The *Oxford and Cambridge* outline syllabus has a European History option but gives no details except the periods from the reign of Constantine onwards and 1450–1954.

The Oxford Local (8835) *British and Foreign History* only has one option out of ten on a modern period but even that is limited (1815–1939). A better syllabus where Europe is concerned is *University of London Historical Studies* (826) which has seven alternative topics, several with a modern European dimension especially *Agencies of World Peace and International Co-operation in the Twentieth Century.* This syllabus has a more varied content than most with topics such as *Race Relations and Minority Problems in the Twentieth Century*; *Society and Technology since the middle of the Eighteenth Century*; *Women in Society*, and *the Nature of Revolution from the middle of the Eighteenth Century.* Only one other 'A/O' syllabus includes an attempt to diversify the content: the SUJB which specifies that links should be made with 'other special sciences, literature and art'. This is almost exceptional in a history scene devoted almost entirely to political and economic concerns.

GCE 'O' Level Examinations

Sixteen syllabuses have an integral modern European element and eight have an optional European section. The following courses offer the greatest opportunities for study of contemporary Europe: *Oxford Local British and Foreign History* (2834) which has three optional periods — 1870–1919, 1919–1950 and 1870–1950, and a very detailed syllabus content which inevitably includes a number of European topics; *Northern Ireland 'O' level* which has topics on International Relations, the Second World War, Western Europe 1919–1965 (Italy, Spain, Germany, France) and Russia 1917–1964.

Other syllabuses which have a prescribed and detailed modern European content are the following World History courses: *Oxford Local World History* (2836); *JMB syllabus G Europe and the Modern World* (1870 to the present day); *AEB syllabus 4 World Affairs since 1914.* (This syllabus has been revised and the new version — *World Affairs from the Russian Revolutions to the Present* (146) was to be examined for the first time in 1983); *University of Cambridge* 2108 *World Affairs since 1919*; and *University of London syllabus C, Modern World History.* All of these are strongly Europe-oriented with detailed syllabus sections and topics covering the major events in Europe in the twentieth century including at least one section on modern Russia, its recent history and internal policies. These syllabuses also have alternative sections on some or all of the following: USA, Africa, the Far East, the Middle East, the Indian sub-continent, but the European element predominates.

Another World History course with considerable modern European potential is the *AEB syllabus 6058 History of World Powers and World Events in the Twentieth Century*, which has a very flexible structure and includes coursework, project work and internal assessment. For this syllabus various 'threshold' topics are suggested. This course could provide excellent opportunities for work on modern European history topics.

Some of the new *AEB 'O'* level syllabuses to be examined from 1983 have increased the European content: *syllabus* 145: *European History from the French Revolution to the First World War*; 150: *European Building from the Renaissance to the Present Day*; 152: *Medicine and Nursing in the Western World from early times to the present.* The last two have important nineteenth and twentieth century sections and indicate a move away from political and economic concerns towards more diversity of content.

Other syllabuses with a potential important European content are WJEC (Oe) *European History* 1870–1957); (Og) *History of the Modern World from 1919*, and Oxford local *Foreign History* (2833) which covers the period 1848–1950. However the syllabus outline details are very scanty in all three cases and there appears to be no prescribed content.

Of the two SCE 'O' grade courses, the *traditional* has an integral modern European dimension in section 6, International Affairs: *British History from 1890 to 1964.* The balance of this section is in favour of European history and since it is a compulsory section (i.e. one question has to be answered from it), the chances are that some modern European history will be studied. Indeed, according to a Scottish historian, out of ten questions set six or seven are usually on Europe.

The *Alternative 'O' grade syllabus* has two topics with a limited modern European dimension: *Russia in Revolution — 1904–1924* and *Britain at War 1914–1919.*

The GCE 'O' levels in which the modern European section is optional are British and European (or Foreign) history syllabuses which offer a very wide range of periods for study. For example, the Oxford and Cambridge *Outlines of European history and other Outlines* offers seven period options ranging from A.D. 800 to 1975.

In the *JMB syllabus A, Aspects of British and Foreign History from c. 1500 to the Present Day* the twentieth century is the fifth of five period options. Within that option are detailed the main political events of the twentieth century.

SUJB syllabus B (modern history) has its British and European sections divided into two optional periods: 1485–1815 or 1815–1964, however, it would be possible to bypass the European section completely since candidates are permitted to concentrate on only one part of either section.

In all of the courses mentioned there is scope for some study of modern European issues but because half of the work is on British or English history, and because of the range and scope of options, the modern European section is inevitably limited.

From this survey of GCE and SCE courses available in 1980 it seems that the most common 'O' and 'A' level courses to combine a major section on English history with a section on European history. The main features of the syllabuses as a whole, besides their pervasive nationalism, are their concentration on rigid chronology rather than historical themes, and somewhat minimal coverage of recent events. It is common, for example, to find sections of European history ending somewhere between 1950 and 1954. The growth of world history syllabuses, however, is an encouraging sign since these tend to deal with more contemporary eras. This development gathered momentum after 1945 with the intellectual, and indeed moral, justification for traditional history syllabuses coming increasingly under attack. After the war the confident assumption that material progress and international dissent could be properly managed by the major European states began to be questioned:

> In Western Europe . . . the practical adequacy of a national frame of action had been deeply eroded, and the intellectual adequacy of nationalistic history seemed plainly to be contradicted by events. The idea of progress, discredited since 1914, was not revived by the technological marvels that continued to pour forth from research laboratories. Political anguish was too widespread, social strains too acute for such an optimistic vision of mankind's career on earth to have such appeal.[5]

From these crisis points, particularly the two world wars, European consciousness began to change in the ways so eloquently described in M Stuart Hughes' work on *Consciousness and Society* (for the years 1890–1930). Hughes discerns a growing vision of common European culture, of a common political, intellectual and social consciousness.

> As European influence in the external world waned and began to retire, so the political societies of Europe, despite, as well as because of the ravages of two world wars, began to grow together. A European elite began to emerge, in the fringes of the underground resistance at first, but sufficiently able for its non-revolutionary wing to be carried into office at the end of the 1940s throughout Western Europe. Its forerunners were the diplomatists, politicians and bureaucrats of the 1920s meeting regularly at Geneva for the League of Nations and the International Labour Office, or at Basle for the old Bank of International Settlements.[7]

The growth of European consciousness and the severe questioning of nationalistic frames of explanation has important implications for the development of history curricula and syllabuses. McNeill feels that:

> The resultant disarray of historical understanding is likely to prove extremely fruitful. New patterns for the comprehension of the past are

> urgently in demand; and it seems probable that in the course of time suitable patterns will indeed be found. To be at all satisfactory these new patterns will have to embrace the history of all branches of mankind in a far more adequate sense than has been done ... by European schools and writers.[8]

Thus, since the Second World War there has been increasing emphasis on historical scholarship devoted to world issues. One of the first 'O' level courses to be developed with this approach was the London syllabus *From 1919 to the Present Day.*

Besides sections on Asia, Africa and the Middle East, Russia and Eastern Europe and the Americas, this syllabus deals in some detail with 'Western Europe, including Britain'. The movement away from nationalistic themes is confirmed by the emphasis the syllabus places on the history of peace-keeping organizations and disarmament.

More recent World History syllabuses have concentrated on skill-based approaches. AEB's *History of World Powers and World Events in the twentieth Century* is a good example. World history was chosen for three reasons: firstly, 'in an increasingly interdependent world, it gives the background and perspective necessary for an understanding of current problems from a global rather than national or continental view'; secondly, 'it was chosen because there is ample evidence of its increasing popularity in both schools and colleges of further education'; and, thirdly, 'because it lends itself particularly well to a study of an essentially interdisciplinary nature'. The syllabus offers considerable scope for the coverage of European themes since the topics and themes can be chosen by the teacher and half the examination marks are awarded for projects and teacher assessments. A large number of projects on European issues have been submitted to the Board and the first aim of the syllabus clearly indicates the emphasis that is favoured. The Regulations stress that the aim is 'to foster the understanding of change and continuity in history'. For example they note: 'a study of the rise of Hitler and the Nazi Party would be a limited one if on the one hand it took no account of the possible existence of certain recurring themes in Germany's history or gave no consideration to the problem of national characteristics; or, on the other, if it failed to recognize the effects of the First World War upon Germany and Europe'.

The considered treatment of 'problems of national characteristics' in European states indicates the potential that world history syllabuses offer in moving away from the traditional patterns of nationalistically-oriented and confirming syllabuses.

A salient feature of all history syllabuses is their predominantly political and economic emphasis. Inevitably the two World Wars and events preceding and following them are a major modern European focus. Typical topics are: *Totalitarianism in Germany and Italy in the Twentieth Century* (AEB 630); *The Triumph of Nationalism (1919–1939)* (University of London syllabus B and JMB Historical Studies); *The Origins of the Second World War* (Oxford Local

9836 and *the Spanish Civil War* (JMB syllabus 9; Oxford Local 2836; Cambridge World Affairs; and British and European History).

The 'O' levels with the most extensive coverage of modern European history — the world history syllabuses — inevitably have a strong political orientation. They all deal largely with the events leading up to and following the first World War; peace treaties; the League of Nations: rise of dictators; the events leading up to the second World War and its political effects; the Cold War and European moves to unity. All have additional sections on the USSR and political developments from the Revolution onwards.

Very few courses have a wider cultural dimension although the new AEB 'O' levels show the start of a welcome change of emphasis. Syllabus 145: *European History from the French Revolution to the First World War* has sections on social and religious developments, while syllabuses 150 and 152 (on Building and Medicine respectively) show a change to more cultural topics. There is also a new AEB 'O' level syllabus on European Agriculture but this is restricted to earlier periods of history.

Two of the 'A' levels — *JMB syllabus A* and *Oxford 9830* and several of the 'A/O' level courses — notably London *Historical Studies* and SUJB *World Affairs*, attempt to introduce elements from the other social sciences and the arts.

The predominance of political and economic material in GCE history syllabuses is accounted a weakness by W.F.J. Inglis.[9] He had analyzed in detail the content of the British and European history papers set by two Boards and found that 'politics at home and abroad — primarily including the actions of governments and their main opponents predominate in all cases.' The only variation he found was that papers on European history 'lay more emphasis on foreign politics than those on British history and the papers on British history are more concerned with domestic than foreign policy.'

To discover how typical of British and European history examination papers these findings are, Inglis surveyed papers set by other Boards including SCE and concludes that 'the broad trends identified in these papers would be substantially replicated in the papers of other British Boards'. As large numbers of candidates take British and European history papers he claims this duplication has serious implications:

> The applicability of the findings of this study to the papers set on modern British and European history by other Boards is of considerable importance, since papers of this type are taken by thousands of candidates at 'A' and 'O' level. In the case of the JMB and Cambridge Boards over 70 per cent of the candidates take papers on modern British and European history; that is over 20,000 at 'O' level and 9000 at 'A' level. This tendency is replicated among the other British Boards, papers on modern British and European history being selected by between 50 and 70 per cent of their candidates at 'A' and 'O' level. Thus the content of the papers outlined in this study, even if confined

> to the JMB and Cambridge Boards, is of importance to thousands of candidates and their schools each year. In addition, if, as is probable, it is common to papers set by the other Boards it is of general significance for the majority of 'A' and 'O' level candidates and for the teaching of the subject throughout Britain.

Commenting on the predominance of political history in examination papers, Inglis expresses surprise at the lack of diversity of content that this represents despite the number of examination boards and the choice of papers available:

> The questions could emphasise any aspect of history from the cultural and social to the economic, political and religious, yet with all this potential freedom the papers set by the two Boards are virtually identical. This similarity raises an interesting question. If the majority of the 'A' and 'O' level candidates for these two Boards take these papers which are so nearly identical and it is likely that other Boards set papers that differ little in content, is there not a certain amount of duplicated effort amongst the Boards? Indeed if the similarity between the papers set by the Boards were to be extended to other papers, for example, imperial and social and economic history as was the case with these types of paper set by the JMB and Cambridge Board then an apparently decentralised examination system would be acting to a large degree in a centralised manner as far as history is concerned.
>
> This lack of variety is also evident when the 'O' and 'A' level papers are compared and when the content of papers on British and European history is analysed. As has already been pointed out even the tendency for papers on European history to favour foreign politics and for those on British history to emphasise domestic politics is only a variation within Category A, both sets of papers following the familar trend of emphasising political as opposed to other types of history. The sameness of these papers has serious implications. Pupils whose special interest is history, some of whom will take degrees in the subject, are being required to take papers at 'A' and 'O' level with virtually the same content despite the opportunity for variation that exists within the subject.

According to Inglis, the duplication of content gives several grounds for concern: the syllabuses largely omit other types of history pupils should have access to such as social history, religious history and cultural history, and they contradict the consensus of opinion among historians themselves that all types of history are worthy of equal consideration. Moreover, purely political history could give pupils a distorted view of past society by concentrating on the activities of a small ruling group, and it could also give them an oversimplified view of the influences which contributed to past events.

Finally Inglis points out that the papers fail to deal with the nature of history which is a serious weakness. Teachers of modern British and European history could draw on a wealth of sources such as building, literature, art and documents of all types, but this has not been fully exploited by the Boards.

The study of historical methods and use of sources mentioned by Inglis has become a part of some history syllabuses notably some of the 'A/O' levels and the new AEB courses and the Schools Council 13–16 Project but it has not yet extensively affected British and European history syllabuses probably because of the amount of material to be studied under those two headings. Nevertheless it is difficult not to agree with Inglis's final comment:

> On a number of counts, therefore, the syllabus of papers on modern history appears to be in need of revision, particularly to bring it into line with history as it is studied today and to give both pupils and teachers scope for variety, choice and experiment.

However, the chances of a greater diversity of content within history syllabuses appear slim. One of the examination Boards (AEB) during discussions about the revision of history syllabuses, notes that 'the GCE Boards are currently contemplating moves towards a greater degree of inter-Board comparability of syllabuses in each subject, in terms of aims and objectives, and perhaps, ultimately, of content'. The same Board refers to the 'increasingly popular, progressive approaches to the study of history for 'O' level examinations' which are not being 'fully developed at 'A' level'.

According to our syllabus survey, the majority of history 'O' level syllabuses do not appear to demonstrate a 'popular, progressive' approach. Very few, for example, have any school assessment, the exceptions being the new AEB 'O' levels which have an optional project and *AEB syllabus* 6 (058) *History of World Powers and World Events in the Twentieth Century* which has a project and teacher assessment. (This syllabus was partly designed in response to the increasing popularity of Mode 3 syllabuses and, according to a spokesman for the Board, 'the newer type of people are channelled into this syllabus'.)

Other 'O' levels which have the possibility of internal assessment are *JMB syllabus A* and *Oxford and Cambridge* which have an optional coursework element and an optional project respectively.

The Schools Council Project 13–16 which began in 1972 represented, perhaps more than any other syllabus, an attempt to adopt a new approach to 'O' level (and CSE) history and to develop a more varied approach to assessment. In this syllabus, coursework accounts for 40 per cent of the total marks.

The other 'O' levels and the vast majority of syllabuses at 'A' level are assessed by terminal examination only. The exceptions are the *AEB alternative 'A' level* which has an internally assessed Personal Study and oral test (25 per cent of the total marks), *University of Cambridge* (9020) which has an optional project, and *SUJB* which has a optional course work essay.

At 'A/O' level there are two syllabuses which have considerable coursework elements: *AEB World Powers in the Twentieth Century* (50 per cent of the total) and *JMB Historical Studies* (45 per cent).

The more innovatory history syllabuses such as *AEB 058* and the Schools Council Project which have greater flexibility and variety of content and assessment, represent models for history syllabuses of the future. The challenges these newer syllabuses present to the teacher, and their potential for teaching about modern European history, are illustrated in the following extracts from case studies based on interviews with teachers who are either already involved in a more progressive history syllabus or considering changing to one in the near future.

School Case Studies

A number of case studies were undertaken to examine how more innovative Europe-focussed history courses were developing. The range of problems discerned in the school case studies can be distinguished as: (a) general problems of introducing innovative courses which seek to re-define curriculum practice and (b) specific problems relating to the Schools Council project.

The Problem of Innovation

Of the first category of problems we can do little more than provide one episode to characterize the general barriers related by innovative history teachers. The implementation, and indeed the study of innovation is enormously complex and the problem cannot be dealt with at length.

Paul is Head of History in a boys' 11–16 comprehensive school (roll 1100). All pupils study history which is part of the Humanities Department. Within Humanities only two members of staff are history specialists, Paul himself and one colleague, while most of the others are geographers.

Paul is a young and committed teacher of his subject. His conversation betrays a deep dissatisfaction with existing styles and methods of history teaching throughout the education system. Ideally he would like to introduce a radical change in his school not just in the content of history courses but also in teaching techniques to combat the stagnation he feels has set in:

> I'm afraid we have spent most of the last decade trundling along in the traditional manner. Fossilization is fast creeping in on us. Our teaching techniques are rather fossilized and I am keen to change our approach radically.

Nevertheless he is aware that change involves risk. The way things are, the subject is successful in the school; the exam results are good and many pupils opt to do 'A' level history at sixth form college, 'thus we start from a happy position and would like to avoid any nose-dive'.

He has tried to introduce the new Schools Council history course but has met deep resistance. He attributes this to a strong conservatism among school teachers in general and believes their hositility to enthusiasm and change stems from a sense of academic failure:

> Most teachers do not want to see too much innovation. There is a massive resistance against it both in particular and in general. I will be brutal about it. The problem with most teachers is that they failed in the academic world. Even if some were bright people they did not do as well as they should have done. So they are not keen on anybody still being keen. There is a sort of conspiracy of mediocrity.

Paul feels that conservatism and hostility to innovation account for a general lack of vitality in teaching practice in schools, something with which he expressed frequent dissatisfaction throughout the interview:

> In teaching the discrepancy between the ideal and what is actually happening is appalling. Most teaching is the intellectual equivalent of school dinners: You are dishing out lumpy, mashed potato.'

Paul's own fear of stagnation; of reproducing the same course year after year, is one of the strongest motives underlying his wish to change the content and method of his teaching:

> I just do not want to get up and have to *explain that* again. It is the fossilization I fear. I am very concerned with that. You get to telling the same jokes again and you kill the material by over-use. I must adapt it in some way because I actually like teaching history. I am committed to the subject. But it is difficult to see yourself. There is no evidence for good teaching practice apart from certain people who in their own way get through the stuff, and maybe that is the only way you are going to work at your particular level.
>
> In education we are not geared to actually improving pupils' performance and reasoning at different levels of history. We *are* geared to posing as the authorities in the classroom in front of a captive audience. I have done that and I still do it and that is really why I want to change, otherwise I will go the same way as everybody else.

Hence Paul would like to change the teacher/pupil relationship so that the latter adopt a more active enquiring role — something that he hopes a new syllabus will help to encourage. He finds, however, that pupils accustomed to the traditional 'captive' role find it difficult to adapt to a different one. In addition, although he has encouraged a more relaxed relationship with his 'O' level groups, several factors such as their experience with other teachers, and the fact that history is timetabled for the end of the afternoon, militate against their more active involvement in class:

> I have discussed this with the fourth years here, what the new ideas are and why it should make them less passive and more active as pupils. But I know that they have got used to the old system and they do not think it is going to work that way. Part of the problem is that I see them for the last two periods and after they have had an ear-bashing for four hours already that day the last thing they want is to think up some smart ideas to impress me and the group around them.

Another problem is the 'O' level pupils' considerable workload. In a school which Paul feels is in danger of becoming an 'O' level crammer', the high ability pupils are encouraged to take as many subjects at 'O' level as they can manage. Consequently although he seems to have had a certain amount of personal success in increasing interest in history among his fourth year pupils through formal and informal contacts, he is very aware that he is competing for their time and commitment with a large number of other subjects:

> The Fourth year is the high-ability intake year which I take every year. By the time they have reached the Fourth year things are very informal. The lesson itself is formal but at lunchtimes a lot of them will drift in to have an essay marked. Often at odd times during the day people will come up and chat to me, perhaps even for an hour after school. That really has made a difference. Time is a problem. We have two hours a week invariably at the latter end of the day and the boys may be doing about ten other 'O' levels. It's not as though it's only history that counts and all the other subjects are also-rans. It's not like that. The Headmaster wants a lot of 'O' level results and some are doing about twelve subjects so there is not time for much relaxaton in a serious sense.

For the putative teacher-innovator lack of time and a heavy workload create particular problems. A new course, especially one which is flexible and school-based, involves a vast amount of preparation. Foreseeing this Paul has allocated part of his summer holiday for the task but realizes that to do so would be less possible if he had a family:

> you have to allocate your own time to preparation. This Summer I'm going to spend a fortnight at a University library. It's a bit weird at this stage in your career to have to spend a fortnight in a University library during the summer to prepare the 'O' level course. It ought to be all buttoned-up according to the old-fashioned teaching style where you get your stuff together and that's it for the next thirty years! I'll enjoy it, but I'm a bit nervous about a new course because I foresee that it will involve hours and hours of work. And I'm not married and haven't got a family.

The Schools Council Course

The research looked in particular at the Schools Council Project 13–16 which began in 1972 and constitutes a different approach to history from the traditional chronological survey of events. According to John Bold it has developed into 'one of the most far-reaching revisions of traditional practice to take place in any school subject'.[10] The project seeks to instil historical attitudes and skills rather than retention of facts, consequently it encourages teachers to participate in an active learning situation rather than just transmitting information to passive pupils.

Two strategies undertaken by the developers of the project have been the production of exemplary materials and the development of a varied approach to the examining of history at GCE 'O' level and CSE. The course is composed of an introductory section *What is History?* designed for the whole ability range in the secondary school third year, and the main 14–16 syllabus for both GCE 'O' level and CSE candidates, the examining of which is jointly operated by the Oxford, Oxford and Cambridge, Cambridge and Southern Universities examination boards.

The 'O' level examination syllabus has several elements: a Study in Development (*Medicine through Time*); a Modern World Study (for which there are four options: *The Irish Question*: *the Rise of Communist China*; *the Move to European Unity since 1945*; *the Arab-Israeli Conflict*); and an Enquiry in Depth (three options: *Elizabethan England 1558–1603*; *The American West 1840–1895*; *Britain 1815–1851*). Pupils are also expected to be able to understand and evaluate historical sources. There are two terminal examination papers, each weighted 30 per cent and course work accounts for 40 per cent.

Of particular interest is the Modern World Studies section of the syllabus which aims 'to help pupils to understand their modern world through a selection of sample studies which attempt to set contemporary events in their historical perspective'. One of the sample studies included deals with the events and personalities involved in the development of modern Europe: *the Move to European Unity*. This aims 'to give an understanding of the historical background and development of the move towards European unity as it affects the contemporary world, and Britain in particular'. The enquiry focusses on certain 'basic questions' to do with the extent to which the recovery in Western Europe since the Second World War is linked to the movement towards unity; the reasons for this movement; why there are divisions between East and West in Europe (thus preventing any real European unity), and Britain's role in Western European unity. Currently, there are two elements in the course that are closely informed by present events: the significance and implications of British membership of the various European organizations, and in particular the EEC; and secondly, from a European position, the future development and survival of unity.

The course deals consistently with the issues of peace and unity and in this sense echoes the earlier aspirations of those seeking antitodes to 'drum and trumpet' national history. This focus is noted in the introduction in the pupils' book where the following questions are posed:

(i) What were the origins of the post-war European unity problems?
(ii) What have been the results of this movement?
(iii) How united is Europe?
(iv) What has been Britain's part in this movement?

The concept of European unity is then examined as an aspect of mutal defence; as a means of creating prosperity, and as a means of eliminating old rivalries and suspicions.

The converse side is stressed by analysis of new rivalries and suspicions and of other factors working against unity. Nevertheless the course is more broadly conceived than as an induction into visions of unification and the following pupil outcomes are stressed: an understanding 'that the reasons for change are complex'; 'that nationalism is still an important force in the modern world'.

Case Study

The case study was conducted at a school where the 13–16 course had been introduced and established by an enthusiastic and committed teacher, who described his first encounter with the project as follows:

> I first came across the Project when I went on a one-day course at which the research team who had been chosen to set it up showed a publicity film about it. And they talked about it and the materials which would be available and I thought this is worth having a look at. In fact, the Schools Council History Project is marvellous. I felt it was the best thing since sliced bread! This is Real history that's what it is! It's getting away from the old examination of five essays in two and a half hours; it's getting away from the memory test. That's not history! It's a diabolical system! This course takes topics and it poses historical tasks. I think all the newer, better history syllabuses are indebted to the Schools Council Project.

However a wide range of problems were described with reference to the *Move to European Unity* option. Teachers commended the well-chosen sources and the fair and unbiased approach they felt encouraged more reflective and balanced attitudes in pupils. They also liked the use of cartoons which were found stimulating and valuable in putting across viewpoints and sustaining interest. Teacher's Guides and filmstrips were thought much less valuable than the pupil materials. A basic problem was not the style of the materials however but the content. Again and again teachers came back to the fact that as one put it 'Europe is utterly BORING.'

> The move to European unity involves very few dramatic incidents. It is basically the story of the growth of the EEC ... Europe since the war

is boring. Its only interesting if they've been to Spain or Italy or Greece on holiday. It *needs* a great deal of impact in the way it's put across Now the simplest way to do this is to basically act in front of the youngsters.

All this simply means is that we use the force of our personalities to put Europe across. When it seems that you've got a boring piece of material you've got to drive the essential points home. So how do you make something like this more interesting? The Coal and Steel Community! Well, it's very difficult isn't it? But somehow you've got to put this across as being the first real major step towards European Unity, and you've got to get them to sympathize ... no more than that ... to empathize with Robert Schuman and the situation in Europe in the late 1940s and early 50s. To do that you've got to have looked at things such as the state of Europe after World War 2. There is an element of drama there and if you could show a photo like the one of Rotterdam, utterly devastated, and if you could concentrate on sources such as the War dead.

In spite of the lack of drama discerned in the European option it is clear that teachers found ways of developing interest among the pupils. This interest could undoubtedly be further nurtured if better visual aids such as photographs cartoons and filmstrips were available. But unfortunately the expense of the course is already a limiting factor.

If we have the money I'd expand it even more. The sheer cost of the School's Council history project is a limiting factor. Now compared with setting up a creative studies course of art, metalwork, woodwork or the sciences, it is not expensive, but these subjects have an obvious demand for school resources, whereas something like history tends to create in a planner's mind .... Well, you need four walls and a blackboard and a stick of chalk and that's it. Whereas we need a lot more resources. Now for the *Move to European Unity* we have got to buy a book for each individual pupil. They have *got* to have the books to do the homework; these are the only materials we have got. So I *have* to limit the numbers doing this course.

Cost is a severe limiting factor because a number of teachers have said to me, 'look, I like the sound of your course. It sounds really interesting but isn't it rather expensive?'

Well, you can get a set of books for a Social and Economic course say at £2 each, say £60 for 30 if you are talking about a group of 30. Now for S.C.H.P. multiply 30 by 15. At the last calculation it was about £15 per candidate just for books alone! I bet it's more than that now. For what you get it's reasonable, but you have to set it against the background of £200 capitation per year and that covers the Third, Fourth and Fifth years. I have not spent anything on the Third year for years! Now I have had £200 for the last three or four years and I have

> got £200 for this coming year. With inflation the purchasing power of £200 is considerably less than it was.'

A further problem affecting all aspects of the course content is that the syllabus is considered 'too loaded and tightly-structured'. Consequently even if there were supplementary materials and visual aids for the European Section there might not be the time available to use them. One teacher spoke of the problems that his pupils faced:

> Well, it is alright for whizz-kid teachers who get promotion and kudos, to do all the work, but when it comes down to the youngsters that we are aiming the work at, there is far too much work to expect them to do with two Modern World Studies and Medicine! You have to get them through three books in one term dealing with the history of medicine from the Stone Age right up to the 1970s. You're dealing with the contribution of the Egyptian Civilization, the Greek, the Romans, the Middle Ages, the Renaissance and the Modern age especially the 19th Century and the 20th. Not only are they studying medicine but they are also studying the interaction of all the developments in mankind and their relationship to the development of medicine. Consequently there is a lot to learn there. We get them through it but it's a mad dash. Time is at a premium. It's not so much a physical but a mental impossibility to cope equally efficiently with all of this course.

The ambivalence about Europe; the perception that it is boring (found commonly among teachers as well as students) the lack of visual aids, all act to ensure that the *Move to European Unity* option seems destined to lag behind the other options in popularity. Only a sustained programme of teacher development and curriculum development (especially of visual aids) could promote this option as a more popular choice.

Conclusions

Most people would agree that some study of twentieth century history is an essential part of children's education; that it will help not only to promote understanding of the events and forces that have shaped the contemporary world but also to counteract the sometimes misleading, oversensational versions of modern history put across by television, the cinema and popular fiction.

Any history of the contemporary world must incorporate a sizeable European element, modern European history having played a unique part in influencing and determining events and trends all over the globe. Some knowledge of recent European history should be part of the cultural baggage of anyone who claims to be educated. Many of our examination syllabuses, however, end their European sections around 1954 or even earlier. Unfortunately the majority of GCE courses were drawn up some time ago which leads to a problem of time-lag. Thus history syllabuses can themselves be historical artefacts.

Nevertheless this is a uniquely fruitful time to try and persuade examination Boards and history teachers that changes are necessary, particularly since history has been suffering in recent years from a gradual decline in popularity, a process which apparently began to accelerate in 1976.[11] This trend has been attributed to a perceptible switch in schools to the sciences and more practical subjects:

> The demand for more time for practical subjects and sciences has threatened to push history into combined humanities course, along with geography and religion, in the early secondary years and into the optional extras for the senior years.[12]

To an extent the development and growing popularity of world history courses could be a reaction to this. These courses embrace events, problems and issues related to the contemporary world, thus their broader scope and greater relevance combined with more flexible methods of study and assessment render them more appealing and of more practical use to pupils. According to a researcher,[13] they are also more beneficial than other history courses. For seventeen months he studied a group of pupils following a modern world history course combining study of documentary and other sources, project work and class discussion. At the end of the course the target group were better able to deal with historical evidence and less likely to hold sterotyped racial and nationalist views than pupils in the same ability range in a control group who had not followed the same course.

Some areas of modern world history, however, may not be easy to put across in the classroom. Whereas young people may be fascinated by the Third World or by modern history of a colourful and dramatic character, they do not immediately empathize with modern European issues. Modern European history therefore, needs some care in the way it is presented and taught as seen in case study.

One possible way of dealing with contemporary European history is through a detailed comparison of pupils' own local community with an area or several areas in continental Europe. The Local History Classroom Project, for example, has reported an initiative of this kind: a comparison of the English community of Barrow with the French community of Marcillé-Raoul. The aim of the exercise was 'for pupils to write some history about their local comunities in the past and exchange the results of that work with their counterparts. The project coordinators suggest that work of this nature could lead to a fruitful collaboration between history and modern languages teachers.[14]

This is one way in which modern European history can be made relevant and interesting: by comparison or contrast; by starting with a local or national perspective which can then be used as reference point in a wider historical context.

An example of a textbook that demonstrates how pupils can be drawn into looking at history from a national perspective gradually enlarging into a European one, is supplied by R. Ben Jones' *Social Economic History of Britain 1770–1977*,[15] for 'O' level candidates. The first edition appeared in 1972, and its economic section ended with Britiain's entry into the EEC. The second edition goes much further and includes economic and social data from 1978. Europe features prominently in the later sections, which have been completely re-written.

If the whole book is covered in a course, then the pupils will be introduced to the concept of a developing economy, and go on to see Britain as the workshop of the world, commanding her markets. But as the twentieth century is covered, the concept of the interdependence of advanced industrial nations is brought out, and the point is pushed home by the illustration of the price of prairie wheat directly affecting the cost of a loaf in Britain. As the evolving position of the British economy during the 1960s is outlined, the economic case for joining the EEC is presented. The consequences are touched upon and the problem of agriculture receives a reasoned treatment, showing as well as problems such as high prices the advantages derived from the Common Agricultural Policy. The impact of membership upon government and administration is considered and the process of decision-making in the Community touched upon. Thus the volume carries the reader from a developing economy to a major industrialized national economy, and so through to the interrelated, European-oriented economy of today.

In social history the work portrays the changing life styles of different social classes in Britain, but ends with an outward-looking European Britain, with readers encouraged to look critically at the changing social world about them.

The importance of developing people's awareness of the interdependence and interrelated concerns of the different nations and races of the world has been given increasing attention in recent years, for example in the influential Brandt Report.

The specific contribution that history can make to this aim is stated in the HMI document on the curriculum 11–16:

> We live in a world of increasingly interdependent countries and in a multicultural society, so local and national history must be related to a wider context, not only Europe but in America, Africa and Asia. So within five years of compulsory secondary education, some balance must be established between local, national and world history.[16]

This expresses the most convincing rationale not only for the inclusion of European history in courses but also for the perspective in which it should be placed as part of a wider world context.

The Inspectorate's working papers on the Curriculum 11–16 provide a background for current considerations about a new core curriculum for English and Welsh schools. An essential part of these discussions is the projected emergence of a new common examination. For this new examination courses for the whole ability range will be developed by examining bodies composed of groups of combined GCE and CSE Boards.

This development provides a unique opportunity to influence the content of examination courses. Since history has been identified as the most important subject for study of modern Europe it is essential that those promoting wider perspectives in history courses set about defining their approaches now. It is unlikely that such a good opportunity will present itself again for another decade.

Notes

1 DANCE, E.M. (1967) 'Bias in History Teaching and Textbook' in SCHÜDDEKOPF, O.E. (Ed.) *History Teaching and History Textbook Revision*, Strasbourg, Council of Europe, pp. 80–1.
2 *Ibid* p. 85.
3 HEATER, D.B. (1979) *Essays on Contemporary Studies*, Ormskirk, G.W. & A. Hesketh, p. 12.
4 SCHÜDDEKOPF, O.E. (1967) 'History textbook revision 1945–1965' in SCHÜDDEKOPF, O.E. (Ed.) *op. cit.*, p. 41.
5 By modern, the period referred to is from c. 1870 to the present day.
6 McNEILL, W. (1970) 'World History in the Schools' in Ballard Martin (Ed.) *New Movement in the Study and Teaching of History*, London, Maurice Temple Smith, p. 21.
7 STUART HUGHES, M. (1979) *Consciousness and Society: the Reorientation of European Social Thought 1890–1930*, Brighton, Harvester Press, p. 394.
8 McNEILL, W. *op. cit.*, p. 21.
9 INGLIS, W.F.J. (1980) 'A Content Analysis of 'O' and 'A' level papers on Modern British and European History set by two GCE 'Examination Boards', *British Educational Research Journal*, Vol. 6, No. 1, pp. 43–51.
10 BOLD JOHN, *Times Educational Supplement*, 24 April 1981.
11 *The Guardian*, 24 January 1979.
12 *The Observer*, 1 February 1981.
13 BOOTH, M. (1980) in *Educational Review*, Vol. 32.
14 LABETTE, B. (1976) *The Local History Classroom Project*, Norwich, University of East Anglia.
15 JONES, R.B. (1979) *Social and Economic History of Britain 1770–1977*, London, Longmans, 2nd edition.
16 Her Majesty's Inspectorate (1977) *Curriculum 11–16*, London, HMSO, 1977.

4 Geography

In the *Europe in the School* Survey (and in earlier surveys examined) geography is consistently rated the second most important subject in the school curriculum for teaching about modern Europe. Because the scope of the subject is so wide, comprising both physical and human sides, geographical studies can include not only the physical features of an area but also up-to-date demographic and economic data and important contemporary issues such as environmental problems.

In the document *Geography and the School Curriculum 11–16* (HMI 1981) the authors argue that geography should:

> help pupils gain a perspective within which they can place local and distant events, develop their own attitudes and make their own decisions. The subject can also help prepare them to take an active interest and become positively and responsibly involved in community life and affairs and in the affairs of the larger society of which they are members.

There has been continous debate among geographers in recent years about the relative importance of the human and physical sides of geography and the appropriate balance between them. The debate intensified in the 1960s and since this point some fundamental changes have taken place in both the content and methodology of geography courses. In particular what became known as *New Geography* developed in the US, Britain and Sweden in the late 1950s and early 1960s partly in response to university geographers' concern to acquire for their subject the status of a scientific discipline. New Geography heralded a swing away from regional geography towards scientific methods on the model of descriptive natural science: spatial theory, quantitative data and model building. Strongly promoted though they were in some universities, the new developments were not wholeheartedly welcomed by all geographers, many of whom considered regional geography to be the proper domain of the subject. More seriously, the creation of data-and concept-based courses in universities led to a growing rift between secondary and tertiary geography programmes and this aroused anxiety about disparities in the definition and content of the subject.[1]

The new methods became more generally accepted around 1967 and by the 1970s they had been absorbed into courses at both secondary and tertiary levels of education. Since the early 1970s, however, there has been resistance to the quantitative approach although it has remained strong in both research and teaching.[2] Some geographers, for example, now believe that the change has been too extreme. During an interview conducted as part of the research case studies the Head of the Geography Department at a Scottish college of education (where graduates are trained for secondary school teaching) expressed such a view:

> Scotland has gone overboard for New Geography but we're now retracing our steps a little. At the University of . . . , for example, the staff went overboard for New Geography but there was a very strong resistance to it from students there and in other universities. They wanted study of place instead of ideas and concepts for their own sake; they want *regional* Geography!

This lecturer expressed some scepticism about geography courses in universities and concern that students, in his experience, 'no longer seem to have the basics: they don't know how to apply data'.

Another professor of geography recently complained that universities are turning out geographers who know 'all about mathematical techniques and methodology but nothing about the world — or the country they live in'. Facts in geography, he claims, are regarded as less important than ideas and techniques: 'this is bound to seep down into schools as young teachers, having had no regional geography in their training are reluctant to teach what they do not know or come to regard as inferior'.[3]

In an article written for *Teaching about Europe* Michael Williams, has described the teacher's dilemma in terms of a debate 'in which one side argues that "knowing how" is more important than "knowing what".' This debate (which is very relevant to teaching about Europe in geography) can be seen as part of the perennial concern over the respective emphases to be placed on 'content' and 'process' in curriculum planning: firstly is Europe an end in itself or a means to an end? Secondly, is the way Europe is studied more important than what is learned about Europe by the pupil at the end of study?

> Some geographers argue that the selection of which places to study is a secondary matter to follow on a prior decision regarding the kinds of knowledge, attitudes and skills pupils ought to acquire. The selection of place will be made on the basis that the places will most usefully serve the process of learning already determined. Thus, European places will be set alongside other places and these European places will not have any intrinsic value simply because they are located in

> Europe. The alternative argument follows from the decision to choose a place first, say, Europe, and then examine that place critically in order to decide which geographical lessons can best be taught from Europe. This debate has certainly not been resolved and it was one which was certain to emerge as soon as the regional basis for syllabus construction was removed. The 'region' was attacked principally because it emphasised the uniqueness of places and because it led to the replication from region to region of the same study techniques.[4]

Paradoxically, therefore, one of the side effects of an approach which replaced emphasis on regions with emphasis on concepts, statistics and data, has been a reappraisal of the place of regional studies within the subject.

New Geography also stimulated fresh attempts to redefine the subject as a whole. Indeed the term 'New Geography' is not currently used in higher education circles since it is no longer 'new', and has been superseded by other approaches. A number of responses occurred between the 1970s and the present to displace quantitative geography. Briefly, such alternative approaches have been labelled — 'behavioural geography', 'liberal geography' (making new geography more relevant), 'phenomenological geography', and 'radical geography'.

Radical geography involved the injection of human or social content into a subject which seemed to be growing increasingly abstract and scientific:

> Out of the tension between the mundane focal interests of the 'new geography' and the urgent need for social relevancy and political involvement came the first stumbling moves towards a 'radical' geography . . .
>
> What emerged from the practice of radical geography was an interest in two types of issues: among academically-oriented geographers an effort to change the focus of the discipline from what was seen as eclectic irrelevances to the study of urgent social problems; among action-oriented geographers, the search for organizational models for promoting social change.[5]

Radical geography and, subsequently, Marxist geography have been influential in the US and, particularly, in Great Britain. In this country it has had an impact in developing a more significant concern with problems of a social, economic and political nature.

It is possible, therefore, when inspecting school geography courses and examination syllabuses, to discern the influence of several recent approaches to geography. The more recently-devised courses often consist of a combination of the quantitative approach and behavioural and radical approaches — attempts to encourage pupils to develop awareness of urgent social, economic and environmental issues, and to think of possible solutions to them.

Since the choice of regional illustrations within the newer courses, more often than not, is left to the teacher it can be extremely difficult to pinpoint what and how much geography of Europe is actually taught in schools. Moreover, there are a number of problems inherent in any attempt to identify not just *what* European geography is taught but what European geography *should* be taught. As pointed out by Williams the answer to these questions will depend not just on the syllabus chosen but on the resources available and, in particular, on how teachers define the aims of the subject: some for example will select content only to further the process of acquiring specific predetermined knowledge, attitudes and skills and to them selection of place will be of secondary importance. Others may first select regions for study and only then decide what geographical knowledge and skills can be derived from studying these areas: 'the place of Europe in any balanced study must be viewed in the light of the academic debate within the subject and the implications of this debate for the teaching of geography in schools.'[6]

An additional obstacle to be confronted in any attempt to assess how much European geography is taught is the relative freedom British teachers have to construct their own courses albeit within the conventions and traditions of the subject and according to the resources and constraints existing in individual schools. This freedom inevitably leads to enormous variations in selection of content, aims and objectives, teaching methods, forms of assessment and choice of resources. Thus one can agree with Williams:

> Strangers to the changing world of school geography teaching must come away bewildered when they find teachers disagreeing in a fundamental way about definitions of school geography, the meaning of Europe, the appropriate curriculum models on which to base syllabus design, and the place of geography in curricula.[7]

The bulk of secondary school geography teaching takes place in years 1–3. For all the reasons mentioned and because these are not the years terminating in external examinations, it is impossible to measure the extent and nature of the European dimension in courses for the 11–14 age groups. One course that appears to be popular with teachers for this age group — the *Oxford Geography Project* — may give some indication of the kind of geography that is *likely* to be taught in years 1–3. Developed for the first years of secondary education, the Project is defined, in its Introduction, as:

> A foundation course which embodies the new thinking in geography and new teaching methods. By stressing the acquisition of essential geographical skills and concepts at progressive levels of difficulty, it provides a base on which any CSE or 'O' level course can be built higher up the school (. . .)
>
> The emphasis is on precision and prediction and on applying geographical knowledge to a swiftly changing world. Throughout the course pupils are asked to participate in making decisions about recurrent contemporary problems and planning possible solutions to them.[8]

This, then, is a course in which emphasis is placed very firmly on new geography and radical geography methods and content. It ensures that there is adequate use of regional examples by being divided into three units: *the Local Framework*, *European Patterns* and *Contrasts in Development*. Thus, the *Oxford Geography Project* is an example of a course for years 1–3 in which recent methods and approaches to geography are set within a balanced framework ranging from the local to the global. Its important section on Europe examines the themes: settlement, rural land use, urban problems, ports, industry, employment and communications. Pupils following this course are therefore likely to study a considerable amount of European geography, albeit not of the traditional 'capes and bays' kind.

Syllabus Commentary

In the upper years of secondary school the kind of geography taught depends largely on the external examination syllabuses available. The following commentary based on a detailed analysis of GCE 'O' and 'A' level and SCE 'O' and 'H' grade courses available in 1980, identifies the syllabuses with the greatest potential for study of European geography. (In this section Europe should be taken to mean continental Europe).

There is no compulsory Europeans content in any of the Geography GCE syllabuses available in 1980. Where there is a specified European element it is always an option to which the USA (or North America) is invariably an alternative. The syllabuses with no specified European content usually offer some scope for European examples to be studied but leave the choice of region to the teacher or pupil. This is particularly true of the revised syllabuses such as the AEB 'A' level which is concept and skill-based rather than region-based. In two of the SCE geography syllabuses, the *alternative 'O' grade* and the *traditional 'H' grade*, there is a compulsory European dimension in the regional geography section.

GCE 'A' level Examinations

In six out of twelve syllabuses there is an optional European content and in all cases the US is one of the alternatives. In one syllabus (*WJEC 0015*) the European option is also set against the British Isles; in another, (*University of Cambridge 9050*) S. America and Africa, while the regional geography section of the Northern Ireland 'A' level offers as alternatives: USA and Canada; The Monsoon Lands of S. and S.E.Asia; Africa, South of the Sahara, or Field Work in the British Isles.

The main areas of Europe listed are limited in most cases to a small number of countries in western Europe. Three syllabuses specify the EEC and in two of them certain regions of the Community are to be studied (*JMB* (*C*): S.E. France, Scotland, N. Rhine Westphalia; *University of Cambridge 9050*: British Isles, France, W. Germany, Benelux, Denmark, Italy. In only three cases (*Oxford Local 9845, 9846 and Northern Ireland*) is the USSR presented as an additional option. Of the syllabuses with an optional European content the one of which this is potentially the most important part is *JMB syllabus C*, a recently developed examination in which the regional section is a third of the total syllabus. The European option is the EEC as constituted in January 1978 and specific case-study areas are identified. In all of the other examinations with an optional European content the regional section accounts for only about one sixth of the total syllabus.

The courses with no specified European content nevertheless offer the possibility of some study of Europe depending on the choice of region or area used by the teacher to illustrate certain topics. Two syllabuses — *JMB* (*B*) and *AEB* (*C.26*) — make no reference to any specific region but are sufficiently flexible to allow for considerable use of European case study examples. Both of these are examples of the newer kinds of geography syllabus offering greater flexibility of content and assessment and an essentially conceptual and thematic approach. The Schools Council 16–19 Project which was being developed at the time of this syllabus analysis, is another example of this trend. Only the *SCE Geography Higher Grade* examination has a compulsory question on Europe: in Paper 2 *Regional Geography*.

'A/O' Examinations

In one out of four, *University of Cambridge 8090*, there is an optional European content to which the alternative is South America. The area of Europe specified is the EEC (British Isles, France, West Germany, Benelux, Denmark, Italy) and if chosen could account for up to one third of the total course.

In none of the other syllabuses is there any direct reference to Europe although there are limited possibilities for the use of European examples in at least one section of each.

GCE 'O' Level Examinations

Eight out of thirteen have an optional European content and in all cases the USA (or North America) is an alternative. Two additional options are Australia and New Zealand (WJEC) (including Japan in one case (*London syllabus A*) and the Developing World (*Oxford Local*).

In most cases the optional European content is Western Europe, usually the countries of the EEC and occasionally Switzerland, Spain and Portugal. The *University of London syllabus A* lists the largest number of countries, fifteen in all, including Finland, and also has an additional option 'the USSR and the rest of Europe'. Two other syllabuses also offer the USSR as an option, *WJEC 0118* and *Oxford and Cambridge*.

Of the syllabuses with a specified European content the ones with the most potential coverage of Europe are undoubtedly the two University of London examinations. Candidates taking *syllabus B* could theoretically spend 50 per cent of their study time on Europe, and those taking *syllabus* A between 25 per cent and 50 per cent. (In 1978 syllabus B was the more popular of the two attracting 19,942 candidates as opposed to 9928 for syllabus A). *The University of Cambridge Local (2200)* also presents opportunities for substantial coverage of Europe. A possible 25 — 50 per cent of total study time could be devoted to Europe for this syllabus which attracted 22,282 candidates in 1978.

In the *Oxford Local syllabus 2845* there is the possibility of spending up to 25 per cent of study time on Europe (23, 949 candidates in 1979), and also in the *Oxford and Cambridge*, one of the more modern theme-based courses.

Of the other examinations with a European option the following approximate proportions of the syllabus could be devoted to study of Europe:

WJEC. 0118 —20 per cent
AEB 033 —16.67 per cent
WJEC Alt. —10 per cent (This syllabus, incidentally, has the most detailed and comprehensive list of European case-studies of all the 'O' level syllabuses.)

Of the remaining syllabuses in which no European content is specified *Oxford Local 2846* has no European possibilities at all while the following offer very limited opportunities for European examples in at least one paper: *JMB. Syllabus A*, *JMB Syllabus B*, *University of Cambridge 2201*, *SUJB* 2208.

The *SCE (traditional) 'O' grade*, has a section on regional and general geography in which the emphasis is on Europe (together with the USSR) although there are a number of other regional options. The *SCE alternative 'O' grade*, in line with the newer GCE syllabuses, is more thematically than regionally-based but in Paper 2 three themes are to be related to, firstly, the United Kingdom and Western Europe and, secondly, World Studies.

In addition to the syllabuses analyzed, three Schools Council Geography Projects have been developed which incorporate some of the newest trends in content, methodology and assessment; these are *Geography for the Young School Leaver* (GYSL); the *Geography 14–18 Project* and the *Geography 16–19 Project*. The following extract from the GYSL 'O' level syllabus (1976) indicates the extent to which the course constitutes an attempt to combine the most recent developments in the subject:

> Geography has seen many changes in recent decades, the most fundamental of which has been a move from descriptions of individual and specific phenomena to a search for repeating and universal patterns and processes. This emphasis on theory, with its generalizations and models on the one hand and its potential for prediction on the

other, is in line with developments in other physical and social sciences. More recently geographers have also been involved in the solution of problems of a social, economic and political nature. This syllabus attempts to translate both the conceptual and the issue-based approach in geography into the school curriculum.

The course (which can be taken to either 'O' level or CSE), aims to prepare pupils to be aware of and involved in important issues relating to the world about them when they leave school. The core syllabus is composed of three key ideas: settlement, economic activity and recreation, which are to be studied in relation to settings on a local, national and international scale. The choice of regional examples is left to the teacher. For the 'O' level course, material on the three core elements is provided by the project developers and schools devise a fourth (on physical studies, regional studies or applied studies). Assessment of the course is a combination of external assessment (a terminal examination 60 per cent) and internal (coursework and continuous assessment 40 per cent).

The GYSL Project is a good example of the more imaginative and flexible approach to geography that has been developed in recent years. 'The New Geography', especially social geography, is very much to the fore, involving analysis of spatial patterns and decision-making in the environment.'[9]

The course has also been very successful. According to Parsons, in 1980 it achieved 'a success unrivalled by any other Schools Council project and this at a time of financial stringency, when the education system has supposedly wearied of innovation'.[10]

This suggests that the newer type of geography course is gaining ground in schools and that a more flexible course is popular with teachers.

The range of examination syllabuses analysed in 1980 revealed a marked division between the 'old-style' geography courses with separate physical, human and regional geography sections and the more flexible recently devised syllabuses which are skill and concept-based and tend to refer to regions less for their own sake than to illustrate particular man-environment themes at scales varying from the local to the global. There is a difference too in methods of assessment. The traditional syllabuses are exclusively assessed by terminal examinations whereas the more innovative ones often have, in addition to these, an optional school-based project, which can be internally assessed.

Where European content is concerned, Michael Williams identified in 1982 the definitions of Europe detectable in school syllabuses and listed them as follows:

1 Pan-European systematic definitions. In these definitions, Europe is sub-divided into major geomorphological, climatic and bio-geographical regions. No account is taken of political frontiers, but the continent is demarcated into physical zones, or regions by isotherms, isobars, contours and other such lines.
2 National definitions. Particular nations are selected for study

according to certain defined criteria. These nations may be subdivided into regions, physical, economic, social or political. Selected regions may be emphasised and studied in greater detail than others.

3 Thematic definitions. Themes may be selected for study and these may be examined at different levels, e.g. the energy problem. This may be studied as a pan-European problem, a Western European problem, a national problem or a local/regional problem. A thematic approach may be combined with case studies.

4 Case Study definitions. The term 'case study' may be applied to the study of a theme. Generally, it is used with reference to studies of relatively small geographical areas which serve to illustrate a theme, e.g. Europort as a study of a major seaport, the coast of Languedoc as a study of tourist development. The precise area is selected because the features evident there are pronounced and distinctive. The location of the case study area within a political, economic or social system is often a secondary consideration and it is frequently neglected.

5 International definitions. These emphasise trans-frontier geographical issues which have been selected to highlight their international significance. These include migration, trade, the movement of ideas and also concepts such as Euregio. It is possible for international groupings such as the EEC, to serve as macro-regions in which national thematic and case studies are made.[11]

Williams points out that all these definitions are to be found in syllabuses with some focussing on one and others on several, according to the choice of subject matter, but that ultimately the teachers make their own selection of content and teaching method.

Schools Council Geography 14–18 and 16–19

To find out the factors involved in this selection process, a case study was conducted in a school where teachers were involved in developing and teaching two of the more recently devised courses: the Schools Council Geography Projects 14–18 and 16–19. Although primarily developed as GCE 'O' and 'A' level syllabuses the two are so flexible in structure and assessment that they can be also used by the whole ability range and have led to CSE and CEE examinations. The two syllabuses are firmly school-based with much of the teaching materials produced by participating schools and a high proportion of internal assessment (14–18: 50 per cent of total marks; 16–19 : 30 per cent).

In their publicity leaflet for the 14–18 Project (developed 1970–75) the Schools Council defines the course as a 'major new development in the teaching of geography (which) was concerned that modern curriculum development should be a school-based activity and an integral part of the teachers' work, rather than a by-product of examination requirements'. The 'O' level examination is administered by the University of Cambridge Local Examinations Syndicate on behalf of all GCE Boards. The course is assessed by a common terminal paper worth 50 per cent of total marks; coursework 30 per cent; and an individual study: 20 per cent (the last two being internally assessed and externally moderated). In the Board's regulations this assessment system is commented on as follows:

> while maintaining standards and comparability of assessment it encourages teachers to:
> (i) draw more effectively on new ideas in geography and education by the systematic and planned development of their individual resources in relation to changing curriculum needs;
> (ii) relate shorter-term subject objectives more effectively to wider, longer term educational aims, particularly by giving more scope for individual study in depth, and constructive feedback to students:
> (iii) participate more fully in sustained processes of curriculum renewal at a time when the subject matter and potential strategies for geography teaching are changing rapidly.
>
> To meet these objectives teachers are actively involved in the evaluation process, through the marking of coursework and individual studies and are encouraged to submit draft questions via moderators for Paper 1.

The 14–18 Project as a whole is concerned with encouraging pupils to take a closer interest in the world about them. It also stresses the development of active rather than passive learning skills: Figures 1 and 2 show the structure of the core syllabus and the system of assessment.

Figure 1 The core syllabus

The aim of the core syllabus is to enable pupils to use important skills, ideas and models drawn on in geography to classify and interpret such everyday experiences as discerning order in landscape and bringing regional and world problems into appropriate frames of reference.

In so doing it is hoped to promote an understanding of:

(a) the geographical character of the local area, and of the British Isles considered as a unit: the use of Ordnance Survey 1:25,000 and 1:50,000 maps.

(b) significant contrasts and similarities in
 (i) other economically-developed regions of the world:
 (ii) less-developed regions of the world:

(c) the working of wider physical and economic systems at a world scale:

(d) the processes underlying landscape and spatial patterns:

(e) environmental inter-relationships considered in terms of systems and sub-systems: and hence with multiple or cumulative causes, rather than simple cause and effect or deterministic explanations:

(f) how landscape and spatial patterns change and may be expected to continue to change, especially in the context of technological change:

(g) the role of decision-making and of the values and perceptions of decision-makers. in the evolution of patterns in human geography:

(h) the importance of the scale at which patterns and systems are considered:

(i) how ideas. models and maps simplify complex geographical reality.

To achieve this aim, schools or local consortia are encouraged to plan their own curricula. Table II below indicates the subject areas which may be used as a basis for curriculum planning and which will be covered by questions in the final common paper.

TABLE I

A Illustrative examples to be chosen from	B Wider systems or contexts to be considered	C Appropriate distribution of examples chosen
(i) Weather and climate	Atmospheric and oceanic circulation	Local and British Isles 40 per cent-50 per cent approximately
(ii) Contrasting landforms	Longer-term geologic and shorter-term geomorphic processes	Other developed regions of the world 15 per cent-30 per cent approximately
(iii) Conoorvation of natural resources	Hydrologic cycle	
(iv) Agricultural land-use (v) Location growth and decline of industries (vi) Transport networks (vii) Economic growth and trade (viii) Settlement patterns between and within towns (ix) Population growth and distribution	Physical Technological Economic Social Political } processes influencing spatial patterns and landscapes	Less developed regions of the world 15 per cent-30 per cent approximately Wider physical and economic systems at a world scale 10 per cent-15 per cent approximately

Figure 2 The Relationship of the Core Syllabus to the System of Assessment

THE CORE SYLLABUS

The core syllabus forms the basis for the selection and development of all learning activities, content, and illustrative examples. *These are chosen individually by schools to develop pupils' general capacity to interpret landscapes, and geographical patterns and trends at local, regional and world scales.* Teachers need to structure and sequence studies to enable pupils to draw upon skills, ideas and models in differing and unfamiliar geographical contexts.

MODES OF ASSESSMENT

Paper 1 — Common Paper

Paper 1 is based directly on the core syllabus and requires structured teaching and learning, usually including case studies.

Past examination questions indicate the balance between 'coverage' and 'depth of study' which the aim of developing pupils' general capacities entails. Pupils will not be required to memorise case studies but will need practice in recalling and reflecting upon their implications; for example, in recognising important ideas and models, and in discussing critically how they can be applied elsewhere.

Paper 2 — Coursework

Coursework units are studies developed from the core syllabus which cannot be adequately assessed under time-limit conditions. They are generally more intensive, specialised or experimental in nature, thus requiring,

(a) flexibility according to the local context;
(b) feedback and interplay between teachers, learners and examiners.

Five units must be completed.

Paper 3 — Individual Study

An in-depth study of a problem of particular interest to the candidate, guided by tutorial advice. It will usually draw on enquiry skills and concepts encountered during the teaching programme.

The 16–19 Geography Project was a follow-up to the 14–18 Project and at the time of the research project in 1980, was still in the development stage. Thirty schools were then involved in piloting the new 'A' level syllabus which was to be examined in 1982 for the first time by the University of London Schools Examination Council on behalf of all the GCE examining bodies. The assessment of 16–19 takes the form of a terminal examination (two papers worth 15 per cent and 40 per cent respectively) coursework assessment (30 per cent) and individual study (15 per cent). Like the 14–18 Project, most of the teaching materials are produced by consortia of schools. The framework of the syllabus on which six core modules (a module is considered to be six weeks' work) and three option modules are constructed, are four 'man-environment' themes: *National Environments — the Challenge of Man; Use and Misuse of National Resources: Man — Environment Issues of Global Concern; and Managing Man-made Environments and Systems.*

As with the 14–18, there is also an individual study, the topic of which is to be chosen by the student.

As the four themes suggest, the 16–19 Project encourages pupils to be interested and involved in the relationship between man and environment. Like the 14–18 Project it is more concerned with enquiry-based learning than the retention of facts.

> The Man-Environment approach to geography is characterised by emphasis on the examination of questions, issues and problems arising from man's inter-relationship with his environment. 'Environment' is used here in its widest sense, to include the physical, socio-cultural and behavioural environments influencing and influenced by man.
>
> As a basis for geography courses, the approach involves drawing out the geographer's distinctive contribution to environmental understanding. This requires understanding of important spatial and environmental concepts in geography and the use of a range of methods employed by geographers in explaining spatial patterns and interactions and in understanding the functioning of human and physical systems.
>
> The approach demands understanding of the way in which geographers can move from description, explanation and analysis to application, commitment and implementation, thus stressing the geographer's concern for and contribution to the improvement of the quality of man's environments and therefore the quality of life.[12]

According to the Schools Council both the 14–18 and 16–19 courses are very successful and have been gaining in popularity each year. Most schools participating in 14–18 have already developed parallel CSE examinations.

The teachers participating in the case study were very enthusiastic about the courses. They particularly welcomed the greater flexibility of syllabus design and content. It is possible, for example, to modify or replace course materials so that the syllabus is in a constant state of development. This in itself creates a far more dynamic course than the traditional geography syllabus which offered little opportunity for change:

> The Schools Council syllabuses are very much more flexible than traditional geography syllabuses. In theory a traditional syllabus may have evolved in the sense that you added bits each year or found out more information about it, but there was rigidity in the things you had to cover. With these projects there's a greater possibility for change.

The teachers also welcomed the chance to devise their own materials in liaison with others, working as a team. They liked too the fairer system of assessment which caters for a wider ability range than the traditional written examination. One teacher summed up the advantages of the projects as follows:

> 14–18 has been very successful. It's caught on well because, I think, of the amount of freedom it gives to teachers to use their own materials and not to feel hidebound by particular textbooks; because it's possible to work together in a consortium therefore you're sharing the work-load; and also, I think, because of the degree of internal assessment. One of the great attractions of 14–18, and I think of 16–19 as well, is that it assesses a much wider range of pupil abilities.

A welcome feature of the projects, according to the teachers in the case study is their stress on *human* geography. In their view 16–19 in particular strikes a good balance between human and physical geography and deals with questions and issues of tremendous interest to both teachers and pupils:

> Physical geography has been grossly over-estimated over the years and a vast amount of syllabuses have been devoted to pure science without any relationship to what man is doing on the earth's surface at all. My view is that 16–19 restores the balance between the two sides. The 16–19 courses aim to teach the physical geography that is relevant to particular questions. And the courses are interesting. Teachers at sixth form level want a fair range of subject matter to teach and they get this with 16–19.

As both Schools Council Geography Projects are essentially thematic or conceptually-based, the choice of regional examples is left entirely to the teacher. The development teams have tried, however, to encourage an appropriate spread of regional examples. With the 14–18 the following proportional coverage of different areas of the world suggested: 40–50 per cent of examples should be local and British: 15–30 per cent from other developed regions; 15–30 per cent from less developed regions, and 10–15 per cent from 'wider physical and economic systems at a world scale'.

The 16–19 is less specific and suggests three scales of examples: small, intermediate and global: 'Courses should ensure a balanced coverage across the range of environments, from dominantly natural to dominantly man-made, as well as a balanced coverage of scales of study, from small scale to global'. To help the teacher keep an appropriate balance between them, these scales are included in a Curriculum Matrix given in the University of Cambridge Regulations and Guidelines. Originally more specific guidelines on regional coverage were given but these were subsequently dropped. The teacher participating in the case study commented on this with some regret:

> The 16–19 produced a guide as to the percentage of examples which ought to come from (a) Britain; (b) Europe; (c) The Third World; (d) The Communist World. They reckoned that this should have been an addendum to the curriculum matrix 'small scale, continental scale, world scale'. They suggested we ought to try and get 55 per cent of regional examples from the Western world; 15 per cent from the Eastern block and 30 per cent from the less developed world. The idea is implicit that you try and get some sort of spread although you can see the Western World predominating partly because a fairly high proportion ought to be local stuff anyway. However they dropped the idea of specific percentages in the later syllabus. It's a pity the guide went because it would have been useful to have it. Now the idea that we should have that sort of spread is implicit rather than stated. The stumbling block was the 15 per cent for the Eastern block totalitarian states. That is so poorly covered by resources. Where do you get the information from?

For one teacher involved in teaching both 14–18 and 16–19 the advantage of the curriculum matrix approach is that it allows pupils to apply the geographical skills and concepts they have acquired to any area, starting with the local and widening out to any part of the world, but he admitted that there could be problems for pupils when trying to relate different parts of the world to the whole:

> If the syllabuses are followed properly they should come out with a good knowledge of their local area, their own country and of various parts of the world. To look at an example of this: we did a theme on Sicily in 14–18. This particular bit was stressing the idea of how land-use will vary as you move away from settlements. We homed in on Sicily for this and students were given a whole load of details for this village; land use at a certain distance from the village; a general description and a lot of information and pictures of the village and similar villages, so that they could start making various conclusions on the sort of patterns in agriculture as they move out from the centre of the village. Now later on, when discussing another part of Europe, you tend to find that that example has stuck in their minds and they think 'can we now apply the same rules to this particular place?' In some cases it works, other cases it doesn't because they think yes, there was Sicily but where *was* Sicily? That is the biggest problem. They know it's in

> Southern Italy but to try and get them to see that in relation to the rest of Europe isn't easy. Having said that I'm not sure whether they see it any more clearly in a traditional syllabus!

In spite of this problem, the teacher felt that the new approach to place is generally more effective than the former comprehensive regional approach: 'rather than plough through every aspect of the EEC you can really pick out what the EEC has to offer in terms of the ideas and concepts you want to put across'. However he admitted that, because of their conceptual nature, the projects may lead to teachers becoming over-involved with ideas and too little concerned with location. This may have happened with their teaching of the 14–18 and he is determined to avoid the problem with the 16–19:

> There is a danger with this and we fell into this trap with the 14–18, of becoming possibly too little concerned with where places are. Because we'd got away from the old type of geography in which you name the countries, label the rivers, draw the main towns and ports, if we weren't careful we tended to concentrate too much on ideas and forgot to train people where places are. What we should have done with 14–18, and what we are planning to do with every module of work in 16–19, is to get a world map with outlines of all the continents, and any place or country or ocean or mountain range or whatever that is mentioned in any unit will get marked on that map so that they have so me idea of the scope and areas they're dealing with.

He also pointed out that the curriculum matrix should help to avoid this problem:

> If a module has been properly constructed using the matrix all the way through, then you are starting off from 'the where' and from that you go on to your concepts. You really are trying to establish location before you do anything else.
>
> What it really boils down to is that regional geography has gone but case study examples from as wide a variety of regions as possible is really what is behind the Schools Council projects.

European Case Studies

In theory, if teachers follow the three scales on the 16–19 curriculum matrix closely, they will use European case studies otherwise the regional balance will be upset. Other considerations that militate in favour of the use of European case studies are the availability of resources, the existing stocks of materials in an institution, and the possibility of Europe having been studied in earlier syllabuses. The case study, for example, showed that teachers selected their regional content according to three criteria: how well the example illustrates the concept/problem being studied; the resources already held at the school, and the areas that have been taught previously by the teacher. Thus although the appropriateness of the example is of paramount importance, the choice of place depends equally on practical considerations:

> If you happen to have a stock of textbooks on Europe, which we have, then you are likely to use European examples. The choice of regional examples also depends to some extent on what one has done before. Schools will tend to take examples from the materials they have already, so as far as regional examples are concerned, these will tend to be the traditional areas. We for example have sets of books on Europe and West Africa.
>
> We were doing this with the Transport Unit the other day for 16–19. We kept saying 'what's a good example of that from Europe?' because Peter has taught Europe; and 'what's a good example of that from West Africa?' because I had taught West Africa. So if we're not careful we shall be biased towards Europe and Africa!

Both the 14–18 and the 16–19 provide opportunities for a detailed European case study in the Individual Study option, although the teachers interviewed found that, on the whole, individual projects tended to be on local themes since pupils are more easily able to get primary data locally. In general the teachers thought that there was sufficient scope in the main part of the courses for pupils to study some parts of Europe in such a way as to be able to apply the resulting knowledge and concepts to other parts of the world: hence Europe would be studied not because it *is* Europe but because it illustrates certain ideas, concepts and situations.

> It might mean in fact that people going through 14–18 may not have covered the whole of the Common Market; they may not have covered the whole of Africa or South America, but they should have studied geography in such a way that they should be able to apply in any situation the concepts and ideas they come across; they should be able to apply those ideas to that situation without having to have done a sort of Cook's tour of it.

Although the new approach initially met with some resistance from both pupils and their parents, the teachers were adamant that it is of more value than the traditional regional method, firstly in that it produces 'thinking, competent geographers as opposed to someone with just a good memory', and secondly, because both students and teachers are obliged to modify their traditional roles and become more active partners in the educational process: Teachers need to work together to devise, produce, adapt or modify course materials; while pupils have to abandon their passive stance and adopt an active, enquiring learning role:

> There was a certain amount of reluctance among students at first. The fact that things were thrown back at them and they weren't told ...

they didn't have to go to books and note and remember things or take down what you say. They had an exercise that they had to work out for themselves and I think they found this a little wearing at first. But once they got used to the idea they said they enjoyed doing it..

Parents would say, "this isn't geography because it's not going through by region. This isn't what geography's about! Why are they studying this?" To which I suppose the answer is: purely because it makes you ask *why* you are studying this; you never asked why you studied the old kind of geography course but you *are* asking now!

Conclusions

Geography is one of the subjects which can best fulfil the fifth educational aim of the six listed in the 1981 DES document on the School Curriculum: to help pupils to understand the world in which they live, and the interdependence of individuals, groups and nations.

This aim is the starting point of a pamphlet circulated in 1981 by the Geographical Association: *Geography in the School Curriculum 5–16*, which was intended as a contribution to the 'current debate' about the school curriculum. If the aim quoted is to be achieved, the pamphlet states, ' then geography must command a place in the education of children between the ages of five and sixteen'. It goes on to list the ways in which geography can increase pupils' awareness and understanding of the contemporary world. Four items which constitute the special contributions of geography are specified. The first of these deals with the understanding and communication of spatial information through maps and other forms of illustration. The other three are the following:

World knowledge. Through studying geography at school each pupil acquires special knowledge, skills and attitudes which are important resources required by adults as citizens of a complicated world. Geography, more than other subjects in the curriculum, helps the pupil to make sense of current events and informed judgements on economic, political, social and environmental issues. This, is particularly important in a country like Britain which maintains its living standards by trading in increasingly competitive world-wide markets. The skills and knowledge acquired in geography classrooms in dealing with world knowledge are useful and vital.

International understanding. Geography has a special role to play in fostering better understanding of different cultures, both within our own society and elsewhere in the world. Geography teachers acknowledge that pupils come to school with their own private views of the world and they seek to provide opportunities for the development of these views.

> *Environmental awareness.* Geography helps pupils to understand their environment and how man uses and misuses it. Through studying physical and human resources at a variety of scales from the immediate and local to the world as a whole, pupils learn to move from the familiar and concrete to the more distant, general and, perhaps, abstract. Geography seeks to satisfy and build upon the child's natural curiosity about the world.

The Geographical Association pamphlet goes on to suggest planned programmes appropriate for both primary and secondary school pupils. The stress is on developing pupil understanding rather than on factual knowledge:

> in modern geography courses pupils gain understanding of issues and problems as well as knowledge of places and people (. . .)
>
> In the past, geography in school was viewed as a subject in which pupils were expected to accumulate large amounts of factual information. The focus was more upon accumulation than progression. Increasingly, geography teachers are endeavouring to match their courses to the development of the pupils' understanding.

The pamphlet concludes with a plea for adequate facilities and resources for geography teaching if the subject is to fulfil its potential for increasing pupils' understanding and awareness of the world about them:

> lacking these resources, pupils will be hindered in trying to make sense of their world. They are likely to leave our schools inadequately prepared to understand the local, national and international environments in which they live and which they will help to shape.

Overall the pamphlet indicates the extent to which recent developments in the subject have been assimilated by geography teachers. The school geography programmes it outlines stress both the New Geography quantitative methods and the active concern with issues and problems which has become associated with Radical Geography. Moreover the strong emphasis the Geographical Association puts in its pamphlet on the broader social aims of the subject and its potential contribution to international understanding, augurs well for the study of contemporary Eruope in future school geography courses. This is not to suggest that Europe should take precedence over other regions but that, as an important part of the globe, it should be an essential component of any course concerned with basic geographical concepts, contemporary issues and problems.

However, as seen in the syllabus analyses and case study, newer syllabuses are often skill and concept-based with no *prescribed* area content. What is crucial is *teacher choice* of regional studies. It is theoretically possible, therefore, for teachers following a recently devised course to omit study of Europe altogether. Nevertheless if they attempt to achieve an appropriate range or balance of case studies to illustrate concepts and topics, there should be close study of at least some areas of the continent of Europe. Ironically this could mean that the newer syllabuses with no compulsory regional content could involve more teaching about Europe than some traditional courses with compulsory regional sections in which Europe is only one of several options and could be omitted altogether. However the inclusion of Europe in school geography courses cannot be guaranteed, especially in the absence of any clear directives or guidelines for its inclusion from any consultative body. In 1982 a consultation exercise was undertaken with geography teachers to define the criteria for examinations for pupils aged 16+. Three documents were circulated to assist them: the report of the Geography Working Party of the GCE and CSE Boards' Joint Council for 16+ National Criteria, the report of the 16+ Working Party of the Geography Committee of the Schools Council, and the report of the Examinations Working Party of the Geographical Association on criteria for a 16+ examination in geography. According to Michael Williams:

> Each of these documents specifies criteria for selecting the content of geography syllabuses but none of them have chosen a regional criterion. Europe is not accorded any special position. Instead the documents contain references to 'a study of the local area, the region in which it is situated, the United Kingdom considered as a whole and as part of various international groups, e.g. the EEC' (the Geographical Association document) and 'some awareness of the United Kingdom's relationships with wider groups of nations' (the Joint Council document).[11]

The geography case study suggests that teachers following more innovative courses are likely to do some work on Europe because it provides good examples of certain concepts and topics; because it is relevant, but also (perhaps even more important), because resources on Europe (at least Western Europe) are readily available. Moreover since some aspects of Europe have probably been covered in former geography courses, the school may have existing stocks of books and materials on Europe — a vital consideration at times of financial stringency. The case study highlighted this practical factor.

Now that the traditional regional geography courses are gradually being replaced by courses of the newer type, it is important to persuade not only geographers but also the people involved in the creation of new examination syllabuses and revision of existing ones, that study of Europe is both relevant and important if pupils are to gain the understanding of the contemporary world that has become one of the central aims of education in recent years. The inclusion in examination courses of a curriculum matrix, as in the Schools Council Projects, is a useful aid to getting a balance of regional examples spread across the globe. By itself, however, it is perhaps not sufficient to ensure that Europe is studied as part of a course.

Several working groups, conferences and projects are currently giving attention to Europe in school geography. For instance, the Standing Conference of European Geography Teachers Association has established a working party involving representatives from eight countries, to examine the European dimension in geography teaching. A bulletin on European geography, *Eurogeo*, has been produced by a working group from 12 European countries. The first issue came out in 1981 and was distributed by the British Geographical Association. It included a questionnaire eliciting information from teachers on the topics in European geography that most aroused their interest. The following topics were specified in order of importance:

Industry (production, location, change, specific industries)
Energy
Agriculture (types, production, changes)
Urban areas (growth, renewal, planning inner city problems)
Environment (pollution, conservation, national parks)
Transport
Regional problems and plans
Trade, port location and functions
Population changes

In the UK individual geographers are also looking into how methods of teaching about Europe in geography should be adapted to take account of the current political and economic situation. This is how one geographer suggests Europe should be viewed in school courses:

> the school geography of Europe once consisted of lists of capitals, capes, bays and products. This changed to detailed studies of the countries and regions and now people are looking at case studies or sample studies which may deal with a problem, topic or theme in a small yet typical area. Games, simulations, and statistical techniques are being introduced, often with a deadening effect.
>
> All these methods may have virtues but isn't it about time that we looked at Europe from another point of view? What do we imagine Europe would be? How do we see it? What do we think about it? How do we feel about it? How has it affected our everyday lives in Britian and how will it influence our lives in the future? Most important of all — how has the EEC changed Europe and how has the growth of the Communist world influenced the geography of Western European nations?
>
> Mountains, rivers, valleys do not have the influence they did. The New Europe is even more man-made than the old. The beef mountains and wine lakes may be more significant in the long run than a real mountain and a real lake, We are living in a more *managed* Europe.
>
> Europe is moving into a new era and its geography is changing whether we like it or not. Amid the heavy note-taking and semi-lecturing often found in the teaching of Europe surely we should introduce at least a few more personal, relevant and realistic appro-

> aches to encourage individuals to find their Europe and their place within it, now and in the future.[12]

Inevitably, there will be marked differences among geography teachers, even those committed to teaching aspects of European geography, in their perception of Europe and its role in the curriculum, and these differences will be reflected in the European topics and areas emphasised in the courses they follow in the classroom. Such differences do not contradict the heartening evidence that a sizeable number of teachers are aware of the valuable contribution geography can make to education about modern Europe and how, within geography courses, study of Europe can be made meaningful and relevant to school children–an important step towards awareness and understanding of the wider world in which they live.

Notes

1 Reactions for and against the development of New Geography are summarized by IVOR GOODSON, (1981) in an article entitled 'Becoming an Academic Subject: Patterns of Explanation and Evolution', *British Journal of Sociology of Education*, Vol. No. 2, pp. 35–52.
2 PEET, R. Ed. (1977) *Radical Geography: Alternative Viewpoints on Contemporary Social Issues*, London, Methuen.
3 BEAVER, quoted in 'Putting Geography on the Map', in the *Times Educational Supplement*, 4 September 1981.
4 WILLIAMS, M. (1982) 'Europe in School Geography', *Teaching about Europe*, Vol. 9, No. 2
5 PEET, R. *op. cit.*
6 WILLIAMS, M. *op. cit.*
7 *Ibid.*
8 *Oxford Geography Project* (1974) Oxford University Press.
9 PARSONS, C. (1980) 'Geography for the Young School Leaver' in STENHOUSE, L. (Ed.) *Curriculum Research and Development in Action*, London Heinemann, 1980
10 *Ibid.*
11 WILLIAMS, M. *op. cit.*
12 WAITES, B. (1982) 'Ways of teaching about Europe in School Geography,' *Teaching about Europe*, Vol 9, No. 2, Spring.

5 *Modern Languages*

Inevitably modern languages will figure prominently in any survey of the European dimension to the curriculum. How much language teaching has contributed to insights other than linguisitic or literary into other modern European cultures is another question which needs to be considered in the context of the considerable changes that have taken place in the subject in the last twenty or so years.

Foreign language teaching in schools has experienced a dramatic change of fortunes since the 1960s. The boom then slump in the subject has been chronicled in detail by Eric Hawkins[1] who describes the stimulus to modern language teaching given by the Nuffield Foundation Foreign Language Materials Project, set up in 1963. The project led to the production of four audio-visual courses: *En Avant, Vorwärt, Adelante* and *Vperyod*! In 1967 the Schools Council transferred the project to the Language Teaching Centre at the University of York where the new courses were to be developed to the level of 16+ examination.

The production of the new materials was part of a wider scheme conducted by the DES, the Schools Council, HMI, the Nuffield Foundation and a number of participating LEAs. This was an experimental scheme in teaching French at primary school level, to the 8+ age group, in the belief that by the age of 11+ they would be ready to begin a second language — German, Italian, Spanish or Russian.

Hawkins describes the 1960s as being a time of growth and change in modern language teaching. He cites as evidence the development of new audio-visual courses and better teaching materials; the establishment of language teacher associations and new in-service courses; the appointment of an increasing number of specialist language advisers (in 1969 there were 30, in 1980 over 130); the growth in town twinning schemes and foreign language assistant exchanges; increased use in language courses of radio, TV, tape-recorders and videotapes; increasing responsiveness on the part of examination

Boards to the needs of all pupils; the introduction into degree courses of a compulsory year abroad, and the growth of exchange schemes for teachers.

After this burgeoning of activity there was a marked deceleration during the 70s. The implications of comprehensive reorganisation for modern language study had not received sufficient attention and this led to enormous problems for language teachers faced with having to teach across the ability range. At the same time the effectiveness of teaching of French at primary level began to be questioned, while the theories of the influential linguist Noam Chomsky began to shake people's faith in audio-visual methods and language laboratories which had not produced the dramatic improvement in linguistic competence that had been hoped for.

As early as 1971 there were signs that the DES, HMI and LEAs were becoming increasingly concerned about the crisis in modern language teaching in comprehensive schools, particularly the drop-out levels in the 5th and 6th forms; the dramatic fall in the numbers of males applying to study languages at universities and the subsequently exacerbated shortage of teachers. In 1976 a conference was called by university language teachers to consider the 'crisis in modern language studies' and in 1977 when the rate of drop-out from modern language classes was causing serious anxiety, HMI produced a very critical study of language teaching based on a survey of 83 comprehensive schools.

Hawkins himself attributes some of the problems in secondary school language teaching to the arbitrary decision by universities in 1967–8 to drop the modern language entrance requirement).

There has been a loss of confidence in what Hawkins terms the 'vertical and horizontal extensions of language teaching' (i.e. down the age range to primary level, and across the ability range at secondary level). As yet, however, no really effective solutions have been found to the problems and in the early 1980s many of them are still in evidence. In 1983, for example, it was pointed out to *Guardian* readers that:

> about 90 per cent of pupils in the first year of secondary education learn a foreign language, almost always French, as compared with slightly more than half in 1965. But by the fourth year the proportion drops to a third, barely higher than in 1965. Moreover the increase over the last decade in the proportion of school leavers who attempt a foreign language has fallen to 3 per cent, particularly among boys; indeed the overall imbalance between boys and girls at all levels is becoming acute.
>
> Only German, popularly believed to be the "masculine" and "scientific" language resists the trend. A further disturbing imbalance lies in the number studying French as against all other languages. Present evidence suggests that the proportions of secondary schools teaching French, German and Spanish as first foreign languages in autumn 1982 were about 98 per cent, 6 per cent and 1 per cent respectively.[2]

One measure designed to reduce the drop-out level has been the creation of Graded Objectives in Modern Languages (GOML) schemes. To a certain extent the development of graded objectives schemes has alleviated the problem of mixed ability teaching, and these have become increasingly popular (in the years 1979–83 the number of schemes increased from 28 to 55).

These tests arose out of dissatisfaction with the traditional examination structure. They replaced the traditional 5 year lead-up to public examinations with a series of tests each with a set of shorter term objectives. The tests were designed as a series of steps leading up to the equivalent of 'O' or 'A' level or beyond, each step being taken according to the pace and ability of the individual learner. The acquisition of each level is seen as an achievement, thus encouraging and motivating the pupil.

One of the principles underlying the schemes is that language learning should be relevant and applicable in practical situations, therefore an important objective is communicative competence in practical situations. This has relevance for the consideration of modern languages as a vehicle for insight into and understanding of other European cultures.

Teaching about Europe

Modern language study is considered by many people to be the most obvious and appropriate context for teaching about contemporary Europe. Indeed it is generally assumed that foreign language courses automatically convey information about foreign countries and the life and culture of other peoples. While it is true that a course in another language will inevitably incorporate some cultural messages and overtones, these depend very heavily both on the kind of vocabulary and language structures taught and on the nature of the course texts and materials used. For example, pupils drilled in the formal grammatical structures of a language and exposed only to a few literary texts such as nineteenth century Romantic poetry, would be ill-equipped to deal with everyday colloquial language situations in the country concerned and would have few insights into the daily life and customs of its people.

There is a growing feeling now that the use of literary texts is inappropriate certainly in the early years of language study, and that the learning of language structures should be allied as closely as possible to their function in authentic real life situations. There are excellent reasons for this. When a language is given an identifiable social and cultural context pupil interest and motivations are enhanced. Increased insight into another race and culture through modern language study is a first and important step towards understanding, tolerance and peaceful co-existence. In recent years this aspect of modern language teaching has received a considerable amount of attention both from linguists themselves and from those concerned with general educational policy and the shaping of the curriculum. The DES in its 1981 *Framework for the Curriculum* pinpointed the need for children to understand the world in which they live and to be aware of the interdependence of individuals, groups and nations. Several years beforehand, in 1977, a statement by the Modern Languages Committee of HMI (*Curriculum 11–16*) made the point that as well as linguistic and social benefits, learning a foreign language 'affords the possibility of acquiring a healthy curiosity towards foreign peoples and developing understanding of the unfamiliar in speech, customs and manners through acquaintance with the people and their way of life and through study of their literature and cultural heritage. It can thus contribute towards the development of international relationships'. But these benefits can only be acquired if the language is taught in relation to its social and cultural context; and later on in the same statement the Modern Languages Committee make this point: 'effective communication in a foreign language demands understanding not only of the language itself but also of the way of life it reflects'.

In the same year the British Association of Language Teachers (BALT) stressed the qualities of understanding, tolerance and empathy that modern language study can engender:

> foreign language learning makes an invaluable and unique contribution to the education of every child, offering him what no other subject can — an opportunity to see into another society and to see his own language and society through the eyes of a foreigner (. . .) It offers pupils an opportunity to view with sympathy and understanding another society and another culture.[3]

Again this appears (somewhat optimistically) to take for granted that modern language study invariably conveys a substantial amount of information about contemporary life and mores in another country.

The integration of language teaching with background information becomes increasingly important as arts subjects decline in popularity and their 'usefulness' to society is called into question. In recent years there has been a noticeable increase in emphasis on the potential economic, political and social benefits to us as a nation of teaching our school children not only the language of another people but also their culture, way of life and institutions. In a paper delivered to the first assembly of the National Congress on Languages in Education in 1975, C.V. James assembled the main arguments put forward in support of the teaching of modern languages in schools and grouped then under four headings: educational, social, political and economic. His paper indicated in particular a growing awareness among political and educational groups of the desirable economic and political benefits to Britain of teaching foreign languages to our school children:

> An early enquiry into the foreign language needs of British industry and commerce found an increasing realisation that the growth of exports depended very much on British ability to speak to the potential customer in his own language, both socially and in business contexts

> (FBI, 1964). Today HMI sees Great Britain as heavily dependent on international trade for survival and uses this as a powerful argument in favour of foreign language learning, The character and quality of education have obvious significance for our national economic efficiency: foreign languages must therefore be considered among the key subjects of the curriculum.
>
> Opinion on this subject is unanimous. In a country which depends for its survival on its trade, it is vital that the British should be able to compete on equal terms, which necessitates a good grasp of the languages they are dealing with (BALT). If we fail to overcome our linguistic insularity we may fail also to secure the future economic well-being of our country (Dunbar). Language learning is no longer merely a vehicle for the educational and social development of the individual, it also has a precisely defined function as a commercial tool on a national scale. This is in turn linked with the political factor: a better knowledge of modern European languages will lead to improved international links, on which economic progress increasingly depends (Council of Europe 69/2)[4]

A more recent statement from HMI (*A View of the Curriculum* 1980) makes the same point: 'the learning of a foreign language offers intellectual stimulus and cultural benefit. It now also has increasing practical value as our links with Europe and the rest of the world are strengthened.

This more utilitarian rationale for modern language learning presupposes (even if it does not state) a combination of linguistic and contemporary background elements.

At a conference on modern language teaching and background studies held at the Schools' Unit in 1980 a participant claimed that the widening of horizons, increased understanding and tolerance that integrated language and background studies can achieve in even the weakest of pupils, is by far the most valid reason for teaching a foreign language in schools:

> Languages for work and languages for intellectual stimulus will always remain for the minority, but language study as a means of achieving what may be seen as a modest degree of international understanding can always be for all. However, if languages are to be taught to a majority of secondary school pupils with the primary aim of attempting to get pupils to shed their national prejudices and to see the world through the eyes of others, the modern languages cannot be taught *in vacuo*. Learning to understand and to make utterances in a foreign language, and learning to read in a foreign language, does not automatically lead to a fuller understanding of the people who speak that language. Therefore, if language learning in our schools is to succeed in bringing about sounder and healthier attitudes towards the peoples of other nations, then an integral part of learning any language must become learning about the people who speak that language,

about the country in which they live and about the way in which they organize their lives. In short, all modern language studies should be accompanied by what, for want of a better name, have become known as background studies.[5]

A number of groups and individuals, therefore, have been putting forward in recent years a convincing rationale for modern language courses in schools integrating instruction in linguistic skills and structures with some study of the contemporary life, culture and institutions of the countries concerned.

Many language courses, packs and materials developed for the first to fourth years of secondary school have manifested the same concern. The Nuffield/Schools Council courses *Vperyod*, *Adelante*, *Vorwärts*, *En Avant/A Votre Avis*, for example, are at pains to set the language in a modern everyday context and to give insights into different European ways of life. A number of commercially-produced courses and books have also been designed to provide language tuition in an authentic modern context. Ultimately, however, it will be the teacher in the classroom and the examination courses followed that will determine how much background material will be studied.

Examination courses vary in the amount of emphasis they put on background elements. An analysis of the GCE/SCE syllabuses available in 1980 indicated some of the changes gradually taking place in modern language teaching in secondary schools.

Syllabus Commentary

GCE 'O' Level Examinations

In general GCE 'O' level examinations had little or no compulsory contemporary background elements in 1980. Some basic knowledge of the country of origin of the language studied might be required for the oral test but even that was not considered essential and obviously it was the candidates' fluency, in the language rather than the knowledge of a country that would be assessed.

In 1980 no plans were envisaged by any of the Boards to introduce contemporary background studies as a significant element in 'O' level courses, in spite of the dissatisfaction with 'O' level courses expressed by such bodies as CILT in their critical analysis: *Modern Languages Examination at 16+* (1980)

GCE 'A/O' Examinations

Some Boards have used the alternative 'O' level papers to introduce important innovations in the direction of topics of contemporary importance and language geared to texts of a topical nature. The *Oxford and Cambridge A/O French and*

German for Business Studies (with Spanish in preparation) has a highly vocational slant with general questions (in English) on contemporary France and Germany. The Oxford Delegacy's Alternative 'O' level concentrates on texts from contemporary plays, novels, short stories, newspapers and magazines. Southern Universities Joint Board (SUJB) and the University of London Board both lay emphasis on aspects of current political affairs and social conditions in comprehension, essay work and oral. French oral topics include: immigrant workers, role of women, role of trade unions. There is obviously scope here for a wider European angle to be represented. The *Joint Matriculation Board (JMB) A/O* is interesting in that it centres on acquisition of skills: examination of and response to materials of varying kinds — statistics, maps, articles etc. Here there are obvious opportunities for comparison within Europe. But it is in the 'A' level examinations that the changes have been particularly startling.

GCE 'A' level Examinations

In 1973 background studies featured rarely in any of the 'A' level syllabuses and literary studies and texts more or less reigned supreme. The change has been spectacular. In 1980 there was not one Board which had not included, or did not plan to include, some study of contemporary social, historical, political, geographical, cultural themes of the country whose language is being studied, (for example, Oxford & Cambridge, Oxford Delegacy and the Cambridge Boards which in 1982 developed joint papers). In some cases deliberately or implicitly, these themes were being widened to include other parts of Europe.

Before reviewing all its 'A' level syllabuses, the JMB canvassed its teachers on the place of non-linguistic components of the 'A' level Modern Languages syllabuses. The general feeling (77.8% of the teachers) was that the practice of requiring literary questions on four set books is too narrow and too literature-orientated. The teachers would prefer themes raising questions of a historical, political, economic or philosophical nature.

Finally, Cambridge was re-introducing French background topics in 1982, setting joint papers with Oxford and Cambridge and the Oxford Delegacy. Whilst few takers were expected at first, and difficulties with getting examiners were anticipated, they went ahead with preparation of similar changes to the German and Spanish syllabuses, thus reinforcing the general trend towards greater emphasis on background studies to reinforce and to contextualise the language study.

The syllabuses, taken as a whole, demonstrate an implicit need to widen out from only national considerations. Topics such as 'Post-war Politics in France', 'German History 1918–1972', 'Spain since 1945' (SUJB) demand some knowledge of what was taking place in the rest of Europe.

The AEB French syllabus deliberately included 'The relationship of France to Germany' as a topic which would give the wider dimension. The same Board's German syllabus included the 'Study of Germany 1949–74'; the Italian syllabus included 'Fascism' and 'Politics and Society since World War II'; and the Spanish syllabus included 'The Spanish Civil War 1936–39'. It is obvious that all these topics cannot be nationally contained.

The Welsh Joint Education Committee (WJEC) prescribed one text in French on the history of European unity (*Histoire de l'Unite Européenne*, Lecerf) and the JMB's prescribed topics for the Russian oral included 'The Common Market'. (One inevitably asks why only the Russian?)

New French papers proposed for the University of London in 1982 were to have less emphasis on literature and more on varied aspects of French life and culture. The language and subject matter of reading and aural comprehension and essay questions would be such as found in news bulletins, newspapers (Le Monde, Figaro, L'Express etc.). Many of these, one imagines, would take some reference to European rather than purely French affairs. Similar syllabuses would operate for German, Italian and Russian. The SUJB works in very much the same way. Translation passages were to be in differing styles: 'colloquial, descriptive, discursive, documentary, journalese, literary and narrative. Knowledge of France and current events may well be an advantage in understanding the passages'. Obviously the study of French current events involves a wide perspective.

Assessment procedures in part define the limits to background studies. Whilst most essays had to be written in the language, some essays on background topics were asked for in English (Oxford and Cambridge Delegacy). Only one Board (SUJB) asked for a project or, as it is called, an individual study (written in English and/or German and assessed by the Board).

A dissertation in English on 'one or more aspects of a topic concerned with contemporary France', part of the JMB examination, was offered as an alternative to one question on non-literary prescribed works. (Some Boards are very fearful of introducing 'project work' because it can be done so badly, particularly when language teachers are unfamiliar with it.)
Where Scottish examinations in modern languages are concerned, candidates are expected to know 'common facts' about the foreign countries concerned at 'O' grade and 'basic facts of the geography, history and customs' of the same at 'H' grade. The CSYS (Certificate of Sixth Year Studies) syllabuses in French, German, Italian, Russian and Spanish have a paper on *Literature and Background Studies* which is worth more marks than any of the other papers.

Graded Objectives

Dissatisfaction with the traditional examination structure led to the development of the graded objectives schemes mentioned earlier. The genesis of these is described in the CILT publication *Graded Objectives in Modern Languages*:

> the basic principle of the Graded Objectives Scheme for Modern Language Learning, as they are at present realised, were first expressed in opposition to the plans for new public examinations to be taken at age sixteen-plus. The feasibility studies carried out with a view to amalgamating CSE and GCE 'O' level produced specimen examinations which seemed just as irrelevant to the most pressing needs of modern language teaching and learning in schools as those they were intended to replace. The uneasiness about performance in modern language teaching and learning then felt has continued to be increasingly expressed at all levels both official and unofficial. The enormous success of schools and teachers in extending modern language teaching from the 30 per cent or so of the secondary school population of the early 1960s (the population of the grammar schools plus a selected few in some secondary modern schools) to be almost 90 per cent in the mid 1970s has been obscured by what appears to be a failure to get much that is worthwhile taught to the majority.[6]

In their book Harding *et al* claim that the GCE and CSE system in modern languages leads to failure for a large number of pupils who are set unsuitable tasks:

> in spite of some attempts to introduce new types of test, modern language examination syllabuses at all levels remained very heavily weighted in favour of the emphasis on formal grammatical accuracy that had always characterised the aims of grammar school language learning.

The authors point out that the large number of pupils who have been deemed incapable of following examination courses do not receive any credit for their two or three years of language learning.

The first graded objectives schemes were produced by Oxfordshire and York in 1976, and both, according to CILT, expanded considerably indicating 'a growing confidence among teachers and examiners in the full potential of the system'.

One of the most important aims of the graded test schemes was to make language learning more relevant to pupils than the traditional academic linguistic and literary approach. According to Harding *et al*:

> the most worthwhile objectives would seem to be the ability to use the language for realistic purposes rather than (. . .) the ability to describe the language or use it for purposes which the actual user would rarely need to employ.

Thus the graded tests schemes emphasize communication skills as opposed to a purely formal, grammatical approach. Most of the schemes attempt to place the language in a meaningful everyday context, incorporating such background elements as would aid the learner to 'get by' in certain everyday situations such as shopping, travelling, eating out, visiting places of entertainment etc. Limited though they are by the different learning levels of the course, the tests nevertheless constitute a greater attempt to relate a foreign language to an, authentic contemporary background than traditional 'O' level courses. For example the topics covered in the Cumbria and Lancashire graded tests syllabuses are as follows:

(i) personal information
(ii) finding the way
(iii) travel
(iv) eating and drinking
(v) shopping
(vi) banks, post-offices and telephones
(vii) illness and emergency
(viii) leisure and entertainment
(ix) greetings and forms of polite address
(x) living in a French/German/Spanish household
(xi) schools and education
(xii) talking about Britain

Another example of an established and successful graded tests schemes is the West Sussex Graded Levels of Achievement Scheme (GOALS) which has submitted to the AEB a level 5, draft mode 3 GCE 'O' level examination syllabus in French for first examination in 1985.

Four levels of GOALS are already being taken in Sussex secondary schools and level 4 was examined by the SREB as a Mode 3 CSE for the first time in 1983 with 161 candidates from four secondary schools. The increasing popularity of GOALS and the need for continuity in teaching approach and style convinced the GOALS development team of the need for a one year course at level 5, for able pupils wishing to pursue their studies at a higher level. The following principles lie at the heart of the West Sussex GOALS scheme:

1 The learner deals with a series of shorter term, clearly defined objectives. Each component of the scheme represents a recognisable level of attainment, of which the pupil is aware, and is certificated. Thus at whatever time the pupil terminates the course, he/she would be able to demonstrate real benefits from his/her language study.
2 The scheme seeks to develop in the learner the ability to communicate effectively in the written and spoken language, by selecting language appropriate to a given activity ('survival' situations, less structured interpersonal activities, etc.), and to use that language in a meaningful way. This is the essence of the Communicative Approach.
3 It seeks to relate language to the socio-cultural context in which it operates, and to give pupils a sense of direction. It emphasizes the relevance of a particular language activity by working through the

medium of authentic materials, related to the age, interests and experience of the particular target group.

Indeed, if language learning is to prosper in the 1980s, this last part is particularly important. Language learning must be made purposeful; foreign languages must deal with *reality*; they must be seen to be *real*, and must have *practical use*.

4 The learner should be encouraged throughout the course to use language independently, to generate his/her own language, and to transfer his/her knowledge to other situations. In order to achieve this, the learner will still need to be provided with a grammatical framework, and knowledge of how the language operates. However, knowledge of a structural system should not be an end in itself, but a means to making meaningful utterances. Implied in all the above, is the freedom of the teacher to adopt teaching methods and objectives appropriate to a particular ability grouping.[7]

Like other graded objective schemes, GOALS has been formulated according to the basic belief that modern language courses should be adequately related to real life. The syllabus is very detailed, falling into the following categories: (A) General Contexts of communication; (B) Register/Relationships (formal, semi-formal, informal); (C) Topic areas and settings (15 listed): (D) Language functions (a great number listed); (E) General concepts and notions (a great number listed); (F) Language Tasks (a great number listed of a 'social' and 'public' nature). Overall great stress is laid on the practical use of contemporary language and 'it should be noted that although there will be no separate test of background knowledge, the cultural element is an integral part of the course and is implied in the syllabus'.

Because of their stress on modern everyday usage of language, the GOAL schemes can be seen as providing an opportunity for pupils to gain some useful insights into another contemporary European culture.

Conclusions

Modern language courses are not European studies courses and should not be considered as such. Linguists can legitimately point out that in courses designed primarily to inculcate language structures and skills, study of the modern life and culture of another country is only one element which must necessarily be secondary in importance to the primary objective of the course as a whole.

Language teaching with little or no reference to a contemporary cultural context has nevertheless aroused criticism from a number of quarters in recent years:

> what worries me is that often a good deal of run of the mill language teaching is completely divorced from any possible relevance to any kind of context that a child could appreciate (. . .) One sees so much of the kind of teaching where a particular grammatical point is taken and

> hammered through in various abstract exercises and this has no relation at all to any aspect of life.[8]

A practising teacher in the research case studies forcefully expressed his dissatisfaction with the constraints of GCE syllabuses:

> at school we made our background studies foreground studies. Quite simply we taught about Europe in French. We said to hell with exams! Obviously the grammar got taught somehow but when we wanted to discuss Germany, Russia etc. we did it in French. And the 'O'-level results at the end of the day were exactly the same as they were before we switched.

Even CILT, not noted for its support of European background studies, criticized Examination Boards in 1950 for their lack of attention to contemporary background in GCE 'O' level examination courses:

> the overwhelming impression gained from an investigation into the examinations is of an intense preoccupation with language structure rather than function. It is not what the language is doing or meaning which is of primary importance but whether it is well formed (. . .)
>
> As we have been made increasingly aware, over the past few years particularly, there is more to learning language than learning language alone. We also learn about the culture of the country concerned, something about our own in contrast or in similarity, and about the more general aspects of contemporary European civilisation. These may sound like pious abstractions but as people like Eric Hawkins have pointed out, they are the way to a liberation of the spirit and, therefore arguably the principal justification for teaching languages to the majority at all.
>
> In that case the examiners have a particular duty to project as faithful an image of contemporary society as possible and at the same time present images with which candidates can usefully identify. One must admit that they are frequently not very good at this.
>
> The view of life suggested in general and in the particular countries concerned is often very peculiar or badly out of date.[9]

A member of CILT expanded this point at the Schools Unit conference on language teaching and background studies:

> We do not see as a central feature of our concern the relation between language and background studies, (. . .) What we are really looking for is surely more enlightened teaching of foreign skills with all that entails, and you cannot teach these satisfactorily except within and against the background and context of the country whose language you are learning. So a lot of the comments we made in our 16+ book related to the trivialising of language in its use in a context which was unrelated to having anything to say of interest about the country, and

many of the examples used in modern language exams are culled from a context which is from fifty to a hundred years out of date in terms both of language and civilisation features.[10]

The situation regarding background studies at 'O' level at the moment seems to be that any initiatives in this direction are left entirely to the individual teacher (as will be seen in the school curriculum study, Chapter 8) or depend, equally arbitrarily, on the reading texts used which, as indicated, may be totally inappropriate and out of date. This is particularly regrettable since the middle years of schooling occur during a crucial period of a child's development; a time when it is vital to heighten his or her awareness of and tolerance towards the wider world and its inhabitants. More than many subjects in the curriculum, modern language courses in years 4 and 5 could go some way towards fulfilling this goal.

In Scotland the situation regarding the background element in modern language examinations is similar to that in the rest of the United Kingdom. Although there is a certain amount of cultural information in the higher grade syllabus and a considerable amount in the Certificate of Sixth Year Studies, the background element is virtually ignored at 'O' grade. Concern about this was expressed at a national in-service course on background studies in modern languages held in Aberdeen in 1978:

> The first major focus (of the national course) was the place of background in courses where the major objective is language acquisition, that is in courses leading to national examinations in the fourth and fifth years. Background has been on the whole very much a cinderella in these courses, although lip-service is paid to in the regulations of the SCE Examination Board. On the whole, however, the amount taught to certificate (SCE) classes will depend largely on the interest, knowledge and predilections of the individual teacher and will be determined, as far as content goes, by the course-book in use. This can mean that very little such information is presented at all even in S1 and S2, whilst in years 3, 4 and 5 background recedes very deeply into the background, as preoccupation with major examination tasks takes over.[11]

Reactions to background studies in non-certificate classes from the seventy participants at the Scottish conference ranged from general acceptance to complete hostility: 'others reiterated the familiar view that it was no part of a modern language teacher's job to teach material which was more appropriate to a teacher of history, geography or modern studies'.[12]

Resistance from modern language teachers to any major change in examination syllabuses is recognized as an obstacle to syllabus reform by CILT:

> The examinations cannot be reformed without the consent of the teachers, and they, it must be said, seem to be the most conservative element in the system. In the three 'O' level boards offering two types

of examinations, one broadly traditional, one within limits attempting to cater for a newer view of language learning, three times as many candidates were entered for the traditional papers as for the new ones in 1978. That is of course a teacher's not a candidate's decision.[13]

Here we return to one of the main problems in curriculum reform: the (understandable) reluctance of many teachers to risk new courses, methods and materials that deviate from the teaching approach to which they have long been accustomed. This is one of the most formidable barriers to the implementation of new syllabuses, particularly in the case of modern languages which, of all the traditional sujects, is the one which has had most difficulty in adjusting to the new classroom needs created by school reorganisation. In spite of the development of livelier audio-lingual and audio-visual methods and materials, many teachers still prefer courses to be specifically grammar-based with emphasis on formal accuracy.

In fact the changed classroom situation has inclined some teachers, particularly those with grammar school experience, to revert even more to the traditional hard-line grammar approach to cope with the greater ability range to be found in comprehensive schools. For example the German language teacher in the school curriculum study (chapter 8), was not convinced that it is essential to increase the background element in either 'O' level or 'A' level work: 'they can get it elsewhere; they can find these things out for themselves'. Instead she advocated a return to 'grammar and sentence structure to compensate for the increasingly sloppy modern teaching methods and generally lower intelligence level of pupils (. . .) teachers these days are more and more forced to teach the cat sat on the mat'. Such a purist approach was unexpected from a young teacher whose own training had been in a multidisciplinary, contextual school of European studies. Nevertheless hers is not an uncommon attitude among foreign language teachers and while such an attitude persists, reinforced by the public examination system, modern languages could remain a subject accessible only to pupils capable of learning a series of grammatical rules and forms of little immediate relevance to everyday life.

The strong emphasis on grammatical forms of speech in language classes has inevitably discriminated against less academic pupils in comprehensive schools. As often as not they have been shunted into hastily-devised 'easier' substitute courses entitled French studies, German studies, European Studies etc. The case studies indicated that this situation is still very prevalent; for example in one of the European Studies case studies a coordinator of the subject could be seen to be trying vainly to upgrade European Studies in his school at the same time as the language department was using it as a dumping ground for their weaker pupils. In the school curriculum study a teacher of German was given the task of keeping the 'delinquent' French pupils 'meaningfully occupied' in a 'European Studies' course which turned out to be nothing less than a remedial English class.

The development of graded tests schemes in recent years shows that some modern linguists are finally facing the challenge of teaching modern languages across the ability range, and with some success according to the Schools Council *Project on Graded Tests in Modern Languages*. An evaluation exercise undertaken as part of this Project indicated that such tests boost achievement and stimulate positive attitudes to language learning in children who hitherto would have been diverted into the substitute courses mentioned above.

Not all linguists, however, are convinced of the value of the graded test approach and in 1981 an article by Harry Redford listed the dangers he believed to be inherent in it as follows:

> the lack of 'generative capacity' in the syllabus based on language 'functions' rather than structures, which without highly skilled teaching can become a mere animated phrasebook; the overly permissive attitude to error (just as deplorable as the old pedantic insistence on strict formal accuracy); the phoney cult of 'learn-as-you-play', pretending that basic competence in a foreign language can be achieved without effort in the artificial setting of a school.[14]

Some advocates of graded tests are equally aware of these dangers. A modern languages adviser, for example, recently outlined his belief that graded test schemes could be very limited if they failed to take into account the broader social and cultural dimensions of the languages taught:

> Even though most graded test projects have placed the emphasis firmly on communication skills and defined explicit criteria for achieving them, of real value to pupils and teachers alike, we should remain aware of the potential danger that such schemes may sometimes be too narrowly conceived, and if confined to 'performance skills' alone and to the so-called 'survival' aspects of communication, they might easily degenerate into mere 'phrase book' exercises, divorced from any broader dimension and with no more educational relevance than the courses they have replaced. The question of factual content, of a body of knowledge or, better, areas of understanding linked to the whole curriculum — is especially pertinent in relation to the GOML movement; since any attempt to develop a degree of 'communicative competence' in young language learners should by definition take fully into account the broad area of contextual or 'background' studies, or it will risk failure by remaining a mere 'code'. Indeed, 'communication' in a foreign language, without a concomitant awareness and appreciation, at however modest a level, of both the nature of speech acts and the social — cultural realities mediated by that language, — the probable assumptions and pre-dispositions of native speakers, for example, and the salient features of their own linguistic and social environment — would appear to involve a contradiction in terms.[15]

Integration of Languages and Background Studies

To avoid this problem of separation between communicative competence and contextual studies, the working group involved in developing graded tests in West Sussex, (GOALS) set themselves the task of devising integral background components for the different stages of the course, with the aid of a small EEC grant. Integration is the key word in the GOALS attempt to develop the background dimension to its graded tests. Likewise the *integration of language learning and cultural context* was a focal point of discussion at the 1980 Modern Languages conference at the Schools Unit. One participant outlined his belief that the inclusion of an integral background component in the graded test schemes would set the pace for change throughout the public examination system:

> If background studies are to have any hope of playing their rightful role in the process of modern language learning, then their importance will ultimately have to be recognised by all bodies concerned with the official assessment of performance by language learners. This means that the importance of background studies will have to be recognised in CSE, GCE and 16+ examinations. Still more important, their value needs to be recognised by those presently involved in devising graded proficiency tests in modern languages, for it would seem that these tests will eventually provide a means of assessment of pupil performance for a majority of secondary school pupils. If the graded test movement fails to come out strongly in favour of the teaching of background studies, there would seem little likelihood of their importance being readily accepted by those responsible for public examinations.[16]

Ironically a greater attempt is made at integration of language and background in courses designed for weaker or less academic pupils. In 1980 this was commented on in an HMC Modern Languages Report by A.J. Leng who outlined the ways in which courses for weaker pupils could pioneer a new framework for 'O' level syllabuses:

> Increasingly the 'educational' justification for languages seems to include, with the requirement of basic skills in speaking, understanding, reading and writing, attention to the culture of the target language. It is perhaps an irony that at present this is only offered as examination material for candidates who sit CSE. For the weaker pupils we should be talking about the comprehension tests, oral communication and a smaller amount of composition work being educationally and practically more suitable, but to this could usefully be added a section on background which would include geography, history and everyday observable phenomena. This may well point the way to a new prescription at 'O' level.[17]

Conclusions

If the importance of contemporary background content is not recognized now when new examinations are being planned, then modern languages will fail to fulfil the role generally attributed to the subject: to engender understanding of other peoples and other ways of life. If this important function continues to be left largely to the predilection of the individual teacher whose classroom objectives are bound to be restricted by the syllabuses in use, then the subject cannot be said to be fully exploiting its potential for widening pupils' horizons and contributing to international understanding.

This failure can only be avoided if certain measures are implemented. The Schools Unit conference on modern languages and background studies concluded with a series of practical recommendations based on the principle 'that modern language teaching should spring from and be informed by an awareness of the "embeddedness" of a language in the culture of the country concerned.' The recommendations included: persuading modern language organizations, educationalists and teachers of the contribution modern languages make to the total secondary school curriculum in widening horizons and increasing international understanding; discussing the implementation of background study proposals at local and national levels; incorporating this aspect into pre-service and in-service teacher training programmes; greater use of exchange schemes and foreign language assistants to keep knowledge of other countries up-to-date and bring the reality of another culture into the classroom.

Above all what is needed is to persuade those involved in developing foreign language courses and materials to *integrate* the teaching of linguistic skills with contemporary background materials. To separate the two would be impractical, for learning another language is demanding and there is little time for extra content; secondly, it would be inappropriate: to quote a further education lecturer at the Sussex conference: 'I belive that if we separate the background or complementary element totally from linguistic studies, then both begin to make nonsense'.

There are, however, several constraints to be considered when discussing the role of modern languages in teaching about Europe: the gradual reduction in the number of languages taught in schools; the much criticised but continuing preponderance of French, and the lack of opportunity for pupils to have contact with native speakers. In the latter case the fall in the number of foreign assistants being employed in British schools is a cause for concern, as is the failure by many schools to manage to provide visits or links with other European countries (although cost constraints are an understandable obstacle in the present economic climate). Nevertheless there are promising signs of concern about the situation at an official level. A consultative paper issued by the DES and the Welsh office in May 1983. *Foreign Languages in the School Curriculum*, expressed concern about the teaching of languages in schools, and suggested that some kind of national policy is needed to rectify the situation.

Discussing this Robert Tate and James Muckle[18] put forward a number of suggestions for improvement, one of which would be the diversification from French towards German, Italian, Spanish and Russian. They also suggest more opportunity for contact with native speakers through greater use of *assistants* and the establishment of more pupil and teacher exchanges; the development of in-service training, and the organisation of schemes to allow teachers sabbatical leave 'to keep them in contact with the target language'. Learning a language should lead to 'the enrichment of life' according to the DES consultative document, and Tate and Muckle comment:

> if a properly integrated programme of foreign language teaching is linked with the foreign civilisation and culture, and with the study of the mother tongue, it should increase understanding and tolerance as well as providing an investment for the nation's prosperity. A national policy is the only way, and means must be found to fund it and back it all the way down from the DES through the LEA to the schools.

The active collaboration of the teacher in any change is crucial. If a 'properly integrated programme of foreign language teaching' is to develop, then attitudes among some language teachers will have to change.

> Too many linguists seem to have failed to realize that the way to achieve better results in modern language learning is to undertake every possible attempt to make modern languages really *live*.
>
> It is not only through turning more to the teaching of functional language skills and the appropriate background knowledge that modern linguists should seek to Europeanize their teaching strategies. It is their clear duty to set about forging for their pupils links and contacts with the foreign country whose language they are seeking to teach (. . .) Far too many British secondary schools still have no links with schools in countries whose languages they are trying to teach.[19]

If language teachers, with the support of their LEAs and their head-teachers, can bring about such links and can ensure that their courses are not divorced from the culture and civilization of the countries whose languages are taught, then they will be making a vital contribution to teaching about Europe in secondary schools.

Notes

1 Hawkins, E. (1981) *Modern Languages in the Curriculum*, Cambridge University Press.
2 Tate R. and Muckle J. (1983) 'Foreign to the System', in *The Guardian*, 11 October 1983.
3 James, C.V. (1978) in *Foreign Languages in Education*, the Report of the National Congress on Languages in Education 1st Assembly, CILT pp. 8–10.
4 *Ibid*, pp. 11–12.

5 PEACOCK, D. (1981) 'Modern Languages, Background Studies and the European Dimension' in *Modern Languages and Background Studies: a European Dimension*, ed. Eileen Daffern, Curriculum Development Series No. 13 the Schools Unit.
6 HARDING, A., PAGE, B., ROWELL, S. (1980) *Graded Objectives in Modern Languages*, CILT.
7 GOALS, level 5/Mode 3 GCE (French) Draft Submission.
8 GARNER, E., 'Background Studies and Graded Examinations', in *Modern Languages and Background Studies: a European Dimension, Op. Cit.*
9 *Modern Languages Examinations at 16+:* (a critical analysis), CILT 1980.
10 MOYS, A., Deputy Director of CILT, at the Schools Unit seminar on Modern Languages and Background Studies, October 1980.
11 *Modern Languages in Scotland*, No. 18, May 1979.
12 *Ibid.*
13 *Modern Languages Examinations at 16+, Op. Cit.*
14 REDFORD, H. 'Language Barriers' in *The Times Educational Supplement*, 8 May 1981.
15 GARNER, E., 'Background Studies and Graded Examinations' in *Modern Languages and Background Studies: a European Dimension, Op. Cit.*
16 PEACOCK, D. *in Modern Languages and Background Studies, Op. cit.*
17 LENG, A.J. (1980) *A view for the 1980s*, HMC Modern Languages Report, No. 2.
18 TATE, R. MUCKLE, J. (1981), *Op, Cit.*
19 PEACOCK, D. (1980) 'The Role of the Modern Linguist in Study of Europe' in *Teaching about Europe*, Vol. 8, No. 1.

6 *Economics*

Economics is a subject with considerable potential for teaching about Europe, although it is not to be found as a specific objective in any of the secondary school examination syllabuses available in 1980. To a certain extent this is understandable. The state and workings of the national economy affect to a greater or lesser degree most areas of an individual's life, therefore pupils learning the subject need to study as a priority basic economic theory and facts about the British economy. This core content must, nevertheless, incorporate some details relating to external factors affecting the national economy such as overseas trade and British membership of international trading blocks such as the EEC. There is also a case for courses including references, however brief, to other economic systems. An element of contrast would allow for more than one perspective, a consideration of some importance given the diversity of economic theories and given too that national economic trends and objectives tend to be modified according to whichever government is currently in office.

The teaching of economics in the UK increased dramatically in the 1950s and 1960s[1] and the subject is now well established in secondary school and tertiary education curricula. This accelerated growth developed along lines subsequently followed in other EEC countries, a process which according to Ryba and Robinson in their survey of the subject in EC Member States, seemed to have its origins in a number of related educational, economic, political and social changes which have taken place in Europe since the Second World War:

> (. . .) what may well have appeared, in each individual country, to be an autonomous development inspired by its own national conditions, and steered into existence by its own successful pressure groups, has in reality been a more internationally based response to broader changes in the structure and content of all European school systems and to the underlying economic, social, and political conditions in post-war Europe to which these broader changes are themselves related.[2]

One important factor that undoubtedly contributed to the rapid expansion of the subject in Europe was the economic growth which characterized many EEC countries in the 1960s and which created an unprecedented need for employees with basic economic knowledge and expertise. Simultaneously in many Member States secondary education was undergoing a major process of reform, the most significent phase of which was the changeover from a selective to a single school system catering for the entire ability range. This development has had far-reaching consequences on the curriculum particularly where the establishment and expansion of newer subjects are concerned. The results in terms of the expansion of economics education in EEC countries have been summarized by Raymond Ryba of the Economics Association:

> The particular significance of these developments for economics education lay in the fact that whereas the former selective secondary schools of Europe have, like those in France, generally resisted curricular change in favour of the inclusion of economics, the new comprehensivised schools were generally much more in its favour. As had already happened in Britain fundamental curricular rethinking inevitably began to take place to meet the needs of 'new' secondary populations extending across the whole ability range. These, unlike their highly selected predecessors, were generally unwilling, and, in the case of the less able pupils, unable, to profit from outdated secondary curricula which had originally been developed in relation to only the most able fraction of each age cohort. In this context, economic studies within the general secondary education curriculum, was either introduced *de novo* or, where it already existed, was expanded in one form of another.[3]

The rapid expansion of the teaching of economics in Europe has undoubtedly been accompanied and stimulated by an increased perception of the subject's value and relevance both to the individual and to society as a whole. Although there inevitably are marked differences in definitions, course content and emphases in the different countries of the EEC, the fact that economics has established itself so quickly and against all odds in secondary education in many European countries in the last few decades testifies to a heightened awareness in society of the subject's importance:

> ... To have breached the barricades around the secondary school curriculum, barricades habitually defended with even greater tenacity, persistence and success than those in higher education, represents no mean achievement. The fact of this development in virtually all nine Community Countries speaks volumes not only for the inherent qualities of the subject and the determination and inspiration, in the face of great and powerful opposition, of the individuals and groups of educationists involved within each country, but also for the irresistible strength of the larger societal pressures at work.[4]

Syllabus Commentary

In Great Britain most secondary economics courses are at sixth form level leading to GCE 'A' level, although there has been a steady increase in the number of schools offering the subject at 'O' level. On the whole, school courses are academic rather than vocational in character, laying stress on descriptive economics and economic theory relating to the UK. Some schools also offer courses in commerce, business or industrial studies which are basically factual and descriptive. Analysis of the examination courses available in all these subjects shows what opportunities school children are offered to learn about European economic systems and institutions.

A survey of GCE and SCE syllabuses in economics, commerce and business studies available in 1980 revealed little real variation between them. The 16+ courses are mainly descriptive with some theory and some commercial application. 'A' level courses focus on economic or market theory and its application to the British economy. Very few make any specific reference to economies and institutions outside Great Britain other than in the context of overseas trade.

GCE 'A' level syllabuses

Only three out of the twelve 1980 syllabuses in these subjects contain a specific European element, albeit in each case a limited one: *AEB Economics (618)* includes references to the EEC and EFTA under one of nine syllabus headings — *International Trade*. According to statistics this was the most popular A level in economics (9094 candidates in summer 1978).

SUJB: Economics (9076) contains a reference to Europe in the context of *International Economics* — the eighth of nine syllabus sections. Again this is restricted primarily to the EEC as 'an example of an economic block in relation to the UK economy'. (1979 statistics show the number of candidates taking this syllabus to be small — 309.)

Oxford and Cambridge: Economics is the only 'A' level in the subject to have a section on comparative economics — in the fourth section of paper 2 *Applied Economics*. For this section pupils are expected to 'show their knowledge and understanding of the economics of a developing nation, a developed industrial nation, a communist country, the EEC, and international economic institutions (e.g. IMF, World Bank, GATT)'. However, paper 2 is optional and candidates can choose in preference paper 3: *British Economic and Social History since 1780*. Nevertheless even this paper provides some possibilities of European content particularly in sub-section 3: *The International Economy*: 'the growth of foreign trade; capital exports; migration; imperialism; Britain's changing position in the world economy'. Paper 1 — Principles of Economics — could also include reference to Europe under sub-section 9: *International Trade*. This syllabus therefore contains more specific and potential European content than the other 'A' levels. The number of candidates for it, however, has been considerably smaller than for the AEB — 2331 in summer 1979.

Of the remaining 'A' levels, *AEB: Business Studies* (655) has an overseas dimension in one of its four main syllabus sections: *Factors external to businesses which affect the attainment of objectives.* This contains reference to the UK's role as a trading nation and its dependence on international trade; the susceptibility of British business to world economic conditions . . . The effect of home and overseas governments' actions and policies on business in the UK.'

None of the other 'A' levels contain any specific references to Europe. The JMB, Oxford, London, Cambridge, WJEC, Northern Ireland and SCE ('H' grade) syllabuses concentrate on basic economic concepts with special reference to the UK but they could all include some very limited European content under certain of the general headings such as International Trade. Of these syllabuses the London and JMB are the most popular, attracting 7955 and 7951 candidates respectively in 1978 and 1979.

GCE 'A/O' Level syllabuses

Of the five analyzed, two have a specified European content — *AEB: Business Studies 176* which refers to the effect on business of international agencies such as the EEC and IMF; and *JMB: Industrial Studies* which has a sub-section under syllabus heading C: *Industrial Relations* specifically relating to the influence of the EEC. This syllabus also has sections on International Trade and 'Other Industrial Systems', so theoretically it could provide several opportunities for study of European economics and institutions. Unfortunately this examination appeared to have a small clientele, only 110 candidates in 1979.

The 'A/O' syllabus with the largest number of candidates in 1979 was the *Oxford and Cambridge: British Economic Organisation.* There is no specific European content in the course but it has European possibilities under at least four of the general syllabus sections.

The remaining 'A/O' syllabuses — *University of London Commercial Studies* (810) and *SUJB Economics and Public Affairs* (8102) have limited potential where European content is concerned except within the context of foreign trade.

GCE 'O' Level syllabuses

Of the fourteen analyzed, only three make any specific reference to European economics. In all cases this is restricted to the EEC.

AEB (syllabus 2) Social Economics (061) has a syllabus section *Britain and the World* which contains a sub-section on *The Social and Economic Policies of the EEC*. This syllabus, which has an internal assessment element, was taken by 3130 candidates in 1978.

Oxford Local: Commerce (7886) has a reference to the effects of the EEC under the heading *Foreign Trade* (4176 candidates in 1979) and the *AEB British Industrial Society (162)* syllabus contains a sub-section 'The effect of EEC decisions on government plans'. This syllabus also has a coursework element but attracted fewer candidates than the other AEB 'O' levels (863 in 1978).

By far the most popular economics 'O' level in 1980 seemed to be *AEB (syllabus 1) Economic Principles (073)* which had 11,169 candidates in 1978. Although there is no specific mention of anything European in the course, some European content could be included mainly in the International Trade section.

The most popular 'O' level commerce syllabus is also the AEB (13,597 candidates in 1978). The course is based on the commercial structure of the UK and there is no prescribed European content although some reference to the EEC could be made in the International Trade section.

The remaining 'O' level syllabuses focus similarly on the UK economic and commercial structure with the possibility of any European content being confined to the International or Overseas Trade sections. This is true of *JMB: Government, Economics and Commerce*; *London: Economics (120)*; *London; Commerce (100)*; *Oxford Local: Economics (2840)*; *Cambridge Economics*; *Cambridge: Economics and Public Affairs*; *SUJB: Commerce (7101)*; *WJEC: Economics (0112)* and *SCE Economics 'O' grade*. Of these the most popular syllabus in 1978–79 was *London Economics (120)* (10,357 candidates in 1978), followed by *JMB Government, Economics and Commerce* (7157 in 1979); *London: Commerce (100)* (5871 in 1978), and *Oxford: Economics (2840)* (5644 in 1979).

There seems to be a considerable amount of similarity between syllabuses in economics, commerce and business studies. Most courses in economics, for example, cover the same ground — basic economic theory, the British economy and the skills of the economist. One 'O' level syllabus, for example, is described in terms which could summarize most of the examinations available:

> a descriptive approach to the main institutions and activities of the UK economy together with an understanding of the nature of the economic problem and an elementary approach to some key economic concepts including price determination in a competitive market.

A similar format — basic concepts and a descriptive approach to UK institutions and commercial activities — characterizes courses in commerce and business studies.

The few specific references to Europe that are contained in GCE and SCE courses are mainly restricted to the EEC and its effects on British trade, although few syllabuses devote any sizeable space to this. Only the AEB 'O' Level (syllabus 2) in social economics has a complete sub-section entitled 'The Social and Economic Policies of the EEC'. A few syllabuses mention EFTA, and organizations such as IMF, but on the whole allusions to European or international economic systems and institutions are extremely rare, the main opportunities for their inclusion being provided by the overseas or international trade syllabus sections or topics.

Only two syllabuses — *Oxford and Cambridge 'A' Level Economics* and *JMB 'A/O' Industrial Studies* — have a comparative economics element, and only the first of these makes specific reference to a communist economy.

Conclusions

Since the 1960s there have been a number of projects and conferences sponsored by the EEC and other European organizations focussing on the discussion and comparison of the teaching of economics within Europe. One of these, a curriculum study on economics education in Western Europe in the early 1970s, was based on research sponsored by the Council of Europe. This study argued the case for an expansion of economics in European educational systems in terms of Europe's need for economic knowledge and expertise:

> The rise of international institutions during this century has been rapid. We may be far away from a world state, and still a little way from a cooperating group of European states, but the European institutions creep steadily forward year by year. These must be staffed by European or international civil servants with loyalties far wider than those customarily acquired by the citizen of any one state. Those international civil servants will be certain to find that, however much they need a knowledge of politics, a knowledge of economics will form a substratum for every consequential international or European decision they take (. . .)
>
> Europe can only maintain its living standards if it keeps its share of world markets, if it encourages innovation, if it manages its economic resources, better than its competitors. There is no better way of achieving these aims than in expanding Europe's economic expertise through the incorporation of economic studies into appropriate levels of its educational systems.[5]

One of the findings of the study was that although the teaching of economics as an academic discipline had expanded rapidly at the upper secondary level in Western Europe (particularly in the UK where the number of entries for GCE 'A' level in the subject 'quadrupled' between 1965–69), none of the countries participating in the research included teaching about Europe as an economic entity in the aims of their economic courses:

> From an expansion of economic studies based on European economic interests, it would follow logically that the aims of teaching economics within European countries should include that of teaching about Europe. In fact, there is extraordinarily little about Europe as an economic entity in any of the aims of teaching economics expressed

> overtly or covertly by the representatives of the various European countries who provided the research material for this Study.[6]

The Council of Europe research involved asking participants which general aspects of economics received the most detailed treatment in their secondary school courses. The topics to be placed in order of priority were:

> (1) economic theory (2) national economic structure (3) world international structure (4) European economic structure (5) political economics (6) social economics.

The report comments on the results of this question.

> If we can generalize the results over the whole of the countries providing the information, we can set out a hypothetical 'European' order of priority for teaching the aspects of economics as follows:
>
> 1 Economic theory
> 2 National economic structure
> 3 Political economics
> 4 Social economics
> 5 World international structure
> 6 European economic structure
>
> The UK falls exactly on this order of priority, while Switzerland, Malta and the Netherlands are very close indeed to it. It is still a little saddening to find confirmation of the view that study of the European economic structure achieves to date the lowest priority of all.[7]

From the syllabus analysis undertaken for the *Europe in the School* project it can be seen that in this respect little has changed, although nearly a decade has passed, and it seems likely that most examination boards would still list the topics in the same order of priority.

There has indeed been some criticism of economics education in Great Britain in recent years[8] although opinions differ as to its specific deficiencies. Certainly the dearth of European content has not been singled out as a particular shortcoming although one senior lecturer in the subject has suggested that the best kind of training in economics in schools '. . . would begin with what used to be called civics, and economic history of a wide-ranging international kind'[9], which implies a belief that school courses are currently too parochial in character.

Whether courses in economics should extend much beyond basic theory and the national economy is, of course, a moot point. The Council of Europe research report nevertheless remarks on the contradiction between the content of courses in Western European schools and the aim, expressed by nearly all of the representatives of the participating countries, to encourage students of the subject 'to acquire through study of economics an understanding of the world in which we live' As the author of the report points out:

> This laudable aim can only be effective through a subject study such as economics if the syllabus specifically goes beyond teaching about the economics of the pupils' own country.

The Council of Europe Curriculum Study makes a convincing case for the incorporation of a section on Europe in economics courses:

> The study of external economies invites a question as to whether all students of economics in Western Europe should study Western Europe as an economic entity. Of course, in a politico-economic sense there is no economic entity of western Europe. However, if we disregard political boundaries, and concentrate on economic activity, it might well be possible to envisage a micro-economic study of Western Europe.
>
> Some of the largest industrial and commercial enterprises already treat Western Europe as one market. Car production firms, chemical producers, oil consortia, plastics producers and air-lines all tend to act economically as if Western Europe were an economic entity. Customs barriers at political boundaries are a nuisance, but even they are breaking down.
>
> The European Economic Community formed its customs unions in 1968. The EEC is in the process of forming common industrial, energy, and regional policies. A single Western European currency with a common currency reserve is a stated aim of EEC countries . . .
>
> It would be premature to assume the formation of a political entity of Western Europe. It does not, however, require more than a limited adjustment of thinking to anticipate in Western Europe an economics syllabus addition entitled *The Economy of Western Europe*.[10]

The Curriculum Study also stresses the usefulness of comparative economics, an element which as the *Europe in the School* syllabus analysis shows, is still generally lacking in most British school courses:

> Comparative studies of economic systems are bound to widen minds, open eyes, and unstop ears closed to the values of any economic system different from that practised in a given country.[11]

The study of contrasting economic systems can be of particular value. The author of the 1972 curriculum report singled out the absence of references to planned economies as a particular shortcoming of economics education in Western Europe:

> If there is one major weakness in the teaching of economics in Western Europe, it is a relative failure to study wholly planned economies. It may be argued that there is enough to learn about capitalistic and mixed economies, but this argument omits to consider the profoundly educational value of comparison and contrast. Comparison and contrast are not easily employed by teachers of economics in western

> Europe for the simple reason that the most obvious comparisons are with similar countries with mixed socialist/capitalist economies. It will be easy to persuade teachers — or educationists in general — that a study of a wholly planned economy should become a standard part of the syllabus in economics of every country of Western Europe.
>
> It is not necessary to look solely to the USSR for a case study of a wholly planned economy. Examples stand beside Western Europe in Eastern Europe. These different economies already exchange substantial quantities of goods and services each year. This exchange process alone should justify a necessity for a mixed type of economic organisation to be taught by constrast or comparison with a wholly planned economy.[12]

The same point was made by a British economics teacher interviewed in a case study undertaken in 1980 as part of the *Europe in the School* project. Commenting on the lack of European content in examination courses, this teacher noted in particular the omission of references to Eastern European economics and claimed she would welcome 'more detailed study of command-type economies and what it is meant by and involved in a command-type economy'.

The analysis of examination syllabuses indicates that currently only the *JMB 'A/O' level in Industrial Studies* and the *Oxford and Cambridge 'A' level* in economics provide opportunities for study of planned economy. The latter syllabus also includes in its Comparative Economics section 'the economics of a developing nation', something which is omitted in all the other syllabuses analyzed although *AEB 'O' level Economics, syllabus 2* has a sub-section on 'Britain's economic relations with developing countries'.

The 1972 Council of Europe Curriculum Study pointed out the interdependence of developed and less advanced economies:

> There is already a sense in which the world is one economy. We would do well to utilise the teaching of economics to enable those with high standards of living to discover that low standards of living exist, and that the two types of economy are interdependent.[13]

The 1980 Brandt Report forcefully emphasized this point. So too, have various official utterances on the English and Welsh school curriculum in recent years. Nevertheless, it is fair to say that the majority of British school economics courses manifest the same national, even insular, bias that was evident nearly ten years ago. Not only do they contain little or no reference to any economic systems outside the UK but few of them make anything but the most cursory mention of Europe of which the UK is a part. Although some syllabuses now have a section which incorporates Europe as a topic, 'questions are rather rare and answers to questions rarer still' according to a member of the British Economics Association. Yet the continent of Europe contains abundant examples of different economic systems and this, combined with the UK's economic and political links with other countries of Europe, provides a rationale for economics courses incorporating a European dimension.

Teachers could argue, of course, that they have insufficient time to teach the basic economic theory and knowledge of our own system that make up the core content needed by students of the subject and that anything in addition to that is a 'frill'. Nevertheless, as has already been noted with history syllabuses, many economics courses are virtually identical differing only in minor detail. Given the number of examination boards and courses available one wonders whether such uniformity is essential and whether the subject would not be enriched by having more scope and diversity of content, particularly in 'A' level courses.

Where the addition of European content is concerned, there have been a number of promising inter-European initiatives in recent years[14] which could eventually have some influence on the content and methodology of economics education in schools. But since most economics courses are examination-oriented the most effective changes have to be made by the examination Boards when they are developing and redesigning syllabuses. They have to be persuaded that there is a strong case for economics courses providing, at least at 'A' level, some opportunity for the study of other systems, which are similar to, or different from our own, if only to fulfil the aim expressed by so many educationalists and politicians in recent years — to encourage greater understanding of the world in which we live. If this aim were acted upon, study not just of economic systems within the EEC, but also of other economic systems in Europe and the wider world would ideally be included in school economics courses.

Notes

1 Details of the development of economics in the UK are outlined by SZRETER, R. (1975) 'Economics Education in Schools' in LEE, N. (Ed.) *Teaching Economics*, 2nd edition, Economics Association/Heinemann Educational Books. Szreter gives the following figures for candidates entering GCE examinations in economics:

	'A' Level	*'O' Level*
1951	1 181	1 593
1961	6 134	6 993
1971	26,454	41,240

2 RYBA, R. (1977) 'The Recent Evolution of Economics Education in EEC countries at the Upper Secondary Level' in RYBA, R. and ROBINSON: B (Eds) *Aspects of Upper Secondary Economics Education in EEC Countries*, Economics Association (on behalf of the EEC Working Committee on Economics Education).

3 *Ibid* p. 25.

4 *Ibid* p. 28.

5 BONNEY RUST, W. (1972) *European Curriculum Studies No. 7: Economics*, Strasbourg, Council of Europe, Council for Cultural Cooperation, pp. 17–18.

6 *Ibid* p. 19.

7 *Ibid* pp. 39–41.

8 See Hallett, G. (1981) 'The Economic Crisis and the Crisis in Education', *The Times Higher Educational Supplement*, 7 August.
9 *Ibid.*
10 Bonney Rust, W. (1972) *op. cit.*, pp. 105–6.
11 *Ibid* p. 17.
12 *Ibid* pp. 105–6.
13 *Ibid* pp. 106–7.
14 Ryba, R. (1977) *op. cit.*, pp. 30–2.

7 *Modern Studies*

So far the research has centred on the main subjects in the secondary school curriculum identified as having the greatest potential European dimension. This section will consider Modern Studies, a good example of a newer integrated or multi-disciplinary subject with a modern European component which has succeeded in establishing a secure place for itself in secondary schools and teacher training institutions in Scotland.[1]

The examination system in Scotland differs from that in the rest of the United Kingdom although some schools may present candidates for GCE and CSE examinations. The Scottish Certificate of Education (SCE) Ordinary Grade is taken at the end of a secondary school pupil's fourth year and Higher Grade is taken at the end of the fifth year. Pupils can also take a separate Certificate of Sixth Year Studies (CSYS) although 'H' Grade passes would be sufficient for higher education entrance qualification.

Most study of Europe in Scottish schools takes place within the traditional subjects history and geography together with Modern Studies which has established itself in the secondary school curriculum over the last two decades. (The first examinations were held in 1962 at 'O' grade and in 1968 at 'H' grade.)

The Modern Studies Association defines the subject as follows:

> A multi-disciplinary study of contemporary society deploying skills, concepts and knowledge drawn selectively from the social subject disciplines to focus on social, economic and political issues of concern to individuals and groups at local, national and international levels. A more concise description might be that it is a course of study about how people in Britain and in certain countries overseas organize their lives and how economic, social and political issues affect them. The essential features are that it is *multi-disciplinary* contemporary and concerned with issues.[2]

The aims of the subject as set out in the new 'O' grade syllabus are the following:

Through the study of contemporary society and issues, Modern Studies aims:

(a) to develop knowledge and understanding of contemporary society, its changing nature, its institutions and the influence acting upon them;

(b) to develop the practical and intellectual skills necessary for the study and intelligent discussion of contemporary issues;

(c) to encourage the formation of considered attitudes of an intellectual, humanitarian, social and political nature;

and thus contribute to the candidate's preparation for full and active membership of society.

There are Modern Studies Departments in the five main Scottish Colleges of Education and, according to the Information Officer for the Modern Studies Association, the subject is taught in virtually all of Scotland's 3000 secondary schools, over half of which have Modern Studies Departments.

Teachers of Modern Studies tend to come from the following specialist subject areas in which they have taken a degree: geography, history, economics, politics, and social studies. They have then acquired a teaching qualification in Modern Studies at a college of education.

Statistics show that there has been a steady increase in the number of candidates taking SCE in Modern Studies particularly at 'O' grade. For example, there were 9410 candidates in 1978 as opposed to 6831 in 1973, and the number has undoubtedly grown since then. A large number of schools have also introduced the subject in the first and second year classes — standards 1 and 2 (S1 and S2) — although there is no compulsory syllabus at this level and teachers are free to introduce topics which they think will best fulfil the aims of the subject and prepare their pupils for the S3 and S4 work.

The SCE Examination Board has also developed a Modern Studies syllabus for the Certificate of Sixth Year Studies and this was examined for the first time in 1982.

To investigate the scope Modern Studies offers for teaching about contemporary Europe, case studies were conducted in large urban comprehensive schools in Scotland. These were co-educational with rolls of over 1,500. The Principal Teachers in the Modern Studies departments of these schools discussed, in a series of interviews, how the subject had evolved in their respective schools; their experiences teaching the syllabuses, and the kind of work on Europe they had been developing within the courses.

Their comments gave some interesting insights into the nature of the subject, the way it has developed over the past two decades, and some of the problems it has encountered in establishing itself in the curriculum. For although Modern Studies is now well established in the Scottish secondary school curriculum, this position has not been achieved without some conflict with the more traditional subjects.

In the case study schools Modern Studies was taught in S1 and S2 as well as to 'O' and 'H' Grade in S3, S4 and S5. Pupils in their third year in Scottish secondary schools usually study English and mathematics; a social subject (history, geography or Modern Studies); a modern language; a science, and two other subjects. It is common, therefore, to find Modern Studies timetabled against history and geography in the third year option groups of subjects, and this was the case in the case study schools. The comments of the Modern Studies teachers revealed that in competing with history and geography for a fair share of pupils, Modern Studies, like many innovatory subjects, needed to shake off an initial 'low status' image and pupils and parents alike had to be persuaded of its academic worth and usefulness. Like European Studies, in some schools it was seen at first as an option for the less able. Now, however, in most schools the subject competes on an equal basis with other subjects in the curriculum and here the analogy with European studies ends. This was the experience of one teacher in a case study school:

> when I first came here, six years ago, Modern Studies had not built up at all. It had been going for quite some time not in S1 or S2 mind you, but in the third and fourth years. But it had a very non-academic status in those days. A few years ago it was always expected that the bright children would take history and geography and the less able would do Modern Studies. That is no longer the case. In fact sometimes now the opposite applies: very mature students, both boys and girls, will go for Modern Studies because they like the politics element. They find it more academic than history or geography.

The same teacher claimed that until relatively recently he was still encountering some hostility to Modern Studies from other members of staff:

> up until last year or two years ago we were still getting opposition from teachers under threat who were subtly trying to devalue Modern Studies, but I think the battles are over now, at least they are here.

The situation regarding acceptance of Modern Studies as a subject on a par with the other social subjects seems to be uneven over Scotland as a whole, according to another teacher who had taught Modern Studies in several areas:

> the low status image of Modern Studies still persists in some parts of Scotland, Renfrew Division of Strathclyde for example, where the subject still lacks encouragement. The position is patchy over the country as a whole but here in Glasgow it's different. It's well established here.

This situation may well be related to the fact that although there are not many Modern Studies advisers in Scotland, there was a very active one in Glasgow in 1980.

Within individual schools the approach, attitude and activities of teachers can also help to determine whether or not a relatively new subject gets accepted by pupils, their parents and other members of staff. One of the case study teachers, for example, prepared a detailed information sheet setting out for pupils and parents the nature of the subject, the content of third and fourth year courses and the benefits of Modern Studies qualifications to pupils. Although there was no overt canvassing for pupils in his school, he felt that this approach, combined with various inherent advantages the subject has over other subjects, succeeded in allowing Modern Studies to compete on an equal footing with history and geography and a fair number of third year pupils opted for it:

> In this school there is no hard sell: we say that all three social subjects offer the same career prospects, therefore, unless you have a very specific career in mind, take the one you like best or do best at. We then have the advantage that our subject has more variety than history or geography: it's more up-to-date and pupils relate to it better, so we often win in that way. I think where it loses out is in schools where the old message is still there: that that it's less valuable than the other two. That used to be the message — that you'd lose out unless you took one of the other two. Modern Studies was not recognized. But once schools give it the same status officially as the other two, pupils feel reassured enough to take it. In this school, for example, we usually draw a third of the Third Year children. This year I've got 110 doing 'O' grade and 50 non-certificate children. That's out of a year group of 400. We are happy to receive a comfortable third. History receives more than us but geography does less well.

In one of the case study schools, therefore, Modern Studies had achieved by 1980 a position of equal status with history and geography. In another, the principal teacher appeared less satisfied with the progress the subject had made. He felt it had not yet completely overcome the handicap of having had an initial low status image and he had encountered some opposition to the development of the subject from teachers of more established subjects:

> The subject has not completely overcome its low status image yet. This year we have come up against some remains . . . children, for example, doing geography because they feel it goes with science, though I do not quite see the connection. To my mind it doesn't matter which of the social subjects a child does in 90 per cent of cases. But people feel that if they are doing a science or a maths-based course then geography is the one to do. We're viewed as an upstart subject. It varies according to personalities. Geography, for example, is taught here in a very traditional way by a very traditional teacher, and he did not like the intrusion of Modern Studies although, strangely enough, he taught Modern Studies himself before I came to the school. But when I came, a separate department was created for Modern Studies and I think he was rather annoyed that the subject had been elevated in this way. That was six years ago. He had been able to teach Modern Studies

> from a geographical point of view, which he could do in the early days before the syllabus was reconstructed.
>
> We have had two head teachers in the time I have been here. The first was fairly sympathetic; the present one — no! I had a great battle to retain our first and second year classes. Her objection was that she thought the concepts we are dealing with were beyond the average first and second year child. There was a very real threat of cutting our period allocation for S1 by half or even cutting Modern Studies in the first year altogether. Fortunately it did not come about. I don't know whether she was impressed with my arguments, but I certainly had a lot of long arguments with her where I thought I wasn't getting anywhere, and eventually we managed to retain our position partly I think because of staffing difficulties. She had no option but to leave the children with us because there were no extra staff in any other departments available to give them extra maths or anything. That was when she came three years ago and since then she has not threatened us again.

The politics of the curriculum are much in evidence here. Advocates of a new subject have to be strong and persistent to overcome its 'upstart' or low status image and hostility from other teachers. When, as in this case, there is also opposition from the headteacher whose support is crucial for curriculum development or expansion, then it is obvious that a teacher will need energy, resources and forcefulness beyond the norm.

The same teacher in the Modern Studies case study had experienced strong competition between the three social subjects for third year pupils and he was not altogether happy with the numbers attracted by Modern Studies:

> We are in direct competition with history and geography. There are some unwritten rules: there are things we do or do not do to try and attract children, for example we do not go all out with propaganda to try and tempt them; we do not try and persuade parents. We do, however, present parents with as much information as we can about the subject. Even so we have had some flare-ups with the three principal teachers involved.
>
> The numbers are fairly evenly spread between the three subjects. One year we did best; last year geography did best; this year history did best, so it does the rounds. But this year we happen to have done badly. There are reasons for this. I have narrowed it down to the following factors: devising our own syllabus in the first and second years; then we have to allow for things like the influence of various teachers. Then there is the attractiveness of our subject — that's something else ... (If we knew what motivated children in their choice of subjects we would not be trailing in the numbers we are attracting); the nature of the material being taught: I think that's a major reason why we have done badly. I think we have got a lot of

> work to do restructuring our first and second year syllabus. We have got a big revision exercise on our hands. Then there is the status of the subject . . . that counts for a lot; what they think a subject will do for them in later life. Geography, for example, seems to have a lot of status in our school and elsewhere I think. And we cannot for the life of us think why because it is very traditionally, very mundanely taught, at least that is generally thought to be the case. We, being a relatively new and 'upstart' subject, found it difficult to acquire such status and prestige, though it is beginning to come through children who have done 'O' and 'H' grade in Modern Studies and other children in the family tend to follow suit.

These comments suggest how much commitment and drive are needed by a teacher of a newer subject when that subject is in direct competition with older, more established areas of the curriculum.

Modern Studies was viewed as particularly threatening by geography and history teachers in its early days because the examination courses had a mainly geographical and historical emphasis (including work on ordnance survey maps). In 1977, however, the 'O' grade was restructured and, according to a lecturer in the subject, Modern Studies now has a distinct identity of its own: due to the changing academic background of the teachers of Modern Studies, the subject has acquired a new emphasis and become more politically than historically or geographically orientated:

> The nature of the subject has changed because the background of the teachers has changed and now specialist Modern Studies teachers teach the whole syllabus. The subject has evolved considerably since it started. In the 1960s basically there were no specialist teachers of Modern Studies. The subject was taught by teachers of history and geography and sometimes teachers of English. But gradually, as teachers have come through Colleges of Education or attended night classes or gained qualifications in other ways, they have got a piece of paper saying they are qualified teachers of *Modern Studies* which is significant. As that body has grown, it has included teachers with politics, sociology and economics in their training, so the composition of the teaching body has changed and the subject has swung away from history and geography which are now a relatively minor element in it, whereas politics has increased. If you teach about modern issues and problems many of them have a large political content. You cannot ignore politics.

Because of this change of emphasis, Modern Studies should no longer present a threat to the other social subjects, history and geography. The fact that it is still regarded with some suspicion in academic circles may have something to do with its multi-disciplinary nature. As recently as 1976 the

Scottish Central Committee on Social Subjects expressed doubts in their *Curriculum Paper 15* about the desirability of Modern Studies being taught in S1 and S2:

> The Committee is also aware that, for a number of reasons, a number of schools have, either individually or with the support of their Education Authorities, embarked on trial courses in S1 and S2 with the other social sciences. (. . .) The Committee does not, at this time, recommend multi-disciplinary or integrated courses in Modern Studies or of a Modern Studies type in S1 and S2.[3]

Nevertheless a 1979 survey of Modern Studies courses in S1 and S2 showed that they had increased in number and a subsequent report concluded that, in spite of many problems, these courses are appropriate for the younger age groups and of educational value. The report is worth quoting since it summarizes the stages the subject has needed to go through prior to its establishment in the curriculum:

> The evidence from submissions and from schools was quite consistent in recognising the educational value of courses in contemporary studies, however presented.
>
> If a curriculum development is to establish itself in schools and in the eyes of others then it has to convince suppliers and consumers of its worth. Without their support it cannot compete successfully for staff, time and resources. In this respect Modern Studies at S1/S2 has had distinctive problems. As a 'new' subject it has had to create an identity and demonstrate both its relevance and practicability to younger pupils in common courses. Also, it has lacked consistent promotion from outside the schools, with regional support ranging from the very good to the non-existent, and with expressions of national policy being generally discouraging. So, unlike many other developments it has been thrown back largely upon the persuasiveness and commitment of individual advocates.
>
> Despite the particular and often discouraging circumstances the development has taken root and grown. A subject identity has been created, its appropriateness to younger pupils has been demonstrated, and there has been a steady growth in provision until it now exists in a large number of schools.
>
> Our evidence suggests there is much sound practice, enthusiasm on the part of headteachers and teachers, and value for pupils. At the same time, however, it is apparent that basic necessary conditions for effective courses to operate are not always present, and that in these instances and in the more generally satisfactory situations further support to teachers, whether from within schools or outside, may be needed if improvements in the quality of provision are to take place. The need for such support applies not only to current provision, but

may be more pressing if wider provision across secondary schools is to be promoted successfully.

The issue of promoting wider provision remains highly contentious, for whilst there is fairly general recognition that courses on contemporary affairs are important for all pupils, there is considerable divergence of opinion as to whether they should take the form of the subject of Modern Studies or result from a reconsideration of the nature and organisation of the Social Subjects in S1/S2. We have not seen it as part of our remit to express our opinions on the course of development, but believe it important to note that a substantial and reasonably coherent provision of Modern Studies now exists and that this has not been paralleled by any other consistent alternative to date.[4]

The fact that Modern Studies has expanded in this way and become more than exclusively a third, fourth, and fifth year SCE subject, indicates the increasingly secure position it is establishing in the secondary school curriculum. Clearly the essential step in gaining and maintaining this position was establishing Modern Studies as an SCE subject in the first place. Just as a GCE examination confers status on a subject in the English curriculum, so Modern Studies has needed this to become really established in Scotland. This was conceded by one of the teachers in the case studies:

> Modern Studies has become established by being accepted as an SCE subject that's the main thing. Once you get that established you get a defined syllabus; you get the status of an examination subject; you get the back-up of a College of Education; you get trained teachers. That way you get a subject to stick. There must now be few schools in Scotland which do not now present pupils for Modern Studies, at least at 'O' grade:

The career prospects the subject offers to the teacher also contribute considerably to its strength:

> Teachers in Modern Studies can be reasonably sure of a career structure with promotion possibilities. Forty hours (say 60 periods weekly) of the subject merits a principal teacher: 20 hours an assistant principal. Under 20 hours weekly there would be no promoted posts and the subject would very likely be subsumed under history or geography or the Social Subjects generally.

The professional experience of one of the teachers interviewed illustrates the career prospects offered by the subject. Originally engaged to teach history and Modern Studies in his first school, he subsequently moved on to become Head of Department in his present school where 'the subject has grown so much that I now only teach Modern Studies. It now takes all my time'.

In spite of lingering pockets of resistance to what is sometimes considered an 'upstart subject' and in spite of there being no Moden Studies in higher education, there is little doubt that Modern Studies has a sure and lasting place in Scottish Secondary School curriculum. To quote one of the teachers in the case studies:

> I think a lot of our battles have been fought and won. In other words we're established as a social subject with a Head of Department, with a department structure and career prospects. I would say that Modern Studies in schools is on a par with every other subject. We're accepted for university general entrance qualifications in exactly the same way as other subjects.

The European Dimension to Modern Studies

Modern Studies courses are constructed so as to develop pupils' awareness first of the community they live in then of the wider world about them. The European element has to be seen in this perspective. A teacher of the subject summarized it as follows:

> Modern Studies is concerned with the individual in his community his family and the area where he lives. Then we widen this out to the district and the town; Scotland and the Scottish dimension; the UK dimension; the European dimension; then of course elements of the wider world — America, Russia, China, Third World countries and so on. So we try to see this as a continuum from the individual to the wider world. The European dimension, the EEC component, are only part of that.

The 'O' grade Modern Studies syllabus is the lynch-pin of the subject as a whole. The 'O' grade course determines not only what is taught in S3 and S4 but also, it is probably fair to say, a lot of what is taught in S1 and S2.

The European content of the 'O' grade syllabus, therefore, tends to influence what European Studies go on lower down the school although there is no prescribed content for S1 and S2 Modern Studies courses. At 'H' grade which is intended to be a continuation of the 'O' grade work, the European element does not differ substantially from that of the 'O' grade syllabus. Consequently the European section of the 'O' grade can be seen as the key to the European content of the subject in general.

The SCE 'O' and 'H' grade syllabuses have both been revised. The new 'O' grade syllabus was introduced in 1978 and a new 'H' grade was examined for the first time in 1981.[5]

The European Component[6]

Within the SCE 'O' grade Modern Studies syllabus the European element is contained in a section concerning selected aspects of international relations, which includes such topics as the Cold War; Sino-Soviet relations; Great Power involvement in Africa and the work of the United Nations Organization. The European element encompasses the emergence, aims, operation and achievements of the European Economic Community, relations between Eastern and Western Europe; and the study of the Eastern block countries. At 'H' grade, the coverage is similar but in much greater depth, with considerable emphasis on recent economic, social and political change in both Western and Eastern Europe.

Teachers of Modern Studies have fairly clear guidelines as to what they are expected to teach to 'O' and 'H' grade standard. There are four main areas of study — politics and government, economics, society, and military and strategic aspects — and the main emphasis is very definitely on recent events (the last ten to fifteen years), although the starting point is generally taken as 1945.

SCE 'O' Grade Modern Studies

The SCE 'O' grade examination in Modern Studies, comprises three elements: a written paper (Paper I), an objective test paper (Paper 2), and a project-type Special Study. All candidates for 'O' grade are expected to cover the ground outlined so far. They can expect a number of questions on Europe in the objective test paper (which accounts for 20 per cent of the total examination marks) and may opt to answer one question on Europe in the written paper (which accounts for 60 per cent of the total — candidates answer four questions worth 15 marks each). The written paper is divided into three sections, 'Individual Family and Community', 'International Relations and Organizations', and 'The Great Powers'. Candidates answer two questions from the first, and one each from the second and third sections. Questions about Europe normally appear in the second section alongside questions on the Cold War, the United Nations, the Middle East and Africa, and candidates are required to answer one question from the three or four offered.

The Special Study offers the pupil who is really interested in European affairs, a further opportunity to develop his knowledge and understanding about Europe. This project, which accounts for the remaining 20 per cent of the total exam marks, is undertaken over a two-year period and may involve the study of aspects of a community, large or small, at home or abroad. The potential for developing a particular interest in Europe in this part of the syllabus is obviously enormous.

The project could take the form of comparing the system of local or central government, or elections, in one European country with that of Britain, it could involve an in-depth study of aspects of life in a European city or town, or it could take the form of a young person in a comparable European town. The possibilities are endless, the only constraint being that the project must conform to the definition, aims, criteria, and goals of Modern Studies. So too are the opportunities for imaginative and stimulating exercises forming part of the project. Writing letters to European contacts, visiting resource centres to acquire new information, and even making school visits abroad are enjoyable learning experiences. The Special Study, which is internally assessed, offers a unique opportunity to study chosen aspects of European affairs over a period of approximately two years. When the project has been completed, a report is written and marks are awarded on a fifty-fifty basis for the continuous assessment and the terminal assessment (i.e. the report).

SCE 'H' Grade Modern Studies

At the SCE 'higher' grade, which is normally taken by pupils in their fifth or sixth year in secondary school (17 and 18 year olds), the syllabus concentrates on two broad areas entitled 'Contemporary Britain' and 'International Studies'. Within the latter, Europe occupies a substantial place. Three aspects are covered in detail, Western Europe (EEC membership, institutions, policies, external relations, and economic and political change), Eastern Europe (COMECON institutions and policies, social and political change, and internal and external relations), and NATO and the Warsaw Pact (membership, strategic objectives, strengths and weaknesses, relations within and between the two alliances, and the influences of the USA and USSR). Candidates must answer one question worth 12½ per cent of the total marks awarded for the examination, from this section on Europe. Other questions, worth an equal proportion of marks, are drawn from sections on the UK political system, UK social issues, and the Superpowers today.

The remaining 50 per cent of the marks are allocated to 'Depth Studies' which involve a very detailed study of selected topics, utilizing source material for interpretation, analysis and evaluation. At present, six Depth Studies are offered, from which candidates must choose two. The titles are: 'Devolved Power: Scoltand', 'Industrial Relations', 'The Welfare State', 'The Middle East', 'Race Relations', and 'The Third World'. The omission of a Depth Study on Europe is probably the result of the fact that there are so many possible topics to choose from that several which might have been included have had to be left out in order to produce a realistic and manageable syllabus. Nevertheless the opportunity does exist for the inclusion of a European Depth Study at some future date.

The study of European affairs in the Modern Studies context is not limited to a study of the EEC. Eastern European affairs also feature largely in the syllabus. Generally pupils find the study of the Eastern block countries (including the USSR) very interesting, primarily because of the air of mystery attached to them. Relationships and rivalries between East and West, the roles of NATO and the Warsaw Pact and similar topics have considerable appeal for the age groups concerned. The issues examined here, including the deployment and possible effects of nuclear weapons, the division of Germany and the influence of the Superpowers on European affairs, contain such a wealth of interesting material for discussion that pupils usually approach them with much more enthusiasm than they do the EEC.

To sum up, European affairs can and do occupy a significant place in the syllabuses and examinations in Modern Studies. Europe, is, however, only one of a very wide range of important topics relevant to Modern Studies. The European components of the syllabuses are viewed by many candidates as less interesting than some of the other topics such as Great Power rivalry. But, through the use of varied and stimulating approaches in teaching methods and materials, even the most resistant of pupils can find much to interest them in the study of contemporary Europe.

The Case Studies

The teachers in the case studies indicated that they considered the EEC topic to be the most important European component of the 'O' grade syllabus, although there was a general feeling that this part of the course was difficult and demanding for pupils. All the teachers interviewed felt that, with such a full syllabus, there was not sufficient time available to cover all the topics really adequately. One of them summarized his 'O' grade time-table as follows:

> In the first half of the Third Year we do Contemporary Britain; in the second half we do the Contemporary World. In the Fourth Year we do the Great Powers — America and Russia: then the Special Study; then the more difficult areas of contemporary Britain. That needs the greater maturity of the fourth year.
>
> I've been preparing a new scheme of work for next year and for the EEC Component I'll allocate four weeks. That compares with British Government at the start of the Third Year, I'll spend five weeks on that; then in the International Relations section, topics like the Cold War, the Divided World, I'll give six weeks to that, and the EEC follows on from that. I just feel one cannot go into depth. There just isn't time.
>
> We look too at Eastern Europe partly through Soviet Union Foreign policy, partly in the International Relations section where we're looking at the Divided World. We take the Warsaw Pact and we look at NATO as military alliances, but we look at them in a very basic way: as an alliance system, nothing about life styles or systems of government or anything like that; I don't think there would be the time, which is always the problem, I think, about Europe, both Western and Eastern Europe. There would never be the time to do justice to France or West Germany even. There is not time to do Europe extensively.

Interestingly this teacher admitted that he would allocate more time to the European component if it proved to be popular with the pupils:

> Maybe other schools give it more time than that but we think that's enough because, as I see the 'O' grade, it's not the number one topic in terms of popularity!
>
> If I felt Europe was a more popular topic I would give it six weeks. But I sense that pupils don't like it.

The comments of teachers participating in the case studies implied that the EEC content of the 'O' grade syllabus is virtually the least popular part of the course with the pupils and, although they did not say as much, probably with the teachers as well. One of them (who sets some of the SCE examination questions on Europe) attributed this unpopularity mainly to Scotland's distance from the continent:

> The perspective on Europe is different in Scotland than it is in the South. The continent of Europe is much closer to you! If you look at the regional vote in the Referendum on the EEC you can see that the vote 'For' became progressively smaller with distance from the Channel. People here do not automatically look towards Europe.

But other teachers' comments suggested that there could be other reasons for pupils' lack of interest in Europe. One claimed that the European concepts he had to teach were basically too demanding even for his fourth year students and very difficult for the teacher to put across:

> Europe is one of the most demanding parts of the Modern Studies work at 'O' grade particularly, and I would say that the Fourth Year, that is sixteen-year-olds, are struggling with some of the concepts. They find it difficult and because of this it is a less popular area of the course, though it does have lighter parts, its enjoyable parts. But when you begin to get into things like CAP it is very difficult to teach and for them to pick up. Free trade, price mechanisms ... we have great problems in trying to get these points across.

In another school, another Modern Studies teacher was having similar problems with putting across European institutions to his S3 and S4 groups:

> You get these topics and you think they're tremendously relevant; they are happening all the time and we're living with these things and you would think that they would respond really well and they do respond up to a point, but they tend not to get as much interested response as other topics. I suppose it could be due to the teaching, it could be due to the material: the EEC and institutions; the worker moving through trade barriers; CAP and what it's trying to do — these things kids tend not to respond too well to.

According to all the teachers interviewed, the strongest reason for the

EEC topic's general unpopularity with pupils seemed to be its basic dryness; it's lack of human interest. Because of this some teachers tended to reduce some of the time they had intended to spend on study of the EEC and concentrate on more popular areas of the syllabus. One of them expressed this strategy as follows:

> You don't want to deaden pupils' response. I think the Third World goes down slightly better. It's the material. They understand things like population explosion; disease; the problems of the Third World. We had a marvellous film recently on Cambodia and they responded trremendously to people's suffering. It's the human element in these kinds of studies. It's more interesting.

All the teachers in the case studies felt the need to enliven the European topics by using additional material. Although they had adequate access to good text books and documentary material, they all tried to make the courses more immediate and relevant by using slides, films, TV magazines and newspaper reports. According to one of them:

> We try and make the material as visual as possible and try and bring in as many issues as we can; issues that they could find mentioned on T.V. or in the newspapers. There are usually plenty — butter mountains, that kind of thing. Although they may have been struggling with something like CAP up until that point, they're willing to discuss the raging issues. They're angry that we are selling cheap butter to Russia for example. Plenty of visuals in the text books is important. I use the overhead projector a lot; map work, flags, backgrounds, and we get booklets from various Community agencies. Fortunately these were sent to the school, we did not ask for them. We borrow slides and EAV tap-cassette sets and film strips from resource centres. We also use magazines such as the Economist a lot. There is no problem finding resources. There are too many to choose from.

These comments suggest that the conscientious Modern Studies teacher needs, when dealing with European issues, to supplement the available textbooks with whatever he or she can find or create that will render the material more interesting and relevant to pupils. In the subject's early days, production of one's own resources was essential because of lack of books. In the last few years, however, several suitable books have come on the market including two published by Oliver and Boyd specifically for Modern Studies: *The Contemporary World* by Jim Cannon, Bill Clark and George Smuga, 1979; and the sister volume *Contemporary Britain*.

In spite of the existence of good textbooks the teachers interviewed were still developing many of their own resources and worksheets, partly out of the need to keep up-to-date with contemporary events and issues, partly because financial constraints in some schools was making it difficult to acquire a sufficient number of sets of books to cater for all the pupils taking the 'O' grade course.

The case studies indicated that a significant constraint affecting the teaching of the European elements of the 'O' grade course was the examination structure: teachers following an examination syllabus need to cover in their course work topics that are likely to come up as questions. The Modern Studies teachers interviewed readily admitted that this concern was uppermost when they allocated time to different topics:

> We try to be economical with our use of time. We *know* they will get questions on the Community in various exams so we stick to the Community. The teaching is definitely geared to what is likely to come up in exams.

There is, nevertheless, a more flexible part of the 'O' grade syllabus where there is no prescribed content and pupils are free to choose their own topic: the Special Study. In 1980, however, no pupil in any of the case study schools had yet chosen a European topic. This could be partly because the Special Study lends itself more to projects of a more local or national character, but it could also reflect a general, resistance to study of European issues aroused by the difficult and rather dry EEC topic. The fact that no European Special Studies had been undertaken by any of their pupils did not surprise any of the teachers concerned. As one put it: 'I don't think that even at the best of times we would have any pupils opting to do Europe. I think the initial feeling is that it is rather dry.'

Another teacher has also found Special Studies on Europe to be rare:

> In the 'O' grade pupils can study European affairs in considerable depth. A pupil could, if he or she chose to answer a question on Europe in Paper I, and chose a European topic in the Special Study, be in a position where more than one-third of the answers attempted (in terms of marks allocated) were concerned with European affairs. This rarely happens however, partly because pupils are encouraged to choose questions from a wide area of the syllabus, and partly because few are so enthusiastic about Europe, and about European affairs.

The comments of Modern Studies teachers on their experiences teaching the 'O' grade syllabus show that although they consider Europe an essential part of the course (one would teach the EEC topic even if it were not prescribed content), they all had problems with the nature of the material and finding the best approach and teaching techniques to stimulate and arouse a more interested response in their pupils. In their attempts to enliven the subject, however, they were severely hamstrung by constraints of time and the nature of the examination. The main difficulty seemed to be the total 'O' grade workload which all the teachers mentioned frequently as an obstacle to any attempts to experiment with content and cover aspects of the syllabus in greater depth.

Higher grade in Modern Studies is a continuation of 'O' grade work. It is take in the fifth year after pupils have taken their 'O' grade exam at the end of the fourth year. Thus competition between subjects for candidates for 'H' grade is not as acute as it is lower down the school for 'O' grade. The chances are that a good proportion of pupils who have attained 'O' grade in a subject will continue with it to 'H' grade:

The European content of the 'H' grade syllabus in similar to that of the 'O' grade. Paper 1 Section C has sub-sections: (1) Western Europe (which is largely on the EEC); (2) Eastern Europe (which is on Comecon); and (3) NATO and the Warsaw Pact. Although it is possible that older pupils might find study of Western Europe more interesting than they did in S3 and S4, two of the case study teachers omitted this section. According to one of them there are practical reasons for this:

> There is a huge amount to do for higher in only two terms. It is possible to avoid Europe for Higher. Normally we do a study of a country like the Soviet Union or the USA then the European Community. This year we just did the USA and the USSR and cut out the European Community.
>
> A child who pursues Modern Studies right through from S1 to higher will come across modern Europe twice, maybe three times, so we don't always pursue it at Higher because we think they have done it so thoroughly at 'O' grade. Maybe we are too demanding of the children at 'O' grade. I think we are. I have discovered that some of our material for 'O' grade does Higher candidates as well without supplementation.

Another teacher expressed the view that, even more than the 'O' grade, the higher syllabus needs to be taught in such an examination-oriented way that a demanding section on Western Europe does not stand a chance. He finds that studying the Eastern European section of the syllabus is a more practical proposition:

> The thing about the EEC is you don't know what is going to come up. They could throw some beauties at you so you are looking at the paper at a purely practical level. I always do the Great Powers, for example, because you can be sure of getting questions on America and the Soviet Union. And I do things like the United Nations and perhaps China because they are more tightly structured in terms of examination and you can get through that, so, sadly, Europe gets squeezed out, in my case anyway.

Modern Studies in S1 and S2

The constraints presented by the examination is obviously a crucial factor determining the amount of Europe studied for 'H' grade Modern Studies. Not all Modern Studies courses, however, lead to examinations and, as noted earlier, the subject is now widely taught in the first two years of secondary school in Scotland. There is no prescribed syllabus for these years so teachers are free to select and experiment with course content.

One of the teachers interviewed had done some project work on European countries with his first and second year pupils and had found considerable enthusiasm for study of France:

> in S1 and S2 when we do project work we offer them countries. We offer them France and Italy along with the Great Powers — America, USSR and China, and it is interesting: to be democratic we say, 'which one would you like to do?' to a class, and sometimes all the hands go up for France. Whether it is just the link-up with the language which they are just starting, I don't know, but they're very keen to learn about life in France . . . life on the Continent. I think by the time you get to the Third year they become a wee bit cynical about everything!

There was an opportunity here for the teacher to capitalize to this enthusiasm by devising a more varied and 'humanized' European section for S2. Nevertheless, with an eye to the future S3 and S4 workload, he structured a course for S2 which followed very closely the topics to be covered in the 'O' grade syllabus, with sections on the Third World, The Divided World (Cold War, NATO, Warsaw Pact) and the EEC.

In another school, work on Europe in S1 and S4 was also structured mainly around the countries of the EEC. The programme included an introductory section on Europe and a special study of an EEC country, West Germany. As part of the introductory section pupils worked on various different aspects of Europe: flags of EEC countries, map work, capital cities, currencies etc.

The principal teachers in all the case study schools felt that it was important to start preparing S1 and S3 pupils for the demanding 'O' grade course, and their worksheets and assessment schemes indicated a considerable amount of work on general EEC topics.

In practice, therefore, although Modern Studies in S1 and S2 offers opportunites for broader, more extensive work on Europe, teachers tend to keep largely within the confines of the 'O' grade European sections with their strong emphasis on the EEC. However, the kind of work initiated by the teachers in the case studies — projects on different countries, comparisons of standards of living, studies of families engaged in specific industries in Europe, work on different currencies — denote efforts to render work on Europe in S1 and S2 appropriately varied and stimulating for the younger age group.

Conclusions

The general impression given by Modern Studies is that it is a large and developing subject which, because of its size and comprehensive aims, is very demanding both of teacher and pupil.

Like most subjects Modern Studies has needed to be tied to the existing examination structure in order to establish a secure place for itself in the school curriculum and achieve the status of the traditional subjects, but, as in so many cases, the examination structure has turned out to be rather a mixed blessing in that it acts as a limiting and restraining force on both course content and teaching initiatives.

It is a subject which imposes a great deal of work on the teacher partly because of its size but also because of the fact that it deals with contemporary issues and therefore needs constant updating.

Modern Studies is a wide-ranging subject to cover in the two years available for 'O' grade and the restructuring of the syllabus in 1977 seems to have exacerbated this according to one of the case study teachers.

> It's a big subject, Modern Studies, and it has not really got any smaller with the revised 'O' grade. It is still very demanding. I think the subject is too big. There are things I'd love to just chop off. There is an expanded syllabus document for the 'O' grade syllabus and it is meant just to be teachers' guideline headlings, but it is an awful lot of material. I think if you picked that up you really could not get through it all. So I like to go through trying to highlight what I think are the really main points. Some things have to go.

The case studies indicated that the problem could be more acute at 'H' grade where shortage of time and the exigencies of the examination could result in areas of the syllabus being ignored altogether: 'the syllabus is very extensive. If schools do Europe at higher, for example, this would push out something else'.

Modern Studies also requires the teacher to deal with lingering attitudes of suspicion and hostility towards it as a relatively new subject which, being integrated or multi-disciplinary, departs from the established single discipline curricular norm. So that it can compete fairly with other more traditional subjects it may need to be periodically reassessed and justified to pupils, parents and other members of the teaching staff.

All of this means that the Modern Studies teacher, unlike the teacher of more well-established subject, frequently has to enage with the *raison d'être* of his subject, its aims and its priorities. This has positive results: the subject itself remains vital rather than stagnant since it is constantly being reviewed and modified, while Modern Studies teachers need to be committed, energetic and extremely competent.

> It's vital to keep up-to-date. The nature of Modern Studies demands a lot of work just keeping materials up-to-date.
>
> It's frustrating when you know that other teachers such as maths teachers can churn out the same course material year after year. We're constantly revising and updating. It keeps you stimulated but it is very time-consuming. It needs a lot of preparation of materials, a lot of research ... taping broadcasts and things like that.

The European content of the Modern Studies programme comes after the UK sections as the next step in developing pupils' awareness of the wider world. The Western European sections of both 'O' and 'H' grades, however, obviously suffer from having a strong emphasis on the EEC. Significantly when talking of Europe in the 'O' grade syllabus, teachers often tended to mean the EEC section. Nevertheless in the case studies the EEC topic was the most unpopular area of the syllabus as a whole and this could be typical. In general the teachers interviewed felt that the topic was a problem to teach and difficult for pupils to grasp. This should not be an insuperable problem. One teacher suggested that a different approach to the EEC section such as family or worker case studies might stimulate a more positive response in pupils. An additional advantage of teaching about the EEC in such a way is that it would reflect with the definition of Modern Studies work as a 'continuum from the individual to the wider world.' It might conceivably lead also to more European work being done for the Special Study or for 'H' grade.

Since the Higher syllabus virtually duplicates the Western European content of the 'O' grade it is not surprising that some teachers were avoiding it altogether and concentrating on the USSR. It seems unfortunate, however, that the new Higher has at present no Depth Study on any aspect of Europe in the International section of Paper II.

In the light of teachers' experiences teaching the Western European sections of the Modern Studies syllabuses, it is interesting to read extracts from the Chief Examiner's reports on candidates' examination performance in recent years. The comments of the SCE Principal Examiner on the performance of candidates at 'O' and 'H' grade highlighted consistent weaknesses in their responses to SCE questions on Europe. For example, on the 1976 (old) 'O' grade examination:

> There was no marked improvement in candidates' answers to questions in Section B, a worrying feature of performance over the last few years. Candidates who had shown ability in Sections A and C did not sustain their performance into Section B. Excepting the Cold War question and parts of the question on China, disquiet must be expressed about the level of response. Shallow knowledge was revealed in answers to the questions on the USSR and a marked decline in awareness of the institutions and issues of Western Europe was evident elsewhere.

The examiner noted a similar weakness in answers about Europe in the 1976 'H' grade:

> Paper II continues to elicit weaker answers than Paper I and there is room for considerable improvement in this area. The more recent moves towards détente in the Cold War were not known by the majority of candidates, nor were the post-1945 economic policies of the USSR. This lack of knowledge concerning the last decade or so was evinced also in the question on West Germany's political and economic

policies. There has obviously been a decline in the study of Western Europe; candidates are able to understand the institutional features of the European Communities but the issues and processes behind the Institutions seem beyond their conceptual level.

In 1977 the Examiner was less dissatisfied with candidates' general performance in the European sections although he remarked again on the weakness of answers about institutions and economic issues. For example he made the following comment on the 'O' grade papers:

> The disquiet expressed last year about Section B has to be modified in view of the better responses this year to the questions on international affairs and Rhodesia; however the topics relating to agriculture in the European Economic Community were again dealt with superficially.

His remarks about the 'H' grade results for the same year were similar:

> The standard achieved in Paper II was markedly higher this year. Contemporary information was employed in answering the questions on the latest stages of East-West relations, dissidents within the USSR, political changes in Western Europe and their impact on NATO, and excellent answers were produced on Southern Africa. Questions on the constitutional and economic aspects of the EEC, the United Nations and China continued however to receive poor responses.

By 1978 the New 'O' grade syllabus had come into operation alongside the old and the Principal Examiner noted a continuing weakness in candidates' responses to European questions in both:

> *Old 'O' Grade*
> As usual, answers in Section A on Britain were better than those in Section B on World Affairs and Section C on the Nominated Topics, with those in Section B being generally weak. The quality of answers on European topics was also a matter for concern.
>
> *New 'O' Grade*
> In Section B on International Affairs, candidates showed only a superficial knowledge of the European Economic Community with little knowledge of its organisation or economic and political aims and achievements. In Section C, on the Great Powers, the overall performance of candidates was notably weak.

Once again the higher grade papers displayed the same weakness:

> It was most disquieting to find that the examination revealed many candidates with little knowledge of topics central to Modern Studies such as the EEC's Common Agricultural Policy, North Sea Oil revenues, Regional Development Policy in the United Kingdom, the American Constitution and European affairs in general.

These findings suggest that teachers are right to feel some concern about the Western European content of the Modern Studies syllabuses and pupil's lack of response to it. Unfortunately, however, pupil resistance and subsequent poor examination performance may have little to do with the quality of the teaching. All the teachers participating in the case studies had obviously put an immense amount of work and effort into the European sections and had tried to vary their approach and create more interest with audio-visual materials. It has to be conceded that some types of work are inherently far more interesting and stimulating than others; and that with the exception of recent European history in the *Divided World* section, the Western European content as a whole suffers from the drawback of being concerned largely with institutions and organisations, topics which understandably do not fire pupils with enthusiasm. This was confirmed in the Principal Examiner's comment on the 1978 Special Study submissions: 'the most exciting work resulted from investigation of issues rather than of organisations'.

Modern Studies courses for the younger age group, since they are not subject to the constraints of an examination syllabus, offer teachers perhaps the best opportunity to arouse pupil interest in Europe. In fact this may be crucial since such courses are increasing in Scottish secondary schools and, as one teacher's experience suggests, the nature of S1 and S2 work in Modern Studies can determine how many pupils opt to take the subject in S3 and how they are disposed towards certain sections of the 'O' grade syllabus.

The S1 and S2 Modern Studies programmes constructed by case study teachers suggest that teachers are likely to include content that prepares the ground for the intensive 'O' grade work, consequently the same problem with the Western European section can apply. Nevertheless it is possible for study of modern Europe in S1 and S2 to stay within the confines of the 'O' grade syllabus but be presented in a more imaginative and stimulating way through some of the methods already used or suggested by the teachers interviewed. Moreover it might be possible to capitalize on the interest in Europe aroused in younger pupils by their initial contact with modern languages, by integrating modern language and Modern Studies work.

The 1979 enquiry into Modern Studies courses in S1 and S2 undertaken by a group appointed by the Scottish Central Committee on Social Subjects, suggested that the Western European section of courses was not generally considered a high priority by teachers of the subject. In a survey sample schools provided information on specific syllabus content. This evidence was categorized under broad headings, with the following results in order of frequency of mention:

(i) Local Community — environmental and social issues
(ii) Government and politics, including local government
(iii) International affairs — a wide range of issues
(iv) Individual and family, including consumer affairs
(v) Third World studies

(vi) Mass media
(vii) Energy studies
(viii) Great powers studies
(ix) Economy and industry, industrial relations
(x) The United Kingdom in Europe

This again shows the unpopularity of the EEC topic as compared with other wider European issues.

Fortunately, once pupils have done four years of Modern Studies, say from S1 to 'O' grade, they should have been exposed to at least some important current European issues and the nature of British economic and political contacts with the Continent. Does that necessarily make them better Europeans — or European at all in their own estimation? One of the case study teachers doubted it:

> I suppose a few years ago when I was teaching I thought maybe here is a subject with a terrifically relevant content. It would be marvellous if they all went out and found out how many MPs there are and so on. I have really now come round to the view that, well, maybe only a certain amount of work we do over the two years will really be meaningful in that time, but if they go out into the world equipped to be aware, to be critical, to be able to think for themselves, to read the newspapers, then I would be happy, even though you cannot measure it.

Such skills are vital if pupils are to become more aware of the contemporary world, and they are particularly important in relation to understanding of modern European issues and Britain's place in Europe. Thus the practice Modern Studies gives in these skills, as much as the content of courses, makes it a very appropriate subject for broadening the interests and horizons of secondary school pupils.

Notes

1 DUNLOP, O.J. ed, (1977) *Modern Studies, Origins, Aims and Development*, Macmillan.
2 Modern Studies Briefing Document, 1980.
3 Consultative Committee on the Curriculum, (1976), *Curriculum Paper 15*, Paragraph 46.
4 *An Inquiry into the Teaching of Modern Studies in SI and SII, occasional paper*. 1979 Report of a Study Group appointed by the Scottish Committee on Social Subjects.
5 The whole Scottish examination system will be undergoing a major restructuring during the four years from autumn 1983. 'O' grade courses and exams will be replaced by 'standard grade' courses and exams, and 'H' grade exams are also under review.
6 CLARK, B. (1981) 'Teaching about Europe in Modern Studies', *Teaching About Europe*, Vol. 8, No. 2, Spring.

8 A School Curriculum Study

To test the findings of the national survey and subject case studies a single English secondary school was selected for a curriculum study. The choice of school was arrived at in the following way: a number of LEAs were sent details of the *Europe in the School* project and asked whether they could assist in finding case study schools. As a result of this initiative a subject adviser in one Authority offered to circularize schools in his area, asking whether teachers in any of them would cooperate in the project. He received several positive replies. All the schools in which heads and teachers agreed to cooperate were visited and one of them, a large urban comprehensive, seemed the most suitable choice for a brief cross-curriculum survey for the following reasons: the school has a sixth form, therefore caters for the entire secondary school range and has a good spread of subjects; in the 1970s it was reorganised following the amalgamation of the local grammar and secondary modern schools, consequently the school has encountered many of the problems which have bedevilled state education in recent years, and which inevitably affect the curriculum. For these reasons this school seemed an appropriate choice for illustrating current curricular practice in secondary education, and some of the problems and possibilities relating to teaching about modern Europe.

The school has a roll of about 1100. As a result of the amalgamation in 1977, it currently has what one teacher referred to as a 'bloated fifth form and an even more bloated sixth form of three hundred pupils'. In years two and three, classes are mixed ability, but further up the school practice appears to have fluctuated in recent years as a result of the reorganisation, staff cuts and timetabling difficulties. The wider ability range of pupils resulting from the amalgamation of schools has led to banding problems for teachers of examination classes after the fourth year. One of the ex-grammar school teachers indicated that the situation ragarding ability groups has not yet stabilized:

> in the second and third year we take them in form groups which are mixed ability. We're quite happy to do that in the second year, but not

so sure in the third. In the fourth and fifth year we try to get them banded. Again, it depends on the timetable situation. One year we couldn't and we thought that that was rather reflected in the results. I'm not too keen on taking examination classes which are unstreamed.

Options

In the fourth year there is an ostensibly free option system, although as one teacher put it, 'they have to choose so many subjects that once they've got their maths, English, a language, perhaps a science and so on, then it really comes down to history, geography or sociology as choices. So, in a way they have to choose between subjects which have a modern European element'.

Most subjects in the fourth and fifth years can be taken to both CSE and GCE 'O' level. Pupils in the fourth and fifth years who are not taking examination courses or who drop a subject for any reason, are able to do supervised Study Assignments or projects which involve research skills and the ability to work on one's own. All pupils have free access to a very well-equipped Study Assignment area. This is in fact a resources centre where information packs on a variety of subjects are stored, and where tape recorders, film and slide projectors and video-cassette equipment can be used by groups or individuals. The director of this centre complained that her resources were under-used by many subject departments and attributed this in part to the fact that the service was imported from the 'other school' (the secondary modern school which moved to the former grammar school site). To some of the former grammar school staff her outfit, she claimed, was still an 'alien presence'. This comment highlighted the lingering stresses and tensions brought about by the amalgamation, the trauma of which is still being felt. 'The staff have been like they were suffering from flu', said one member of staff and others made frequent references to the reorganisation in tones reminiscent of people just recovering from the effects of the last war. The ex-grammar school teachers were still obviously having difficulties adjusting to the wider ability range and choosing the most appropriate courses and syllabuses. Many of them referred to the problems presented by the existence of lower ability groups particularly in the sixth form.

The cuts in teaching staff resulting from the amalgamation, and subsequent economic cut-backs, have had inevitable repercussions on the school curriculum, and one of the principal effects has been a return to a more traditional teaching pattern. As one teacher put it: 'we find it more difficult now to experiment with courses than before in the grammar school, because staffing has become very much tighter for various reasons'. Another teacher confirmed this view: 'With the economic cut-backs staff cuts, all those problems, nobody's into experiments now. (. . .) The whole climate of opinion here is in favour of what is tried and known to work. This is the result of the staff going through a very difficult period'.

It is against this background of change and contraction, symptomatic of the stresses now taking place in many schools as a result of current economic measures, that the European dimension in this school's curriculum should be viewed. For example one of the casualties of the 1977 reorganisation was a course of study on modern Europe entitled *Britain and Europe*, the brain-child of someone 'very committed to the European ideal' according to the present head of history who explained that the course was initiated by the former head of the history department at the time of the Referendum on entry to Europe:

> Before my time the head of department was in fact very, very keen on Europe and the EEC. She did a big promotion job on the EEC and spent a lot of the course on it. She used to like doing it as well. In the sixth form we have got a General Studies programme — quite an extensive programme, and she organized a whole European Studies course within it which involved team teaching. We used to have lead lessons on various things and then we used to split off into groups: someone would do this week in Europe; someone else did geography of Europe, someone else politics in Europe and so on. In fact, we've been trying to revive the idea but since the school has been re-organised and gone comprehensive we've had all these timetabling problems and it has been difficult. But we've always been very keen on teaching about modern Europe here.

Other teachers expressed enthusiasm about this course and regret at its passing: one attributed the discontinuation of the course to staff cuts: 'it stopped when we reorganized. It was a very good course but it involved a great deal of organization by the staff'. Several members of staff expressed a desire to see the course on Europe revived, but think it unlikely because of all the problems mentioned. One teacher referred to the whole climate of opinion in education as 'reverting towards the subject boundary situation' and away from the multi-disciplinary approach employed in the course on Europe.

Since 1977 therefore, most teaching about modern Europe in the school curriculum has taken place within separate subjects — history, geography, modern languages, economics, politics and sociology with general studies providing a context for any additional modern European material in the upper school. Teachers of these subjects were asked to give details of the modern European content in their courses and express their views on Europe's place in the curriculum.

The young head of the history department, Mike, sees the current trend in history teaching to be towards world history rather than national or European history:

> I think that in the future the trend will be world rather than European history. I personally think that the syllabuses nearly always reflect the political trend about one or two years later. Europe's place in the world is just following on. You can see this very clearly in cases like China, for

example, in the text books. Back in the 1960's China was a terrrible place. Now it's all changed! We're friends with them now!

We very much try to put both Britain and Europe in a world perspective. In a way we have always been very keen on playing up the effects, both good and bad, of European influence on the rest of the world, and I suppose we make quite a point of the decline of European influence as well.

Throughout the lower and middle school history is studied in a world perspective:

> We do the London *Twentieth Century World History* course and the SEREB *Twentieth Century World History* CSE course within which we do quite a lot of European history. The whole syllabus here is geared up to world history. We come onto European history in the second year. We do explorers and things ... we are concerned with Europe in terms of the clash between European culture and the places Europeans went to in Africa, Asia, America and so on. Then in the third year we concentrate much more on British and European history. We do things like the Industrial Revolution and a certain amount of nineteenth century European history. By then we hope they will have gained a fair background both of Europe and the world as a whole so we move straight into the fourth and fifth year world history course.

Mike pointed out, however, since there is only one question on Europe in the 'O' level examination, it is really more practical to work on other sections for examination preparation purposes:

> In this syllabus C history course, Europe now only appears in the essay paper in particular. You see the essay paper is divided into sections and three questions have to be done altogether, one from each section. There are sections on Asia, Africa and the Middle East, Russia and Eastern Europe, America, Europe, and a general one. Europe is only one sixth of the paper and only one question can be done on Europe. So although we do spend quite a lot of time studying Europe, from the point of view of exam preparation and so on that may not be wise now. It's often better to spend more time on things like Russia which is one section or America which is one section.

According to Mike, Europe is still an integral part of the course but a gradually diminishing one, and the same reduction is happening where British history is concerned:

> You can't miss Europe out completely because there's a multiple-choice paper there, and Europe is very important in things like International Relations, so you have to do a fair amount on it, but I would say that, on the whole, the course is becoming year by year less

Eurocentric, while more and more emphasis is being put on China, Russia and America.

Since we've been doing the world history we've found that Britain constitutes such a small part of the paper that if anything goes in fact it tends to be Britain! In other words, our first priority these days tends to be Super Powers, then Britain.

So although Mike has been spending a fair amount of time on Europe with his pupils, the actual scope and period of modern European history covered is limited, mainly because of the exigencies of the exam. Because of this restriction the European component of the world history course does not extend much beyond 1945:

The modern European history we do is, perhaps wrongly, less of the modern period and more pre 1939. We concentrate rather heavily on old favourites like Hitler and Mussolini and so on, but we do cover post-war history as well, particularly France, Germany, Italy.

We don't do a lot of work on Europe post 1945. For instance you might get one question out of thirty on, say, France or Germany after 1945. They've done Hitler and Mussolini in a lot of detail which you would normally do anyway, so they don't need to do post 1945 so much. We always do the EEC. That's as much as we do on Europe in the context of World history.

The EEC part of the syllabus is something which his pupils consider useful for examination purposes but which does not arouse a great deal of enthusiasm or understanding generally:

We tend to get to the EEC some time in the fifth year when they have the exams coming up and they see it as one of those things where you can actually learn all the different parts of it and parrot it back. They tend to think it's relatively easy so they go for it. But they do get confused with all the names and institutions, expecially when you do the founding of the EEC and you tell them that it all stems from the Marshall Plan and you get the OECD and various treaties of Rome and it's easy to get confused by the initials involved in this. The thing you don't get with Europe is the fantastic enthusiasm, the for and against feeling you get with something like Russia. It doesn't tend to arouse them quite so much. It's because it's about institutions and also it's hard for them to appreciate some of the things that the united Europe is working towards. The whole idea for instance that an economic union might eventually lead to political union, it means nothing to them really. They don't see what the EEC is getting at.

In the sixth form the only modern European history studied does not go beyond the origins of the First World War:

We have very big 'A' level groups so in the sixth form we are running three different courses. For one of these are two parts: English social conditions and, as a background for that, modern European history. We generally only go up to the origins of the First World War. There's a reason for this: a lot of them have done the Twentieth Century World History already so we only go up to there. We also do the French Revolution as a special subject. That's a different syllabus altogether. If they do that they do a modern English history background. The other course is also two papers: Normans in England with a medieval European history background. So I suppose we do a fair bit of European history altogether.

Mike does not think that there should be more modern European content in his history courses. The world perspective, he believes, is not only the fashionable one these days but the right one, a view which is apparently shared by his colleagues. He feels too that the world history approach gives his pupils the right historical perspective and helps to make them less narrow in their outlook and attitudes:

We have felt the world history approach is the right one. Since we have all done twentieth century history I suppose we are pretty well clued-up on current affairs, and I think it's just the perspective you get look ing at the News now. Less and less News is European-centred except of course now through the EEC and things like that.

Even if people don't want to go on and become historians as such, world history gives them something they will not lose — knowledge of the twentieth century and so on. The other thing that's important is that they *do* get a sense of perspective about Britain and Europe and their role in the world today, which I think a lot of children leave school without understanding. They do seem to be more *aware* when they've done the course. They actually tend to be very chauvinistic when we first get them!

This is one way in which I think you do see the effects of the course. If I take them, say, at the beginning of the fourth year before we have done the course and say 'What do you think of the EEC?' They can't understand the concept of it at all. But in fact you do find a change of perspective, I think, once they have finished, and I think that's valuable. I don't know if you call it propaganda or what, but they do get a changing view of things. No, I don't think it is propaganda at all, it's just seeing things as they are.

Like Mike, the head of the school geography department, Robert, has moved away from specifically European or British-oriented work towards a wider perspective. The geography taught at the school is in line with the newer developments in the subject — i.e. method and concept take precedence over regional content:

> Our syllabuses have changed in the last three years. Having had a pretty generous bias towards Europe in the whole of one year we have now moved away from that. It's changed in that our work used to be oriented towards the London syllabus which required you to do either North America or Europe in one section of the paper and we did Europe for that section. Now the syllabus is more general so we choose topics which may or may not include Europe in a particular year.

Within the University of London syllabuses that are taught to 'O' and 'A' level there is no prescribed regional content and the choice of area examples and case studies is left to the teacher. Robert detailed the European examples he has been using for illustration purposes. Without exception these have been limited to parts of Western Europe:

> We concentrate on Western Europe. Eastern European geography would be virtually neglected through lack of resources and also this way we can concentrate on more regions and do them in greater depth.
>
> At 'O' level we do the *University of London syllabus A* which has recently been revised in the last few years. We could do a lot more on Europe if we chose to but in fact we choose to do the British Isles and then venture into Europe: we tie the industry up with the Ruhr area for example, and we do agriculture with Britain, taking Holland and Denmark for contrast. We don't look at the European Community as such apart from the odd lesson tying things together.
>
> With the sixth form it's also a wide-ranging syllabus, the London 'A' level-syllabus. That also is really conceptual ideas and a lot of those are taken by studying various problem regions of Europe, the depressed areas or the growth areas, also we look at the agriculture of Europe as a whole, and selected industrial areas.
>
> None of the regions that we look at are prescribed except that you have to deal with countries of the developed world, and in the other half of the paper with countries of the less developed world. So we choose Europe as one of the developed world areas.

Robert believes European case studies to be important in geography because of their relevance to pupils' lives and general awareness particularly at sixth form level. An additional, more practical, reason for choosing European examples is, however, that he already has a lot of material on Western Europe used in previous geography courses in the school:

> We choose European examples because they're more relevant to their currents of life. I think that in the sixth form geography can help the students' awareness of European issues, but not below that level. We do touch on some of the problems of the Common Market and the effects of the Common Market Agriculture Policy for example.
>
> Also, with the 'A' level syllabus which is fairly new, within the last three years, we use Europe because we used to study Europe or rather

Western Europe as a whole, before it, so we already had quite a lot of material. You tend to go for areas where you have the resources and we have a lot of material on Western Europe.

Relatively small numbers are doing the sixth form geography syllabus, which, according to Robert, is because of its strong statistical component, though the move to a more skill and concept-based syllabus does not appear to have affected the 'O' level numbers:

> We have a lot — a large number — doing the 'O' level, and 28 doing 'A' level, with 20 starting in the Lower sixth. The sixth form numbers are dropping at the moment because the syllabus is mathematically-oriented. Consequently we selected people with a mathematical bias which cuts down the numbers. Many syllabuses now have a strong statistical element.

Another subject which demonstrates a similar swing towards statistics and data is economics which is taught exclusively at sixth form level in the school. The teacher of economics, Enid, described the way in which the subject has been developing in recent years:

> Economics is similar to the geography situation, in other words there has been a change in the syllabus in the last few years. It's much more conceptual in nature now and it's a question of testing out their abilities to apply theory to actual data.
>
> The way that economics is going there is an organization side or application of theory side. There's a very strong element now of understanding your theory first, but the examiners are very specific this, an understanding of theory alone is not sufficient to get you a pass. You have to be able to *apply* that theory.

There is very little specified European content in the economics course taught which, like most economics syllabuses is predominantly related to British data. The course, nevertheless, makes references to the EEC, particularly CAP, since these represent examples of several important economic concepts. Enid described the areas of the examination where European references can be made:

> The exam they are working for has three papers: an essay paper worth 40 per cent, a multiple-choice paper, 30 per cent, and a data-response paper 30 per cent. Now the data the pupils are tested on is almost inevitably British data. The only actual specific European content as far as I'm concerned are ideas relating to the Common Market Agriculture Policy in the study of price regularization and primary commodities. One would almost inevitably have to do that because it's an outstanding example of those things. Then where the EEC is concerned, the study of what is meant by a free trade area would come in in connection with trade, which is sort of side

application, nothing specifically economic. So you don't deliberately set out to do a European element, but because of these two particular topics Europe would come in.

Enid does not envisage sufficient time being available for more study of Europe (by which she tended to mean the EEC) within her courses because of the considerable time need to teach basic economic theory. Nevertheless she would welcome the introduction of more study of command-type economies in Economics syllabuses, which could involve reference to parts of Eastern Europe as examples:

> I would be very happy if we had to do more detailed study of command-type economies from the theoretical angle, and an application of it — what is meant and involved in a command-type economy. You could use Eastern Europe there.
>
> But where the EEC is concerned, the time available for understanding basic economic theory is such that I feel the EEC would need to be a separate study.

The politics course in the school presents a similar picture. Again this is taught only to 'A' level in the sixth form and again the syllabus has recently been revised and expanded from the specific into something more general. Sarah, the teacher responsible for this course outlined the changes:

> There have been two changes in the syllabus fairly recently and with the new syllabus there's much more politics now. It used to be *British Constitution* then it became *British Government Politics*, now it's just *Politics*. There are two papers and the first question in each paper is compulsory and sub-divided so that they have the choice of ten out of twelve short questions which they answer in six or seven lines. That tests their knowledge of the details of the paper and the rest of the paper is an essay-type paper. So they could in fact specialize quite a bit in the compulsory section.

As with the economics syllabus, there is little specific European content: 'they could in fact get away with doing nothing about Europe at all,' but in practice the EEC comes into this course too as a useful example of certain political concepts and systems. Consequently there turns out to be a considerable modern European element in the sixth form politics course:

> For the two year 'A' level course we do the London syllabus and take paper 2 which is *Modern British Politics* as an option, but we do the EEC as part of the syllabus and look at it in terms of the general concept of devolution and problems of that type of larger nation. We look at that in fair detail. I suppose we spend possibly four to six weeks on Europe looking at the EEC from a historical perspective, but particularly in relation to constitutional problems. We also look at the different European electoral systems for comparative purpose which we find quite interesting.

Sarah has found that the existing European content in the course gets a positive reponse from pupils and feels quite strongly that it could be expanded particularly withing the context of comparative politics.

> I think the EEC should perhaps play a larger part in the syllabus. I find the pupils are quite interested in it on the whole. The comparison of the European electoral systems, for example, usually demands a certain amount of individual research and that goes down well in class. We get very useful publications from the European Commission Office in London, and there are free handouts which are quite useful. I think most of us now want a larger comparative element: more could be taught in a comparative way. We use the European presidential system, and of course the different monarchies in Europe is good comparative material for the British Constitution, the British Monarchy and that sort of thing. There are certain references made to the European systems but I think a paper could probably be introduced on Europe, the whole European system. Of course we also use information about the different European institutions, so they are fairly knowledgeable about them by the time they have completed the course.

Only a small number of pupils opt to do the politics course — on average ten a year. Double that number elect to do sociology, also taught by Sarah, who claims that the subject tends to attract more people of average or low ability than economics or politics in the sixth form. Sociology is taught in the fourth and fifth years where a considerable number of pupils take a CSE in the subject, and in the upper school where it attracts over twenty 'A' level pupils a year.

As with economics and politics, there is no prescribed European content in the advanced level sociology syllabus although there are European possibilities in the section on a modern industrial society. Sarah admits that to date only a few students have chosen a European area for the industry section, partly, she thinks, because it is easier to do other regions; partly because of scarcity of information about European industrial development:

> There isn't a European element as such in the sociology course. There is a Japanese element at the moment because we're looking at some Japanese industry. Some students are doing a European area: they all do a project on a pre-industrial or pre-literate society and a comparative project on a modern industrial society, but very few of them choose Europe. I think this is probably because if they were to choose, say, Japan, they could study it also at a pre-industrial level; the changeover was rapid and fairly dynamic; that gives them a lot of interest in just the one country. I think also there possibly isn't as much information about European industrial development as there is about something like Japan, Russia or the USA. We don't have much information about most of the European industrial developments in the school library, whereas we have now got one or two books about

> Japanese developments. Of course there's plenty of information about capitalism in general, but that's usually related to America.

Sarah herself would like to have a greater European emphasis in her sociology classes but finds that there is not enough time available: 'We have very small numbers of teaching periods. We have a ten-day timetable and they have one 'A' level period of 45 minutes per day which isn't a great deal. So there isn't much time for frills.'

She tries therefore to incorporate a modern European element into the sixth year 'Opinion' course. This is a course of lectures, one period a week, for the lower sixth form, mostly given by outside speakers 'from different types of organisations for the Arts, Politics etc', who talk on a variety of different issues. Sarah is hoping eventually to arrange for the local Members of the European Parliament to give a lecture to the Opinion group but 'so far this year we haven't had a political speaker, though we have had occasional speakers who have been rather indirectly involved in Europe'.

The Opinion course comes under the umbrella of General Studies which is coordinated by the Head of History. As the *Britain and Europe* course is no longer running, General Studies provides an outlet for teachers who do not have the time or the scope within their courses to do as much work on Europe as they would like to do. According to the coordinator:

> Various people still do courses on European topics in General Studies. In General Studies we tend to follow our own interest very much; various people have done things on certain historical aspects of Europe, for example, certain geographical aspects and so on.

The economics teacher stated that she too deals with any additional European topics in General Studies: 'We haven't time for frills. Any extra elements we bring in through General Studies. There's study time available there so you can use the material you've got on tapes and television in it'.

The history teacher also employs General Studies time for using additional European resources: 'What I tend to do quite often, especially in my General Studies periods is to get a Panorama programme or something like that and show it, or we use Videos. We've got a whole series of videos on things like the EEC and pre-1939 topics.'

General Studies then, in this school, provides an opportunity for members of staff to teach the things they like or topics they feel have not been adequately covered in their special subjects. It appears to be particularly useful for 'topping up' the European content of various courses and clearly members of staff feel that the European issues they examine in General Studies are relevant and important to pupils' lives. Nevertheless, although it is a core subject for the lower sixth who spend about a quarter of their time on it, General Studies has no specifically structured or prescribed content. According to Sarah: 'It incorporates what the staff are prepared to teach. Some departments have got a bit more slack than others, so who teaches it depends on that'.

There is a danger, then, that the course could end up being a bit of a rag bag. And in fact although the staff seem to like teaching the subject (probably because of the relative freedom they have to experiment with content), the pupils themselves are apparently not enthusiastic about it:

> The staff quite like it but I think the pupils don't really want to spend time on something which isn't going to produce an 'A' level at the end. It's hard work for the staff actually because they are not as well motivated and this means one has to make it really that much more interesting.

Lower down the school there is no subject that can be used like General Studies for topping up or supplementing the European content of other courses. In the lower school teaching about Europe is mainly carried out within history, geography, and modern languages. The modern languages taught at the school are French, German and Spanish. French is started in the second year and Spanish and German are introduced as options in the fourth year.

The examination syllabuses taught are the University of London 'O' and 'A' levels and additionally, in French, the South-East Regional CSE. Until recently pupils could also do a CSE in German but problems of staffing now make this impossible. Jane the German teacher, explained that the modern languages department has been cut by two members leaving only seven. This was due partly to economic measures, partly to a falling school roll. Nevertheless opinion at the school is that the staff cuts are out of all proportion to the decline in pupil numbers.

According to Jane the London modern languages syllabuses have virtually no background element. In any case where the German and Spanish two-year 'O' level courses are concerned the language work is so concentrated that there is no time for anything extra:

> If you do Spanish or German in a two-year course to 'O' level that doesn't really leave you any time to do anything on the background of the country. For 'O' level in two years you're skating on very thin ice. They haven't had the time to absorb the range of vocabulary that they should have. You're very lucky if they know six words to do with the station, the café etc. I do try to get them to read, but it's basically language work.

German in particular is a demanding language to learn for children who have no grounding in basic language work:

> German demnds such a degree of mental concentration and you're teaching children who don't have too much idea of grammar in English. You don't have any time to talk to them about Germany except, just to give a trivial example, for 'O' level conversation where they had a topic — 'a famous German'.

With 'A' level pupils however, Jane has introduced a backgrounds element although it is not part of the syllabus:

> It is my personal choice to introduce it as an extension of the language work. I do a survey of politics, history, the federal system and how it affects quite minor things like dialects, food and drink — that sort of thing. They enjoy this and find it very useful. In fact those who go on to university write to me and say how much they need it.

Jane builds up her sixth form background work with the use of German newspapers, BBC broadcasts, video-cassettes of, for example, the T.V. News *Heute Direkte* and material from the Goethe Institut. The school is also fortunate in having a German assistant 'who puts the kids more in contact with the country'. In addition to this, 'A' level pupils are 'encouraged to go abroad during their course', so the chances are that they get a considerable amount of background knowledge during their sixth form years. The amount of that knowledge, however, is entirely at the discrection of the teacher. This school is fortunate in having language teachers who, in general, believe in the value of European background content. The Spanish teacher is committed to it and the recently retired head of French now comes in part-time just to do French background courses. European background is not, however, a prescribed part of the syllabus, nor does Jane consider that it should be:

> I think basically you are there to teach them the rudiments of the language, and as the syllabus stands you're there to do four set books with them. So as far as the background goes I think it should be exactly that — background — though I believe in it very strongly. But I think some of the more worthwhile things you teach are *not* examined and not on the syllabus. As soon as you put it on the syllabus, in an exam, it's ruined as far as I'm concerned. I'm so sick of cramming knowledge into kids which is then churned out and examined.

Jane, a graduate from a university School of European Studies, finds that fitting her sixth form language work into a cultural context is a congenial exercise since it conforms to the pattern of her undergraduate work: 'It reminds me of what I did at university; it hangs together like my work at university'. Out of choice she also teaches a 'German culture and Society' component (to non-linguists) in the sixth form General Studies course. 'it's a little extra of mine'. Jane is therefore basically committed to teaching about Germany as well as teaching the language, at least at sixth form level. Nevertheless she finds that the pupils' generally low level of culture and knowledge prohibits the use of more sophisticated background content: 'my 'A' level group tend to be most interested in things like politics once I've got them into it. But theses are kids who don't know what 'left' or 'right' means in English let alone in German'.

In her General Studies Culture and Society class Jane faces the same problem: 'In the first class I asked them to read something out loud, a newspaper article, and some of them could barely read ... read aloud that is.

Some of the more intelligent kids in the room looked on in total horror.' It is clear that like many of the former grammar school teachers, Jane has had difficulty adjusting to the wider ability range the school now deals with as a result of the reorganization. She believes that only the top third of any mixed ability group can tackle modern languages work and is consequently dubious about the value of the new graded test systems being developed by various Boards:

> You'll never get less able children through graded tests no matter what you call them or how you devise them. There is a level beyond which you cannot teach languages to less able children.
>
> You *cannot* teach modern Languages to more than about a third of any year group if it's truly mixed ability. I think you could teach about one third to exam level; the second third you could probably teach something like European Studies to, and the bottom third you really can't. It doesn't matter *what* you do, *what* your methods are or *who* does it. From my limited experience I think there is a point beyond which you can't go. They have such a limited range in their own language.

Because of the difficulties of teaching children another language Jane, in common, one suspects with many modern language teachers, sees little chance of there being any increase in background work in 'O' level syllabuses, nor does she feel it is particularly necessary — 'they can get it elsewhere; they can find these things out for themselves'.

With 'A' level groups she views learning about the country as an interesting, stimulating and useful extra but, when pushed, admits that in her opinion it should not be an essential element of the course. Consequently, in the view of this language teacher, there is no real case for widening the scope of modern languages examination syllabuses to include more European background content. Instead she advocates a return to the hard grind of language teaching: grammar and sentence structure to compensate for what she describes as 'increasingly sloppy' modern teaching methods and the 'generally lower intelligence level' of pupils:

> Background studies, or General Studies, whatever you like to call them — peripheral studies — flourish at a time of economic expansion. Now that there's a recession and cut-back, and the intelligence level is dropping, teachers are becoming more and more forced to teach 'the cat sat on the mat'.

For pupils who are floundering in modern languages a European Studies course is being developed. Previously European Studies as a separate subject has never really flourished at the school. Jane started a course for a while several years ago with a third year group but 'though it was very popular it was dropped'. This was because of the problems of reorganisation and because of the general climate of opinion within the school — more conservative and less innovative than hitherto. However, Jane was asked to organize some more European Studies courses for the 1980–1 school year but the nature of the request and the motives behind it reveal the all-too-familiar way in which the subject is generally viewed:

> I was asked to take the bottom division of the third year French children and keep them meaningfully occupied for three lessons a week from September. That's how it happened before. I took a third year non-Latin group so, if one's not careful, European Studies gets a sink label attached to it. It should be an attractive proposition, but it comes in with a low status.
>
> How it happened this time was that Mrs ... (in charge of curriculum) sat in her little room and found a problem and said, 'now who on earth will put up with this? I know ... Jane!' That's how things happen in schools. Then three of the high-ups came to me and said 'we think this would be a *marvellous* opportunity for your career!'

Jane started the course in September, 1980: 'I went to pick them up outside the language lab for the first lesson. They introduced themselves to me as "we're the dunces". We now call them the delinquents!'

She described how she had devised a European Studies course for this group:

> The only way to get their interest is to make the course completely child-oriented; make them the centre of the course. We have to completely pander to their interests. Some of them can't even spell the days of the week! So I devised my own course totally out of my head. It's loosely based on Europe but it's anything I happen to know about or the kids might like to do. We worked on a Russian fairy tale and they drew pictures. Then I got them to all bring in a European fairy tale. We did something on their summer holidays. I went round Europe, the different countries of Europe, and I thought: 'my God, we must think of something for each country!' It's all very casual. We're doing Austria at the moment, discussing what you can do there by day and by night during a holiday. I do it completely out of my head.

As Jane talked it became increasingly evident that she viewed the course as having little to do with teaching about Europe. She sees it primarily as a means to give children with a low self-image a sense of academic achievement that they are unable to gain in other subjects: 'they thoroughly enjoy what I do with them because there's no pressure; no hassle; no exam. I give them gold stars and make them feel they're succeeding'.

Secondly she uses the course for (undoubtedly necessary) remedial work in basic English:

> We're doing Austria at the moment, but what we're really doing, and doing a lot of, is copying English — really old fashioned English. I write

> sentences on the blackboard and they copy them into their books because this is what I think will help them most and they are becoming more courageous with their sentences. I believe in teaching them their own language and this is what I'm trying to do: extra English and discussion. So as long as the course is helping the children, interesting them, and they're happy doing it and practising their writing and learning something, that's all I'm worried about and I think the course is justified.

Not surprisingly, Jane's course has been a success, if not in European Studies terms, at least in terms of keeping the 'delinquents' usefully and meaningfully occupied. The children enjoy the course and the school administrators are delighted: 'It's gone down so well that European Studies could expand. The timetablers have said 'we could fill your timetable up acting as the sinbin for the French department alone.'

The striking feature of this school's European Studies course is that it has *nothing* to do with any perceived need to teach pupils about Europe; if the children learn anything about Europe at all it is probably by default. One suspects that the course could equally well go under any other title and it would make little difference. European Studies just provides a convenient framework for a series of exercises of a remedial nature aimed at improving the pupils' general level of attainment with a few enjoyable exercises — drawing, listening to music — thrown in. Jane defended this as follows:

> I suppose European Studies is too gimmicky: all things to all men — but I think this is its strength because a Head could staff it with anybody. You could call anything European Studies — anything that comes out of Europe at all.

It is clear, from Jane's description of her course, that in this school European Studies does not in any way represent a serious attempt to educate pupils about modern Europe.

Conclusions

One of the striking facts to emerge from this curriculum study is the reduction of teaching about modern Europe that has taken place in the school in recent years. Teaching about Europe in this school's curriculum seemed to reach a peak in the 1970s round about the time of the Referendum on entry into Europe. At this time different subjects such as history and geography were taught with a strong European emphasis and a special year-long course in Europe was organized in the sixth form. By 1980, however, the situation had changed considerably. Although there is still a European content which is fairly substantial in the case of history and geography, its general extent and emphasis, and the perspective in which it is viewed, are now different from hitherto. In addition important teaching initiatives on Europe have been discontinued in recent years.

There are several reasons for these changes: the reorganization of the school combined with economic cut-backs has resulted in an overall contraction: staff reductions, tighter timetabling and a general regression away from innovation and experiment towards a more traditional curriculum pattern. Jane, the German teacher, summed up this process:

> We have been suffering from the amalgamation. We've had such a crippling time. The staff were as though they were suffering from flu, in a daze. With the economic cut-backs, staff cuts, all those problems, nobody's into experiments. I was a pupil at this school in the early 60s and the whole climate then was expansive: let's try this, let's do that or the other — but in these times of cut-backs you tend to come back into your subject compartments. You're bound to. The whole climate of opinion here is in favour of what is tried and known to work, and this is the result of the staff going through a very difficult period.

Secondly, the combination of two schools has led to an increase in the numbers of lower and average ability pupils and this has affected the type of courses taught in the school. The ex-grammar school staff (who appear to predominate over the ex-secondary school staff) have found difficulty adjusting to the broader ability range, a strain which might well be an obstacle to their capacity to undertake new teaching initiatives. In addition to this, the increase in the number of less academic pupils has led to a search for 'sink' subjects for those who have difficulty with more demanding disciplines such as modern languages. One result is that European Studies has been reintroduced in the school solely for the purpose of keeping the less able third-year pupils 'meaningfully occupied'.

Another reason is that the syllabuses in some of the social subjects being taught in the school have a marked tendency now to be less focussed on separate areas of the world and more discipline-centred, concerned with methods, basic skills and concepts. The consensus among the teachers responsible for history, geography, politics and economics is that these subjects have become more general and conceptual in recent years. The modern history courses, for example, demonstrate what the head of department sees as a growing tendency to look at history in a world, rather than national, or purely European, perspective. The geography syllabuses taught at the school, in keeping with recent trends in the subject, have become more general and deal with themes and topics to be illustrated by regional examples of the teacher's choice. This choice is as dependent on what stocks of materials and resources are already in the school as on how relevant the area examples are to pupils' lives. Likewise the economics, politics and sociology courses being taught have become more general and topic-based with the choice of specific regional illustrations being left to the teacher. In economics and politics there is no prescribed European content although teachers find that European examples, particularly aspects of the EEC, are almost inevitable in these subjects. In the sociology courses there is also scope in the *modern industrial society* section for European examples but according to the teacher concerned, better ones can be found elsewhere.

In modern languages the amount of contemporary background study seems to depend almost entirely on the personal choice of the teacher concerned.

All of these six subjects, therefore, are being taught in the school with some modern European content but only in the case of the twentieth century history course is this content prescribed. Where the other subjects are concerned how much contemporary European material is used depends upon the individual teachers. In all these subjects the areas of Europe referred to are limited to Western Europe and these areas are further limited in all but history to EEC countries.

The dominant view among the staff is that some European content in their courses is important and relevant, but that the amount they do is sufficient. Only the teacher of politics thought there should be more specific European content (mainly the EEC), while the economics teacher thought an East European element could successfully be incorporated into her courses in relation to command-type economies.

All the teachers interviewed found that covering the existing European content in detail was difficult because of problems of time, and two teachers referred to detailed work on Europe as 'frills' compared with the basic course material. Anything additional on Europe is therefore dealt with as a 'general interest' topic in the sixth form under the umbrella of General Studies, a subject which has the flexibility and freedom from examination constraints to incorporate additional elements.

An important feature of this curriculum study is that it illustrates the increasing trend within certain subjects to study specific areas of the world in a wider perspective than was formerly the case. According to Mike, one can no longer be exclusively concerned with problems at one's own back door. Great Britain and Europe cannot be viewed these days in isolation from the rest of the world. The 'global' view is becoming more important and it is within this broader framework that the European dimension in education needs to be considered.

Thus in certain respects, the single school curriculum survey confirms many of the overall findings of the research: that European Studies is frequently used (or one should say misused) as an all-purpose curriculum area to cater for difficult or low-achieving pupils; that history and geography, despite their changing emphases and conventions, are the subjects most likely to have a substantial modern European element whereas in modern languages the importance attached to cultural or background content seems to depend very much on the priorities of the teacher. The case study also suggests that more peripheral subjects such as politics, economics and sociology which are first taken as fourth year options have the potential for teaching about Europe but this has not yet been fully exploited. Finally, it suggests that a teacher who feels that his/her subject does not give enough scope to the European dimension may have to introduce it as a special topic or as an extra activity in a flexible, non-examinable curriculum area such as General Studies.

9 *Europe across the Curriculum*

In any survey of Europe in the secondary school, the question arises: what approaches and strategies can teachers adopt to Europeanize the curriculum? Should there be a separate European Studies block or should it form a self-contained unit within an established discipline? Alternatively might the best strategy be to try and attempt an overall permeation of the curriculum involving cross-fertilization between different subjects? Because of the wide differences existing between schools there can be no definitive model for innovation. Any curriculum initiative must be tailored to the individual school; its organizational structure, curricular system, and the personality and attitudes of teaching staff.

This was illustrated in the following case study constructed from interviews held in 1980 with teachers from two different comprehensive schools who had been asked to take on the task of introducing a European dimension into the curriculum.

John is head of modern languages in a mixed comprehensive school. The school has an eight form intake and currently has eighty sixth form pupils. The curriculum is organized within seven faculties:

Communications:	(English, drama, basic studies)
Mathematics:	(maths, computer studies, statistics)
Environmental and Social Studies:	(history, geography, R.E. and business studies)
Science:	(physics, chemistry, biology and combined science)
Languages:	(German, French)
Design:	(art, metalwork, woodwork, textile crafts, domestic science)
Recreational Studies:	(P.E. and music)

Integration of subjects is established in the lower school in two areas: environmental and social studies and science. After the third year separate subjects are taught except for world studies and applied science both of which are designed for less able pupils.

In years 1–3 there is a common curriculum taught to mixed ability groups except for maths and modern languages which are 'set' at the end of the first year. All pupils in years 1–3 study English, maths, environmental and social studies, combined science, a foreign language (which alternates annually between French and German), music, drama and P.E. There are additional half-term courses in practical subjects.

For years 4 and 5, English, maths, P.E. and General Studies (composed mainly of careers education and health education) are taken by all pupils. In addition each pupil must choose a course from within each major faculty area. Languages however, fall within two groups of optional subjects from which pupils must choose two subjects to supplement their basic course. Within these options are French, German and either French studies or German studies according to the year.

In the sixth form traditional 'A' level courses are taught. In addition there is a one-year general course which must include courses from at least five faculties.

There is no planned teaching about Europe other than what takes place in the context of French and German courses. Study of Europe in other subjects is, according to John, 'haphazard and coincidental'.

Dave is head of modern languages and head of sixth form in another large school (roll 1500) which has recently become a mixed comprehensive with the amalgamation of the local boys' and girls' secondary modern schools. In Dave's school the curriculum has a more traditional character and subjects are kept rigorously apart from the first year upwards. In years 3 and 4, the core curriculum includes English, mathematics, P.E. and General Studies, and pupils choose additional subjects from several option groups. General Studies is also a core subject in the fifth and sixth years and is composed of five modules: politics, health, careers, law and home management. As in John's school, there is no planned teaching about Europe except what arises naturally within the context of subjects such as history, geography and modern languages, depending on the courses chosen by the teachers concerned.

The two schools involved in the case study therefore have a very different organisational and curricular structure. The teachers themselves, however, are similar in several ways and their respective situations, at the time of the interviews, were almost identical.

Both are young, enthusiastic, and keen to innovate within the confines of the existing curriculum structure. Both are heads of modern languages in their schools, and have responsibilities for the sixth form. Both had been invited by their headteacher to consider and plan strategies for developing a European dimension to the curriculum, hence one of the first hurdles faced by any innovator in school — gaining the approval and cooperation of the head — had already been eliminated in each case. Both teachers, when interviewed, were at the same initial exploratory stage of their task with a year in which to plan their approach. From their conversation it was clear that both perceived their future strategy as taking the following sequential path:

1 *Rationale:* deciding why the European dimension is necessary.
2 The *aims and objectives* of the European dimension.
3 *Organization:* deciding (a) the most appropriate curriculum areas for the incorporation of the European element; (b) the most appropriate target year groups; (c) which members of staff to approach.
4 *Formal approaches* to other members of staff.

John and Dave were equally adamant that (1), (2) and (3) have to be worked out very carefully well in advance before they make formal approaches to other members of the teaching staff, since cooperation from other teachers was seen by both as absolutely essential to the success of the enterprise.

Rationale; Aims and Objectives

John anticipated resistance to education about Europe in the staff room, therefore he was particularly concerned with formulating strong and covincing reasons for having a European element in the curriculum and a viable strategy for its introduction before approaching other teachers:

> I see my role as first of all planning an overall strategy and then implementing it. The implementation would involve convincing Heads of Faculty of the need and the worth of a conscious European dimension in the curriculum: I need to get everything worked out in advance; *WHY* the concept of Europe in the curriculum is worthwhile; how best to organize it; what knowledge and materials we want to put across. All this needs investigating first. In the final analysis I feel it will run into resistance until most teachers are convinced that there is a congent and pressing answer to the question: 'Why do we need a European dimension in our curriculum?'

Dave, though equally convinced that there is a need to work out in advance a rationale for the European dimension, anticipates less resistance from other teachers and feels, perhaps over-optimistically, that once he has epxlained the need for it, identified the appropriate area of the curriculum and located suitable resources and materials, he will get cooperation, even enthusiastic support:

> I should be able to take my ideas back to school without anyone saying: 'look, what do we need this for? You're just adding an airy-fairy aspect to a structured curriculum. You're axing vital time when we're trying to inculcate certain essential areas of information and develop certain skills'.
>
> I need to find out just how diverse this course can be and still be

> meaningful, intact and controllable once we decide on the best areas to go into — and that may depend on the information and books available — then we can approach dynamic and interesting people, informed people, who could put those areas across.
>
> So if I come up with the areas of study I could probably find the staff interested enough and with enough expertise to put them over in a dynamic way.

Thus the essential preliminary task for John and Dave is to work out a persuasive rationale for the inclusion of the European dimension. This involves deciding why importance should be attached to the study of Europe as opposed to other areas of the globe. Interestingly both teachers referred to this question using identical terms:

> *Dave:* Why Europe and not the world? We really have to determine what is of greatest importance to be tackled in school.
>
> *John:* Why Europe? Is a difficult question to answer — why not the world?

John answered his own question by claiming that while Europe should not take undue precedence over other areas of the globe, there are sound cultural reasons for including study of Europe in the curriculum:

> There are general cultural reasons for Europe. We are after all the result of European experience but then we have all sorts of other links. We do have a European legacy and we contribute to Europe. But I don't think I can go round saying 'you *ought* to be teaching about Europe' and Europe mustn't take precedence over everything else.

An additional justification that John sees for study for Europe is that it would form part of an essential *core* of information he believes young people should have in order to 'equip them for life', therefore he sees it as having a practical application.

> I would envisage a sort of core of knowledge across faculties which is essential information students must have in order to go out into life. I need to persuade people that students need to be provided with this essential core of information, and the justifications I see for study of Europe are that it would form part of this core information. Also nowadays, it's not just a question of finding a job for a child at the end of school but of actually equipping him for life; making children realize that they may have trained for several kinds of job and to be ready to be more mobile than in the past.
>
> It's not so much that every child should then entertain the idea of going abroad but they should at least know and be aware that the possibility of the movement of people from one country to another is something that at least one can expect and not think of as unusual.
>
> With learning about Europe I would argue that it's not the content

> it's the experience. It's not what you learn it's what id *does* for you, and I would argue for European education that it's going to do something for a child that will make that child more able to live its life successfully. That to me is firmer ground than talking about content.

Without going into similar detail Dave justifies the inclusion of the European dimension in terms of its importance, relevance and general interest:

> It's a very important and relevant area of information which is interesting enough to put across with a certain success. I think it would be a very valid contribution to the curriculum and we'll get a lot out of it.

Organization

Justifying the inclusion of a European dimension in the curriculum to other members of staff is only one of many problems confronting the teacher entrusted with the task. He/she will have to decide on the appropriate target year groups as well as identify the best areas of the curriculum to use as entry points. The nature and content of the European element can only be devised in relation to existing curricular practice and the syllabuses — especially examination syllabuses — already in use.

Both teachers have completely ruled out the possibility of creating separate European Studies courses in their schools partly because it would not fit in with their present curricular structure, but mainly according to Mike because of the unfortunate image such courses have:

> I certainly wouldn't have anything called European Studies in the curriculum. It's come to mean something, European Studies!

Working in a school where integration of subjects has already taken place in years 1–3, John is committed to the system and would therefore envisage study of Europe not in a separate curricular slot but as part of a much wider area of study in years 1 to 3. He feels also that the European dimension should not just be part of separate subjects like history and modern languages, but that it should be introduced across the faculties and given particular emphasis in the Environmental and Social Science Faculty:

> There are certain skills children learn as well as reading and writing: speaking, listening, and possibly a foreign language as well. I don't think that European Studies can compete at that basic level of the curriculum at all, which is why I'm not keen myself to have it as a separate slot. I would rather have it *within* an area: *within* a discipline. Standing on its own, as separate, it just doesn't come in on the ground-floor level. If we put European Studies in its own slot then the case is equally strong for putting history in its own slot and for actually then

> getting away from the integrated approach altogether and going back to a subject approach because the argument could be equally strong for other bits and pieces, and I'm sure that teachers of other subjects could say that there's an argument for putting their particular subject in a separate slot as well. So it could end up undermining the whole integrated studies system.

There is an additional practical reason for not having separate teaching about Europe in John's school curriculum: 'We wouldn't get any money for a separate block of European Studies. It would come within the Faculty's capitation'.

John outlined the ways in which he thinks the individual faculties can contribute to teaching about Europe:

> I think the main faculties for European education would be environmental and social studies (ESS), languages and English. I can only justify study of Europe in child development terms if I think in terms of political education, if I equate it with political education. The ESS contribution to education about Europe would certainly be political education. Secondly I think English. I'd be looking for a way into the Communications faculty. I'm not too convinced about literature in translation certainly not in the first three years, and I don't think they'd want to be tied down as regards content, but I like the idea of tape-links because that would be very much in the tradition of our English department which is a progressive one. I can really sell the idea of tape-links to the English department because they're really keen on finding ways of teaching children not just to read and write but to speak and to develop listening skills. Tape-links seems a far more fertile way of getting a European dimension than, say teaching literature in translation.

For years 4 and 5, John's strategy for the introduction of the European dimension will depend on future developments with the option groups:

> It will depend very much on what happens to our General Studies people in the fifth year. There's a lot going on in the curriculum and the option system is going to be changed. It's in that kind of context that I'm trying to think about European education for those years.

In his school Dave has to introduce European education into a more traditional curriculum. Because of the reorganisation he claims it is a good time to innovate. Nevertheless the reorganisation has reinforced the traditional curricular pattern since the school staff are anxious to create a good public image for the new comprehensive and good examination results in the traditional subjects are the best means of gaining public approval:

> It was a secondary modern school which has just gone comprehensive. So what are they trying to achieve? They're trying to achieve academic

> excellence and that is revealed in exam successes. And what better way of achieving exam successes than by keeping subjects totally separate?

Dave, therefore, needs to fit the European element into separate subject areas and has to decide which of these is most suitable. So far he has concluded that General Studies in years 3 to 6 is possibly the best context for European studies:

> I want language and background studies to be divorced from what I'm trying to reproduce here; completely separate. I also want it separate from the humanities as they're taught in years 1 to 5.
>
> I'm thinking of a General Studies context but I'm unsure how to structure teaching about Europe within it . . . perhaps the modular approach with five units but I'd be scared that that might be too fragmented and unrelated. What we're anticipating is having a theme then bringing in individual subject areas.
>
> It isn't going to be hinged around Europe but we could put in a certain European component which means that I'm not committed to feeding in an enormous amount of information but I could try things out from week to week — things which could well turn out to be growth areas. I'm in a good position having a full year to try things out before eventually coming up with a final decision about what the course will be. It could be Europe — it could be world studies — it depends on what would be a balanced amount of Europe for our target group.

Since General Studies combines different disciplines and involves teaching staff from different departments, Dave feels he will be able to devise a European component which integrates different areas of knowledge and different learning/teaching skills and resources without disrupting the existing curricular organization of the school:

> in a school which has isolated subject areas I will have the one and only way of bringing together all those areas and putting them into the child's context as an individual; as a European; as a human being.
>
> This way I won't be impinging on anyone else's area.

Preparing the ground for formal approaches to teaching staff

Dave's final point is an important consideration since the teacher who wishes to innovate has to tread very carefully in order to avoid upsetting not only the school's curricular structure but also separate subject groups who may fear that there will be some trespassing on their preserves. Even Mike has encountered hostility to integration of subjects in a school where it is well established:

> The head of history is the kind of person who isn't too happy about

> teaching history in an integrated system. He'd rather be teaching it separately.

Moreover, where Europe is concerned, the political sensibilities of other members of staff need to be taken into account since often the concept of Europe can get confused with people's attitudes to the EEC. John has already discovered this during informal approaches to other members of staff.

> I have only made informal approaches so far and it is probably fair to say that staff do not regard European education as a priority need.
>
> The head of history, for example, had a very negative attitude, probably because he regards himself as an anti-European, anti-EEC, anyway, politically.

John is therefore cautious about being seen to be 'pushing' European education. In fact he believes it might be wiser to soft-pedal Europe in his formal approaches to teachers and present it as a part of a broader, more general area of study. This, he suspects, will elicit a more favourable response:

> I think the way I'm going to approach my head of ESS is *not* to mention Europe at all but ask him about the political education in his faculty as part of a kind of General Studies ... we can look at it (political education) nationally, then we can look at it as applied to Europe, then we can look at it as applied to the world. This approach would socialize the child. We won't scare him off by mentioning European Studies!
>
> European education must not take precedence over everything else. That's why, when I try to persuade them about the importance of political education, I'm going to ask them what they do about the community; what they do in a national context; European context etc. At the same time I'm going to try and encourage other faculties to do their bit as well, but I'm not going to say to them 'you ought to be teaching about Europe'.

John hopes, therefore, to persuade heads of faculty that the European dimension is an essential part of a broad core education and a natural progression from the consideration of local and national areas and issues. His next step would be to persuade them to change their courses and syllabuses accordingly:

> When I have it clear in my mind I shall need to have a meeting with certain key heads of faculty and, if you like, win their hearts and persuade them that it should be in their interests and in the interests of the subjects they teach to bear in mind the European dimension and in fact, where possible, change their syllabuses. This way every child will get a certain European experience. I will certainly be looking to the ESS faculty to do this. I could probably persuade them that since they're looking at man and his environment (which is the central

theme of their work), if they were to look at the environment locally, nationally and in a European context then I think that's a good way of starting to win their minds. If I can win over those heads of faculty plus other important people in the departments and then monitor what they do and actually get them doing something on Europe, then my first battle will be won.

Dave shares John's worry about 'pushing' Europe at the expense of other areas of the world. He too has reached the conclusion that education about Europe might be more successfully incorporated within a wider world or modern studies perspective than considered in isolation:

> Maybe we should think more in terms of the world studies approach, starting off in years 1 to 3 with themselves and their surroundings; then Europe in years 4–5; — then world studies in the sixth form.
>
> Or maybe we could combine the three elements with each part of the school, only going into greater depth with the more mature age groups. It might be a good idea if we just look at years 4–5 as an entity using the world approach — the individual in your country, then Europe, then the world. It could be more realistic — more fundamental. We might then be able to sort out more realistic aims and objectives than if we just focus on Europe. I think there might be a real place in the curriculum for putting the little individual in a big context.

Dave feels there would be several advantages in incorporating this approach into General Studies: it would bring together a number of different subject areas and relate them in a context that the child would be able to assimilate; it would lead to useful pooling of resources and expertise between departments, and it would be more acceptable to other members of staff than a purely European Studies approach:

> I can't see how anybody would object to such a General Studies or Modern Studies course and our allocating time to it.
>
> We won't be going from specific subjects to generalisations; nor will we be going from the generalisation of an integrated course to specifics. We're going from individual subject areas which carry on as such but at the same time we'll have the pooling of resources, bringing together of all the different areas.

Where making formal approaches to other members of staff is concerned, John again is the more cautious of the two and is preparing his ground very thoroughly before broaching the subject. He is aware that apart from all considerations of subject boundaries, political sensibilities and individual resistance to teaching about Europe, any new curriculum ventures require time and funds that are in short supply. He also feels he should be well informed about syllabuses and resources so as to be able to provide advice and encouragement to teachers willing to be involved in the development. Fortunately he has some responsibilities for the timetable thus can offer a few incentives to interested people:

> I have deliberately tried not to broach it formally or to persuade people because when I do it I want to be successful. I don't want to have a second stab at it three weeks later. That would be fatal.
>
> I think that the 'European dimension' approach is the right approach, but also that it will be the most difficult one to implement because it depends on the enthusiasm of several key members of staff and ultimately on the willing participation of the whole staff. In terms of curriculum development, it will have to compete with several other current developments for resources of time and money.
>
> It's impossible to know in advance how much money would be needed for a European dimension. We'd have to get down to the nitty gritty of books and materials needed. The next step would be to become familiar with their syllabuses and possible alternative syllabuses so that I can provide informed encouragement to departments and faculties to develop along European lines.
>
> Also I think that I can probably get them some more time on the curriculum because we're just about to change our time allocation, our timetable and I'm involved in that. So I would hold out a few carrots.

Dave also feels he should acquire as much preparatory information and material as possible before approaching other teachers but is optimistic about gaining support:

> I don't think that any one person is going to have the energy, the time or, at certain times, the inclination and enthusiasm to come up with ideas for such a course. You need to be a team and you need to be able to write, to or phone someone and say: 'please send me information on this? What resources are there on that?' You need someone who's been involved for a number of years in the discussion of such issues. You need to have so much material to show to teachers before they'll commit themselves.
>
> I need to set up a project to ascertain exactly what components to put into such a course and where our priorities lie. If I come up with a good idea I think we have the staff of the right calibre, outlook and possibilities and we can draw on these people. If I'm enthusiastic and they're enthusiastic we have the makings of a valid course.

Both teachers at the time of interview were seeking ideas and advice from agencies and individuals working the field of European education, about course content, resources, and the best curricular strategies to adopt which would fit their respective schools' ethos and organisation.

Six months after the interviews, the teachers were contacted to see what progress, if any, they had made with their deliberations and plans. Dave's belief that he could bring about the desired change once he had presented colleagues with a strong rationale for the European dimension and ideas for its implementation proved to be over-optimistic. He had experienced a number of setbacks and for several reasons had been unable to coordinate a General Studies course with a European studies component from year 3 upwards. He is now concentrating his energies into putting together a course for a sixth form General Studies programme which he hopes he will eventually be able 'to expand downards through the school'. John's greater caution had paid off. At the beginning of the new school year he had produced and distributed to the relevant faculties an information sheet on education about Europe, as a result of which, he claimed 'we are now moving ahead in the three areas outlined'.

Conclusions

The case study demonstrates several general and specific points which have to be taken into account by teachers wishing to innovate by introducing a European element into the curriculum. The general points are relevant to all school innovations:

1 *Gaining the approval and cooperation of the Head*
Both teachers were at a stage beyond this vital initial one since they had been asked by the Head to innovate in the first place.

2 *Gaining the cooperation of other members of staff*
Without this any development could well turn out to be short-lived. In order to persuade other members of staff of the need for the innovation, certain crucial factors have to be worked out in advance.

3 *The rationale for innovation*
'I feel it will run into resistance until most teachers are convinced that there is a cogent and pressing answer to the question: why do we need a European dimension in our curriculum?'

4 *Advance planning*
The formulation of aims and objectives; identification of the areas of the curriculum to be affected and target age groups; location of resources and agencies to contact for help and advice; familiarisation with courses and syllabuses currently in use in the school and with possible alternatives.

Specific points regarding education about Europe which arose from the case study were the following:

The *European dimension* seemed, for both teachers, more suitable than a separate block of European studies for a number of reasons:

1 *Practical*

(a) *Curriculum structure and timetabling pressures*
The difficulty of inserting a new subject into an already crowded curriculum.

(b) *Financial constraints*
Staffing, materials etc.

2 *Political*

(a) *The off-putting low status image of European studies;* 'Its come to mean something, European Studies!'

(b) *Political sensibilities* of other members of staff:
'He is very anti-Europe, anti-EEC anyway, politically'. 'I think the way to approach the Faculty Head is *not* to mention Europe. We won't scare him off by mentioning European Studies.'

(c) *Possible imbalance* — 'Why Europe and not the world?'

For all these reasons, both teachers were committed to introducing the European dimension into their existing curriculum structure not as a separate unit, but as part of a broader framework of study. The possibility they are exploring is to present Europe as an essential part of a *general* or *core education* set in a world or modern studies perspective: i.e. Europe is to be seen as part of a continuum from the local/national perspective to the wider world.

Adaptation to Existing Curricular System

To be successful such a venture must fit in with a school's curricular system especially at a time when experimentation in schools is contracting rather than expanding. For example in a school where there is already some subject integration, John sees European education taking place within several faculties: *Modern Languages* which will provide a certain amount of cultural information; the *Environmental and Social Science* faculty which will emphasize political information, and the *Communications* faculty which will try and organize tape links and exchanges. In years 4 and 5 when subjects are separated into option groups, he is thinking of General Studies, a core subject, as a possible context for study of Europe.

Dave has to incorporate study of Europe into a separate subject curriculum and envisages General Studies, a core subject from year 3 upwards, as a suitable context because of its flexibility and its potential for integrating knowledge, skills and resources from several different subject areas. Different schools, therefore, offer a different range of possibilities. Because of this there can be no definitive model for the introduction of the European dimension. It can only be successfully undertaken within the curriculum areas or subjects that are most appropriate within individual schools.

10 *Conclusions*

The detailed investigations of school practice and examination syllabuses carried out in the course of the research allow the following tentative conclusions: rightly or wrongly, it is unlikely that European Studies as a separate subject will expand substantially in the near future for a number of reasons: the 'low status' image of the subject arising from its too-frequent use as an 'easy' option for lower ability pupils; the reduction in the number of subjects offered in schools as a result of economic pressures; the difficulties of establishing new subjects alongside the entrenched traditional disciplines, and a growing feeling among educationalists that Europe should not be studied in isolation but should be seen in the context of the wider world. An integrated or multi-disciplinary approach, as exemplified by Modern Studies in Scotland, presents possibly the best framework for study of Europe in a broader perspective, however there is no comparable subject that is widely taught in the English and Welsh secondary school curriculum.

For these reasons, and because we are dealing in general with a system where subjects are kept rigorously apart, it seems that the introduction or reinforcement of the European dimension has to be achieved across the curriculum within discrete subjects. The subjects with greatest scope for study of Europe and where it is most acceptable and appropriate are history, geography and modern languages. Where modern languages are concerned, although there have been a number of positive moves towards inclusion of contemporary background elements, it seems that teachers may still be experiencing difficulty in achieving an appropriate balance between instruction in linguistic skills and exposure to the culture of the country concerned.

The research findings suggest that other more peripheral subjects such as economics, politics (or government), social studies and General Studies, which are usually only taken as fourth, fifth or sixth year options, have a potential for teaching about Europe which has not yet been fully exploited.

The tendency among the teachers interviewed was to believe that Europe should no longer be considered in isolation but be taught as part of an interdependent world system. The Head of the History Department in the school curriculum study saw this trend as indicative of a shift in public attitudes which school courses 'nearly always reflect one or two years later'. The Modern Studies approach, starting with a study of the local community and gradually broadening out to encompass national, European, then world perspectives, was considered by many teachers to be an appropriate and balanced approach to study of Europe, and one which would be more acceptable to colleagues than a separate subject or topic approach.

Staffroom resistance, even hostility, to introduction or reinforcement of the European dimension seems to be encountered not infrequently in schools. One of the teachers in the *Europe across the Curriculum* case study was expecting this as a matter of course:

> Why Europe and not the world?
>
> I feel it will run into resistance until most teachers are convinced that there is a cogent and pressing answer to the question: why do we need a European dimension in the curriculum?

The case studies make it abundantly clear that the prerequisite for the introduction of European components on a significant scale in the curriculum *is* the persuasion of teachers and educationalists in general that teaching about Europe is *necessary*, *relevant* and *worthwhile*. The research shows that there is no consensus that this is the case among teachers as a whole. This undoubtedly reflects public apathy towards Europe and a discernible mistrust of, if not hostility, towards, the EEC (for which 'Europe' was frequently used as a synonym in case study schools). The school curriculum study suggests that although there was a temporary surge of interest in Europe and European issues following Britain's enrolment as a member of the Community in the 1970s, this is now very much on the wane and today teachers with a strong interest in Europe and convinced of its relevance may need great caution, tact and perseverence if they wish to gain the wholehearted cooperation of headteachers and colleagues in the staffroom. In this respect the comment of another teacher in the *Europe across the Curriculum* case study, reveals just how sensitive an issue Europe can be: 'I think the best way to approach the Head of Faculty (about introducing Europe) is not to mention Europe at all!' The need to get the understanding and cooperation of colleagues; to change attitudes but keep the peace in the staffroom, is just one of many challenges faced by the teacher wishing to develop European dimensions in the curriculum.

The research case studies highlighted a number of other problems related to the introduction of Europe in particular and to curriculum innovation in general. All the teachers mentioned practical problems such as the need for space in an already crowded timetable; for new books and materials, against a background of severe cuts in educational expenditure which are making it increasingly difficult to maintain even existing provision and standards.

Another difficulty is presented by the constraints on course content imposed by traditional, often outdated examination syllabuses. The importance of external examination syllabuses in determining course content and emphases in secondary schools cannot be underestimated. The likelihood of questions 'coming up' on certain topics is bound to influence teachers in an education system which, all too often, is judged on the number and quality of external examination results. A number of teachers in the case studies commented ruefully that the amount of European content in a course and the time they alotted to it depended, ultimately, on the structure of examination papers rather than on any personal decisions about its relevance and usefulness.

Where teaching about Europe is concerned all the individual problems faced by teachers are compounded by the fact that specific references to the European dimension are conspicuously missing in recent official pronouncements on the curriculum, and by the lack of consensus among educationalists in general on the need to teach pupils about Europe. Moreover the teacher with European interests has to grapple with the difficulty of putting modern European issues and institutions across in the classroom. 'Europe is boring' according to the history teacher teaching the *Move to European Unity* option in the Schools Councils History Project, while all the teachers interviewed in the Scottish case studies admitted that they had problems in making the European material, particularly the 'dry' EEC topic, 'come alive'. Few teachers will have had special training in teaching about Europe to help them grapple with this particular problem[1] and many of them have to find (or create) more stimulating visual resources or, as the teacher in the history case study put it, 'stand on their heads and play the clown' to put Europe 'across'. In other words, teachers wishing to teach Europe successfully and in a lively manner need a prodigious amount of perseverence, energy and imagination. The case studies suggest that teachers with such qualities exist but many more are needed if future generations are to have adequate education about the wider European society in which they live.

The Politics of a European Element in the Curriculum

One of the main difficulties to be confronted by anyone attempting to introduce or reinforce the European dimension in the curriculum is the fact that Europe, for reasons mentioned in the Introduction, is a sensitive political issue and its inclusion on any substantial scale may thus be resisted by some teachers in some schools. Questions about national identity and political autonomy are beyond the orbit of this book, although it can be repeated that education about Europe need not necessarily be the same as propaganda in favour of the EEC (although many people seem to believe the contrary).

The politics of immediate curriculum decisions is, however, very much the concern of this book. School subjects established as part of school timetables are political preserves and, moreover, preserves which radically affect the way in which knowledge is presented to school students. Because of the vested interest groups (notably subject associations) which build up around school subjects, attempts to promote new subjects are fiercely contested if the new subject aspires to high status. It is vital that those promoting or evaluating curriculum changes understand the manner in which the conflict over the curriculum takes place.

Curriculum conflict occurs against a changing background, both in terms of the organization of the educational system and the broader fabric of the national economy. Within this changing 'arena' the conflict over the curriculum adopts a rapidly changing set of 'rules', and 'weapons'. The secondary school arena which emerged after the Second World War was dominated by a newly-developed pattern of external examinations. The promotion of individual subjects in this arena followed the rules of 'professional' debate among 'associations' in the academic and public arenas and also later, in the Schools Council. Separate subject associations focussed on the enhancement of their subjects' evaluation in external examinations as the major weapon of subject promotion. The definitions of subjects that were promoted embraced those ingredients of school knowledge that were viewed as 'high status' and 'academic'. In this way subject associations were drawn inexorably into playing a 'status game' concerning the nature of the examinable knoweldge relating to their subject. By laying claim to high-status academic formulations of the subject ('O' and 'A' level examinations), the subject associations ensured that the special interests of the members were best served. Equipment, resources, finance, graded posts, teacher training and the nature of the pupil clientele: decisions over these issues all followed from the fundamental struggle over the definition of examinable school knowledge.

The crucial importance of 'O' and 'A' level academic status for teachers' career prospects and working conditions explains the huge resistance to the establishment of examination subjects. It is for this reason that Eggleston argues:

> New subjects have been successfully introduced into the school curricula, but almost always such subjects had to preserve the form and manner of the original high-status subjects, such as English, literature, geography and history, and almost always such subjects had to preserve the form and manner of the original high-status subjects from which they sprang.[2]

Implicitly, Eggleston is suggesting two potential fates for new areas of knowledge: *either* the new area can retain its identity as a separate subject but probably be refused high status in the form of examinations at 'O' and 'A' level, *or* a new emphasis (embodying the major content of the new subject) can be added to the traditionally high status, established school subjects.

The politics of the curriculum therefore confirm and reinforce one of the research conclusions: that the most viable Europeanization strategy is to add a European dimension to traditional school subjects, particularly history and geography. In some senses this would be building on movements already underway within these two subjects. Thus the main recommendations are as follows:

> The major subjects involving significant flows of students at 'O' and 'A' level where the European dimension could be successfully introduced or reinforced are history and geography. In these two subjects a number of innovative syllabuses already provide possibilities for the teaching of a European dimension. In history the content is already prescribed in some of these courses; in geography the opportunity is there if more European examples are selected by teachers and more European resources and materials are provided.
>
> There is a time lag in the replacement of old-established syllabuses. Hence negotiations need to be started with Boards to get European content included. In history this means moving syllabuses beyond the common terminal date of 1954 and moving the focus away from purely national obsessions. Some Boards have already made moves in this direction. In geography it means stressing the need for European regional study and adding more European case studies to the study of generalised patterns and models.
>
> Special training courses in the European dimension need to be established and/or modified for history and geography teachers. New specialists should receive this additional training as part of their initial training; established specialists should be offered in-service training.

In spite of the emphasis on history and geography, it would be misleading to focus too exclusively on these initiatives. The relative autonomy of the English educational system at local and classroom level ensures a deep-seated diversity of educational approaches. For this reason too closely specialized a set of approaches would be misguided. What is plainly needed is 'buckshot' strategy which encourages all manner of initiatives concerned with European education. Hence in some local education authorities or classrooms the primary vehicle for European education might well be world studies or politics, just as, in Scotland, it might be Modern Studies. It is crucially important that *all* initiatives stressing a European curriculum element should be encouraged and supported.

> The addition of European content to world studies, economics, integrated studies, social studies or sociology, politics, and General Studies should be pursued through individual school courses and examination syllabuses.
>
> Training courses need to be established which reflect these new European emphases.

However there are certain factors to be taken into account when considering any broad-based introduction of European elements in the curriculum: for example a subject teacher's career structure is a central concern. It is at this level that the subject associations operate to promote the interests of their teacher members. Widely available examinations and training courses offer the basis and rationale for the establishment of and recruitment to subject departments. By developing examinations and training courses, new curriculum areas or elements are allied to the career interests and structures of subject teachers. Without this alliance, it is contended that no broad-based curriculum penetration is likely. Hence it is to the development of new European-oriented examinations and training courses that future initiatives must be firmly committed.

The Problem of Continuity

One important question that arises is how to render treatment of European issues both *coherent and sequential* through the child's secondary school life. In the first three years of the comprehensive school this is more easily accomplished because most students follow a common core of subjects. In the fourth year, however, the student is normally offered a series of 'options'. Thus if European content is added to the common core in the first three years we can assume coherence and sequence as viable objectives. In the fourth year (age 14 or 15), this assumption breaks down. At this age European content might be included in certain traditional subjects, but the student may not choose those subjects. Thus the scheme of European study might end in the fourth year for significant numbers of students.

To ensure a coherent and sequential coverage of European issues the most logical answer would seem to be found in definition of a scheme of European studies for the full span of secondary schooling. This scheme would be multidisciplinary in that it would treat fundamental European issues through the major disciplines involved. The emphasis would be on bringing disciplinary perspectives to bear on key issues and not vice versa. Chapter 9, *Europe across the Curriculum*, shows how some teachers are devising schemes for teaching about Europe that will fit in with the particular curriculum structure of their respective schools. However, if a school has a traditional option system this is more difficult to achieve. What is needed, therefore, is a common core of subjects possibly including European studies in the fourth and fifth year of the comprehensive school. The common core strategy has been under discussion for sometime within the DES. Advocates of European education need to promote their cause in terms of the common core of subjects that is being defined. Active 'lobbying' of government agencies is also necessary.

There is an overriding rationale for teaching pupils in our secondary schools about Europe and European issues. Although we have seen that this can be achieved within the existing curriculum, our investigation into the possibilities of adding new content to the curriculum has shown that there will have to be a number of significant changes not only in educational priorities and practice but also in public attitudes and expectations if young people in our schools are to receive a relevant and broad-based education rather than one still wedded to an outdated, narrowly academic and examination-oriented curricular structure.

Notes

1 A brief summary of the situation regarding teacher training can be found in appendix 2, p. 194.
2 EGGLESTON, J. (1975) *The Sociology of the School Curriculum*, London, Routledge and Kegan Paul.

Appendix 1: New AEB 'O' Level in European Studies

A number of experimental Ordinary level examination syllabuses in European Studies have existed for some time. Both the Cambridge Board and the Oxford/Cambridge Board, for example, have been responsible for such syllabuses. At the moment a new initiative is underway which promises to build on past progress and to address the contemporary demands for an Ordinary level syllabus. This is because many schools now teach CSE courses in European studies and have increasingly wished to offer an 'O' level course alongside the CSE course to cater for the able students that are attracted to European Studies work. With this in mind the Associated Examining Board has since 1977 been considering this issue and has recently set up a working party to devise an Ordinary level examination. The syllabus will be available for teaching in the school year beginning 1984, for examination in 1986. The aims of the syllabus are the following:

1 to give students a knowledge and understanding of contemporary Europe.
2 to develop an awareness of the movements towards unity within Europe.
3 to foster an awareness of the diversity within Europe.
4 to encourage an understanding of Europe's relations with the rest of the world.

The working party spent a great deal of time discussing the continuing dilemma of how to define the Europe which was to be studied. We were clear that we wanted a broad view to be taken of Europe and one which included not just Western but also Eastern Europe, hence we settled for the following phrase: 'Europe is geographically defined as the area from Norway in the north to the Mediterranean Sea in the south and from Iceland in the West to the Urals in the East'. Chronologically the syllabus deals with the emergence of contemporary Europe since the First World War.

The objectives of the syllabus reflect a series of beliefs about pedagogy and syllabus content. Six objectives were listed: firstly, although not in priority, to recall facts about Europe, and secondly to show knowledge and comprehension of European issues, thirdly to demonstrate an understanding of issues from the viewpoint of other Europeans; fourthly, to evaluate information through comparison and contrast; fifthly, to analyse and assess the range of information presented in a variety of forms from newspapers and periodicals, maps, illustrations, tables and graphs and finally to develop and present logical and systematic responses to set questions.

The examination structures are as follows:

PAPER 1 (2¾ hours) 70 per cent of total marks

Section A will test Section A of the core syllabus and mainly objectives 1 and 2. It will contain about 6 compulsory short answer questions. (30 per cent of total marks).

Section B will test section 2 of the core syllabus. It will contain 1 compulsory question testing mainly objectives 5 and 6 and using stimulus material, and 3 other questions testing all objectives and requiring longer answers of which *one* must be answered (40 per cent of total marks)

PAPER 2 (1¾ hours) 30 per cent of total marks

This paper will test the optional syllabus and mainly objectives 2, 3, 4 and 6. It will contain a choice of 2 questions on each option. *Two* questions must be answered, one from each of two chosen options.

Appendix 2: Teacher Training

Considerable changes and developments have taken place in teacher training since the early 1970s. The teacher training structure that has emerged in the wake of various stages of reorganisation has involved: the disappearance of the three-year Certificate of Education (in 1979); the virtual disappearance of the Colleges of Education (which have either merged with polytechnics and universities or diversified into Colleges of Higher Education), and the validation of pre-service courses being made the responsibility of CNAA and universities.

The two main routes to teacher-training in England and Wales are now three- or four-year BEd courses or a one-year PGCE course which normally follows a three-year degree course. In 1979 there were 4947 PGCE students at universities and 4514 in the public sector. According to a 1980 HMI discussion paper *PGCE in the Public Sector*: 'Over half of the present output of qualified teacher comes through the PGCE route and will continue to do throughout the 1980s (. . .)'

Throughout the last decade there has been much debate about the kinds of programme that would best provide an adequate, comprehensive and economically viable training for a reduced number of students. The popularity of PGCE courses in the early 1980s was considered to have partially undermined the potential take-up of BEd courses outside the universities and the ability of PGCE to adequately train a future teacher has been questioned by many educationalists.

Whatever the outcome of current deliberations it is likely that there are yet more substantial changes to come in the teacher-training system and that a large question mark still hangs over many existing BEd courses in polytechnics and colleges of education in England and Wales. The signs are that there will be no expansion of the induction and in-service training programme for some time. For example, according to the HMI 1981 discussion paper on teacher training, there are several ways in which initial and in-service training can be improved 'but the balance must be in favour of the latter. Certainly the influence of newly trained teachers is highly important but they will form only a small minority of the teaching force until well on into the 1980s. The quality of work in the secondary schools throughout that period will depend largely on those who are already teaching'.

In Scotland the teacher training system is different from that in the rest of the UK In Scotland the colleges of education are the sole agencies for the training of teachers with one exception, the University of Stirling. Secondary teaching in Scotland is a graduate profession and graduates, after completing their degrees, go to colleges of education where they are trained alongside other specialists and primary school teachers in the larger institutions. There are education departments in universities which offer master's degrees but this is purely an academic award which does not qualify the recipient to teach.

There are no polytechnics in Scotland in the English sense although there are colleges known as 'central institutions' which range from schools of art, domestic science colleges to technical colleges. None of these are allowed to train teachers and, again, aspiring teachers go to colleges of education after receiving their specialist qualification.

Because of its different teacher training organization, Scotland has avoided many of the problems and changes that have bedevilled the English system. In 1972 while the DES White Papers indicated that some colleges of education in England and Wales might have to close and others would have to change their role, the equivalent Scottish Paper (SED, 1972) stated only that there would be no significant further expansion in the next decade in colleges of education. Consequently the mergers and diversification which have characterized English colleges in the last decade have not taken place in Scotland, although there are now signs that the situation is beginning to change with the projected (and much resisted) closure of two of the ten Scottish colleges of education.

Due, therefore, to the continuing state of flux and uncertainty in the higher and further education sector, any analysis of courses currently on offer is subject to the proviso that the situation could change rapidly in the next few years and not only in polytechnics and colleges of education: universities are also suffering their share of turmoil, and the resulting changes in course provision could be far-reaching. Multidisciplinary subjects like European Studies, if based in the humanities or social sciences, could be seriously affected by a number of different factors: the expected programme of cuts in higher education resulting in the reduction of student intake and the running down of some subjects (for example some European languages, an area which traditionally feeds into European Studies programmes); the competition for students which may eventually be exacerbated by falling school rolls and fears of unemployment which may lead to a tendency among applicants to opt for 'safe' established subjects or those with a vocational orientation. In addition to these factors, newer, broader courses of study outside or across the established disciplines could well be affected in higher and further education as a whole by such factors as greater stringency of the CNAA and other validating bodies towards course submissions and proposed changes in the organization and possible grant distribution of the Social Science Research Council.

Another development which could affect future provision of arts courses is the 'advice' given by the UGC to universities (summer 1981) to reduce their arts student intake and increase the number studying science and technology. The projected overall cut in university student numbers is estimated at 20,000 by 1984. One immediate result of this policy appears to be an increase in the number of students applying to take courses at polytechnics. The *Times Higher Education Supplement* of 4 September 1981, for example, reported a surge of applicants to degree courses in polytechnics and colleges as a result of cutbacks in university recruitment. The resulting and unexpected popularity of public sector courses, due also in part to the large numbers of eighteen year olds currently leaving school, will, at least in the short term, assuage some lecturers' fears about whether adequate numbers of students can be attracted to the diversified courses. BEd courses in 1981, however, continued to be undersubscribed.

As fewer and fewer teacher training places are becoming available, many young people who otherwise might have entered the profession may be considering following courses which offer a wider range of career options.

The increasing popularity of PGCE courses in recent years suggests that many future secondary school teachers will get the bulk of their study of modern Europe in first degree subject courses rather than in BEd programmes.

Study of Modern Europe in Higher and Further Education

In 1980 few existing teacher training programmes had European Studies *per se* as an option, although teaching about Europe could, of course, be a component of subject options such as history, geography and modern languages. The European studies components then available within teacher training courses were mainly to be found as PGCE options with the following exceptions: Bulmershe College which had teaching about Europe as a third year curriculum elective in the BEd. course; Herfordshire College which offered European Studies as part of the French BEd course, and the New University of Ulster which offered West European Studies concurrently with the BEd degree. Twelve institutions specified European Studies as part of the available PGCE options although in some cases this may have been a modern language option under another guise. In addition to these some colleges and polytechnics had developed a number of degree courses in European Studies which could provide students with suitable qualifications for teaching about Europe at secondary school level.

Where teacher training programmes were concerned, there were a number of problems: because of a certain lack of forward planning or faulty coordination between the teacher training system and schools, there have been increasing discrepancies between demand for teachers with particular basic specialisms and the actual supply. This has been a matter of some concern in recent years and institutions may come under pressure to increase numbers of recruits to teacher training programmes in certain specialisms such as mathematics, physical science and practical subjects and to reduce student intake to others. This could mean the elimination of some less established subjects in initial teacher training, and the introduction of new curriculum areas which are not considered vital may be impossible. It seems that schools and teacher training programmes are expected to respond to social, economic and technological changes in society: for example, new areas of study have been introduced into teacher training programmes when the need for them has been perceived for example, education for multiracial society which in 1981 took on a special urgency. If the need for an area of study is *not* clearly perceived and identified by society and schools, then there will understandably be few attempts to develop that area in teacher training.

This appears to be the case with education about Europe. Since there is no consensus that this should form part of the school curriculum (none of the official documents on teacher training, secondary schooling and the school curriculum produced during the last ten years include any substantial reference to or recommendations on the European dimension), teaching about modern Europe is patchy in schools and this is reflected in teacher education.

Thus the prerequisite for change must be the acceptance by society and, by extension, educationalists, that for all the reasons stated at the beginning of this report, some knowledge of Europe is an essential part of the educational process. If this general acceptance could be achieved, the incorporation into teacher training schemes of course components which encourage understanding of European cultures and states with which Britain has so many geographical, historical, economic and political links would be a natural development.

Since, as argued earlier, it would unrealistic (and probably unpopular) to attempt the establishment at this time of a separate European Studies specialism, the most workable means of ensuring a European dimension to teacher training would seem to be via contributions from specialisms such as history, geography, languages, English (literature), art, technology and music within which there could either be a continuing European emphasis or separate course options.

Ideally, given our links with Europe and our cultural heritage, education about Europe should naturally permeate the curriculum. However separation and a general 'unrelatedness' of subjects bedevils our education system at all levels. As pointed out in the HMI discussion paper *Teaching Training and the Secondary School* (1981):

> The specialist teacher of any subject, at whatever level he operates, is always at risk of confining his vision within its boundaries. However, the contribution of that subject to the pupils' education is weakened if it is not perceived by the teacher and presented to the pupil in terms of its relation to the rest of the curriculum. There are two associated

aspects of this notion. One is the extent to which the teacher sees his subject as part of the curriculum as a whole and as contributing to it. The other is the explicit making of links between subjects in such a manner that the skills and ways of thinking in a particular subject are given opportunity for development in others.

The discussion paper sees the subject-centred approach as a vicious circle which it is difficult for teachers to break out of:

> It is quite possible that the student entering teacher training has never been invited to consider his subject as one element in an educational process which should make sense as a whole for pupils; to see it in the context of the whole school curriculum. The subject-centred approach is very deeply rooted, both in the students who enter BEd and PGCE and in the attitude of most of the schools where they will have their teaching practice and their early experience as teachers. To break this circuit is no easy task.

While this separateness between subjects persists it will be difficult to ensure that permeation of education about Europe takes place within the entire curriculum. As long as official guidelines and prescriptions for treatment of European issues are lacking, it will be up to committed subject specialists to make sure that the European dimension is present in their contributions to teacher training courses either as optional or compulsory course units or as a general and continuing area of reference.

Within each specialism in teacher training the incorporation of the European dimension should be based on to the following considerations:

- the information, concepts and skills that pupils should acquire through study of Europe;
- the appropriate methods for teaching about Europe;
- how much time to allocate to the European aspects of each discipline;
- how the European element relates to the curriculum as a whole.

These are important questions which must follow the recognition that the European dimension is an essential part of the education process.

For Product Safety Concerns and Information please contact our EU
representative GPSR@taylorandfrancis.com
Taylor & Francis Verlag GmbH, Kaufingerstraße 24, 80331 München, Germany

www.ingramcontent.com/pod-product-compliance
Lightning Source LLC
LaVergne TN
LVHW010602110826
845149LV00003B/740

9781138321601